The Perfecting of Nature

The Perfecting of Nature
Reforming Bodies in Antebellum Literature

Josh Doty

The University of North Carolina Press CHAPEL HILL

© 2020 The University of North Carolina Press
All rights reserved
Set in Merope Basic by Westchester Publishing Services
Manufactured in the United States of America

The University of North Carolina Press has been a member
of the Green Press Initiative since 2003.

Library of Congress Cataloging-in-Publication Data
Names: Doty, Josh, author.
Title: The perfecting of nature : reforming bodies in antebellum literature / Josh Doty.
Description: Chapel Hill : University of North Carolina Press, 2020. |
    Includes bibliographical references and index.
Identifiers: LCCN 2020010713 | ISBN 9781469659602 (cloth : alk paper) |
    ISBN 9781469659619 (paperback : alk paper) | ISBN 9781469659626 (ebook)
Subjects: LCSH: Human body in literature. | American literature—1783–1850—History and
    criticism.
Classification: LCC PN56.B62 D68 2020 | DDC 810.9/3561—dc23
LC record available at https://lccn.loc.gov/2020010713

Cover illustration: Edward Williams Clay, *Roper's Gymnasium, 274 Market Street, Philadelphia*
(Philadelphia: Childs and Inman Press, ca. 1831). Courtesy of the Wainwright Lithograph
Collection, Library Company of Philadelphia.

A portion of chapter 2 was previously published in a different form as "Digesting *Moby-Dick*,"
Leviathan: A Journal of Melville Studies 19, no. 1 (Spring 2017): 85–101. It appears here courtesy
of Johns Hopkins University Press.

For Katie,
"best of wives and best of women"

Contents

Acknowledgments ix

Introduction 1

CHAPTER ONE
Transcendental Self-Culture and the Horizons of Bioplasticity 16

CHAPTER TWO
Governance, Race, and Alimentary Selfhood in Melville 42

CHAPTER THREE
Sculpting the Body Electric 74
Exercise and Self-Fashioning in Walt Whitman

CHAPTER FOUR
Tricks of the Blood 101
Heredity and Repair in Oliver Wendell Holmes Sr.

Coda 130
Literature and Neurological Selfhood

Notes 133
Bibliography 155
Index 165

Acknowledgments

It is a pleasure to thank those without whom this project would not be possible. My greatest intellectual debt is to Jane F. Thrailkill, who introduced me to the study of nineteenth-century literature and science. She remains a model of scholarly generosity and rigor. Eliza Richards patiently taught me how to craft a sustained argument (not an easy task) and encouraged me to write with concision and energy. Matthew Taylor has long been a wonderful advocate and sounding board. Tim Marr helped me think through my work on Melville, and John McGowan offered wise counsel. Philip F. Gura taught me much of what I know about the transcendentalists, and I first gained a grasp of antebellum reform culture in his classes. Don Wehrs has long been an advocate and friend. Erich Nunn did much to help me learn the ropes of the profession. The late Noel Polk taught me to take my writing and my ideas seriously.

I began this project at Spring Hill College; I thank my colleagues in the English Department there for their kind support. I finished the book at St. Mary's University in the company of terrific teacher-scholars, all of whom I thank for their graciousness and hospitality.

Funding provided by Spring Hill College's Mitchell Family Faculty Scholarship Grant allowed me to travel to archives that proved essential to completing the book. I wish to thank Jeffrey S. Cramer at the Walden Woods Project's Thoreau Institute Library and the librarians at the American Antiquarian Society and the Houghton Library for their kind help finding archival material. I also wish to thank the librarians at the Rare Book and Special Collections Division at the Library of Congress for their assistance.

Lucas Church at UNC Press has been an exemplary editor, and I could not have asked for a better person to guide my manuscript through the publishing process. I am grateful to my anonymous readers, who provided feedback that was critical to the shape of my argument; their interventions pushed me to think in unexpected directions, which has enriched the book immensely.

My parents, Danny and Diane Doty, have long supported my journey to academe and have been cheerleaders of this project. I thank my in-laws, John and Jean Meersman, for all the scotch and for so often allowing me to use their basement as a writing studio. Colleen and Stew Miller, Kathy Theofel,

Chris Theofel, Pat and Debra Guyton, and the rest of my family strewn from Mississippi to California kept the good times rolling. My friends Corey Bishop and Erin Clyburn have been lifelines since our undergraduate days.

I could not have completed this book without the companionship of my dog, Darwin, whose insistent reminders that I take breaks to play punctuate almost every page you hold. He passed away as the manuscript neared completion, but I will forevermore happily associate this project with him. My son, Jack Doty, arrived a few months before my deadline for the final manuscript; his direct, frank engagement with the world and his astonishing capacity to learn have kept me mindful of the seemingly unlimited potential of the human form.

My greatest thanks are to my wife, Katie Meersman, who pulled double time as a parent to give me the time to finish this book and who has moved from the Deep South to the Carolinas to the Gulf Coast to south Texas for my career. (I promise we won't move again.) I dedicate this work to her.

The Perfecting of Nature

Introduction

> What is man but a mass of thawing clay?
> —HENRY DAVID THOREAU, *Walden*

In September 1838, social reformer and Unitarian minister William Ellery Channing stood in front of a crowd of Boston laborers to tell them that they could become whatever they wished. The topic of his address, an examination of what he called "self-culture," was to introduce the Franklin Lectures, a series of addresses "attended," as he noted, "chiefly by those, who are occupied with manual labor."[1] His lecture urged these men to find within themselves the "means of improvement, of self-culture, possessed no where else."[2] Channing identified "two powers of the human soul," "the self-searching and the self-forming power," that make self-culture possible.[3] The self-searching power allows one to observe and thus become aware of one's abilities, and the self-forming power enables one to cultivate those abilities. "We have the power of not only tracing our powers," he said, "but of guiding and impelling them; not only of watching our passions, but of controlling them; not only of seeing our faculties grow, but of applying to them means and influences to aid their growth."[4] Our capacities are, in other words, in our own hands. By titling his lecture "Self-culture," he took as his subject "the care which every man owes to himself, to the unfolding and perfecting of his nature."[5] In this formulation, self-culture is a form of self-directed "care" available to every man; because it allows a man to engage in "the unfolding and perfecting of his nature," he "owes" himself the pursuit of self-culture. It is at once the freedom to perfect oneself and the responsibility to do so.

In the decades that followed Channing's address, the human body emerged within popular cultures of reform as a potent subject of both the self-searching and the self-forming power. Health reformers invented not only systems of self-searching that trained Americans to monitor and assess their physical states but also systems of self-formation that asserted the body's ability to be both reformed (refined, improved) and re-formed (modified, remade). Literary authors, as I argue in the pages that follow, assessed reformers' ideas about these emerging conceptions of bodily change by giving them imaginative form; in doing so, they intervened in the morphing body of reform itself. Literary scholars tend to frame the nineteenth-century body as fixed, ossified; as proof, they point to the rigid skulls surveyed by craniometrists and the facial features analyzed by physiognomists. But *The Perfecting of Nature* considers literature's engagement with another set of ideas—including popular medicine, dietary reform, physical training, and, perhaps surprisingly, phrenology—that construed the human body as endlessly changing and changeable. "We are not potted and buried in our bodies," Ralph Waldo Emerson asserts in his lecture "Reform" (1860), "but every body is newly created from day to day, and every moment."[6] This book recovers the place of the "newly created" body in the antebellum literary imagination.

I argue for the importance of ideas about the human body's malleability to antebellum literary expression by examining how and why bodies change in works by Margaret Fuller, Henry David Thoreau, Nathaniel Hawthorne, Herman Melville, Walt Whitman, and Oliver Wendell Holmes Sr. I show how ideas about bodily change that emerged in the decades leading up to the Civil War offered Americans new ways of thinking about the body's capacities, albeit in different ways, to different degrees, and for different reasons. Scientific and medical ideas about the changing body are traceable back until at least Galenic medicine and humoral theory, and Christian Science and other self-forming projects of the late-century United States developed them further, but I take the antebellum era as my focus because it was a period of especially profound interconnection between literature and reform. Far from being the mere recipients of the ideas of others, the authors this book studies participated in vigorous debates about what changeable bodies might mean for the fledgling nation. Indeed, as figures such as Whitman and Holmes remind us, the roles of "reformer" and "writer" are not always easily distinguishable. For instance, Whitman took a turn as a health reformer between the second and third editions of *Leaves of Grass*, published in 1856 and 1860, in his recently recovered health series "Manly Health and Training" (1858). In "Manly Health," as in his poetry, Whitman celebrates the body for its beauty and its capacity for affection, but he also describes how the interdependence of the human body's diverse anatomical features and physiological processes means that there are a number of ways to change the body *"for good and bad,"* as he puts it; new ideas about the body's malleability thus suggested, to health reformers, physicians, and writers alike, new worlds of promise and peril.[7]

Antebellum health reformers, whose utopian verve and tireless application of medical concepts to social problems place them alongside literary writers at the center of this book, circulated emerging ways of understanding the body through a rich and dynamic print culture. Historian Charles Rosenberg writes that cheaper paper, printing, and binding methods made it easier than ever for reformers to publish their ideas, and emerging national markets facilitated an "increasingly accessible universe of print" for Americans interested in staying abreast of new developments in phrenology and homeopathy.[8] What they discovered was that, as Daniel Harrison Jacques puts it in *Hints toward Physical Perfection* (1859), "*the already existing and even matured physical organization may, under certain conditions, and by the use of perfectly legitimate means, be modified, both in its internal conditions and in its external forms, to an almost unlimited extent.*"[9] Reformers used a range of terms—including "physical culture," "self-cultivation," "physiological reform," and "hygiene"—in addition to "self-culture," to name their efforts to educate others on the means (*"perfectly legitimate,"* as Jacques assures readers) by which to mold their *"internal conditions"* and *"external forms."*

Reformers differed in the particulars of their systems, and their disagreements form one of the themes of this book. But taken as a whole, they viewed emerging ways of altering, healing, cultivating, and intervening in the human body as catalysts for national renewal. Historian Regina Morantz-Sanchez writes that in the decades preceding the Civil War, "self-help in health matters, public hygiene, dietary reform, temperance, hydro-therapy, and physiological instruction merged as ingredients in a coherent and articulate campaign to save the nation by combating the ill-health of its citizenry."[10] For example, dietary reformer Sylvester Graham, confronted by a national population he believed to be pathologically drained of its vital energies, invented the Graham cracker as a food so bland that eating it would not harm the body, as he believed spiced foods did, and a good deal of his immensely influential system of dietetics comprises ways to bolster "vital energy" through a restricted diet, cold-water baths, and daily exercise. How something like Grahamian dietetics might reform the United States was an open question even for its adherents, and literary historian Philip F. Gura argues that reformers focused on ameliorating problems at the scale of the individual rather than of society could not "imagine a different, more ameliorative, more pragmatic approach to the nation's problems" than self-improvement, "particularly through legislative enactment."[11] Because of reformers' emphasis on the renewal of the individual self, he writes, "the social harmony they sought eluded them."[12] Yet even the most seemingly self-oriented (and, as skeptical contemporaries noted, self-congratulatory) practices often went hand in hand with radical political sentiments. William Tyler, a boarder in Asenath Nicholson's Graham Boarding House, so named for its adherence to Grahamian dietetics, writes in an 1833 letter to his brother that his cohabitants seek to better not only themselves but also their nation: "The Boarders in this establishment are not only Grahamites, but Garrisonites—not only reformers in diet, but radicals in Politics. Such a knot of abolitionists I never before fell in with. Slavery, Colonization, etc. constitute the unvarying monotonous theme of their conversations except that they give place to an occasional comment upon their peculiar style of living."[13] In Nicholson's boardinghouse, Grahamian interventions into the human body sit at the table with abolitionist interventions into national politics. This sense of the continuity between the reform of individuals' bodies and that of the nation inflects practically every health reform discourse of the antebellum period.

Literature shaped the cultural reception of these ideas by depicting how they transformed Americans' understanding of what sort of creatures they were: in flux, open to being affected by others and the environment. Antebellum writers created imaginative spaces that foregrounded the possibilities and limitations of the sorts of embodied subjectivity this flux created, and literary elements such as plot, figuration, and characterization enabled readers to reflect on their own embodiment. Here I have in mind Sari Altschuler's term "imaginative experimentation," which she uses to describe "both the various ways in which doctors and writers used their imaginations to craft, test, and implement their theories of health and the role literary forms played in developing that work."[14] Antebellum writers' literary creations—Thoreau's ascetic persona, Melville's dyspeptic sailors, Whitman's vigorous athletes—are, similarly, ways of assessing the potential of the human body. In addressing the intersection of nineteenth-century American literature, science, and medicine, *The Perfecting of Nature* joins a number of recent studies by Altschuler, Justine Murison, Kyla Wazana Tompkins, Michelle Neely, Kyla Schuller, Britt Rusert, Jane F. Thrailkill, and others that have recovered the importance of scientific ideas and disciplines such as mesmerism, nerve physiology, phrenology, and dietary reform to the nineteenth-century American literary imagination.[15] What this book adds is an emphasis on how, by offering readers opportunities to engage imaginatively with the changeability of the body, literature participated in the creation of subjects aware of their ability to change (or be changed) at the most fundamental physiological levels. If literature is, as Emerson writes in his essay "Circles" (1841), at once "a platform whence we may command a view of our present life" and "a purchase by which we may move it," then part of its role in the antebellum decades was to show readers both who they were and who they might become.[16]

By attending to how antebellum Americans could turn to literature as a way to understand their somatic capacities, *The Perfecting of Nature* positions the reading of literature as a tool for self-cultivation alongside such practices as exercise and dietary management. Attending to literature's engagement with ideas about the changeability of the body alerts us to antebellum Americans' sense of the power of the written word to shape the world. I agree with Rita Felski, who, in her argument for methodological alternatives to critique, asserts that rather than searching "behind the text—for its hidden causes, determining conditions, and noxious motives—we might place ourselves in front of the text, reflecting on what it unfurls, calls forth, makes possible."[17] My contention is that part of what antebellum literature "makes possible" for its readers is a variety of ways to think through the pleasures, dangers, responsibilities, and demands of the changeable body. To understand literature this way "is not idealism, aestheticism, or magical thinking," as Felski argues, "but a recognition—long overdue—of the text's status as cofactor: as something that makes a difference, that helps makes things happen."[18] This book argues that in antebellum America, literature was a vital "cofactor" in giving cultural form to emerging forms of embodiment.

The Past and Present of Plasticity

In the course of remaining attentive to the rich and varied history of the antebellum epistemological structures that gave shape to the different ways Americans could understand their embodiment, I resist reducing multiple, contesting ideas about the mutability of the human body to a simplified cultural phenomenon that I can then "complicate." No such phenomenon existed, and the ideas I engage are complicated in their own right. Instead, in the chapters that follow I seek to understand what did exist: the individual yet profoundly interconnected figures, concepts, disciplines, texts, and practices from which diverse ideas about the human body's changeability emerged in the decades before the Civil War. In this study I use the term "bioplasticity" to refer to the basic assumption these ideas shared: that the human body is, to some degree, malleable. Antebellum Americans themselves did not use the word "bioplasticity" to refer to bodily changeability, preferring instead to speak metaphorically in terms of clay, as Henry David Thoreau does, or fluidity, as Margaret Fuller does, but they did use the word "plastic" to describe it, as Jacques does when he asserts that "the human form is plastic."[19]

Despite the historical usage of the word "plastic," I use "bioplasticity" advisedly, for when we refer to "plasticity" today, we typically mean neuroplasticity, or twenty-first-century ideas about the ability of the brain specifically to change its neural makeup. Although the historical particularities of antebellum ideas about the body's capacity to change are foundational to this study, the way I think about bioplasticity owes much to debates in science and technology studies on the social, philosophical, and political implications of neuroplasticity. The work of Catherine Malabou, Nikolas Rose and Joelle M. Abi-Rached, and Brenda Bhandar and Jonathan Goldberg-Hiller, in particular, asks what concepts of the plastic brain mean for how we in the present day constitute selfhood. Are we "flexible" selves, "malleable" selves, selves that can be one thing and then another? Yes, but not quite: neuroplasticity means something more than mere flexibility. As Malabou writes, the difference between neuroplasticity and something like "neural flexibility" is that neuroplasticity is to be understood as referring to not only the brain's flexibility but also its capacity for self-creation: "To be flexible is to receive a form or impression, to be able to form oneself, to take the form, not to give it. To be docile, not to resist. No scientist would ever speak of neural flexibility. The scientific concept is neural plasticity, which integrates creativity as an objective dimension of the brain."[20] Malabou understands this creativity as an engine of resistance against hegemonic forces that would otherwise impress themselves upon our brains. Considering the political possibilities of neuroplasticity, she writes, "To talk about the plasticity of the brain means to see in it not only the creator and receiver of form but also an agency of disobedience to every constituted form, a refusal to submit to a model."[21] In the antebellum context, physiologists, writers, and reformist thinkers of all stripes similarly understood the body itself as having not only the qualities of impressibility and flexibility but also the quality of self-creation, the perfecting of nature.

In drawing this comparison, I am less interested in making a claim about any sort of historical continuity between bioplasticity and neuroplasticity than I am in pointing out the ways that attending to the antebellum period's emphasis on the malleability of the body enables reimagining twenty-first-century thinking about plasticity in contexts that are—rather than solely neurological—alimentary, skeletal, pulmonary, nervous, and muscular. For example, we might inquire whether and to what extent literary depictions of bioplasticity enable a similar sort of "agency of disobedience" that Malabou finds in neuroplasticity; in doing so, we orient ourselves toward the rebellious potential of historical modes of embodiment. But here I wish to use a light touch. Even as this book looks to thinkers like Malabou to unfold the multifoliate potential of bioplasticity, it keeps within sight the many factors that distinguish past and present intellectual and cultural contexts. Compared to neuroplasticity, bioplasticity is an indeterminate concept; it is an assumption about the human body, not a discrete physiological process in and of itself, as neuroplasticity is thought to be today. Consequently, and perhaps appropriately, its form changes depending on how it is expressed and what uses it might serve. This is to say that conceptions of bioplasticity are themselves plastic: never finished, always in the process of taking form.

One of the goals of this book is to identify what literary critics and historians might miss, or have missed, by neglecting antebellum theories of bodily change. To give one example, the early decades of the nineteenth century saw the emergence of diverse conceptions of eating and digestion, the most well-known of which is Graham's dietetics. His anxieties about sexuality and racial difference are easily identifiable by our reading practices, so that is where our attention tends to focus. But scholars have been less attentive to the ways that Grahamian dietetics, and antebellum dietary reform more generally, articulate a vison of human life that is, to use Thoreau's phrase, "startlingly moral."[22] The devoted Grahamian lets not a morsel past her lips without considering the role it might play in the moral ecologies of both her body and the world; her sense that what she consumes might dramatically alter her physical makeup and mental well-being situates her in a mode of embodiment that is anxious, even paranoid, but also hopeful for physical, emotional, and moral flourishing. In the same vein, we tend not to notice antebellum conceptions of the spiritual and religious aspects of materiality, but theorists of new materialism could well benefit from attending to the stubborn presence of the immaterial and transcendent within antebellum modes of embodiment. Most of all, bioplasticity orients us toward the human body in its entirety—muscle, bone, blood, guts—as a site of change, growth, spiritual renewal, and political action. In sum, it offers another way to think through the relationship between the human body and culture.

The insights we might draw from antebellum ideas about the human body are most available when we resist the urge to understand them using solely the terms, concepts, and disciplinary habits of mind available to us in the present day. This is not to advocate for "defamiliarizing" bioplasticity, which is already less familiar than we might suspect. I would suggest instead a disciplined attentiveness to the alterity of the antebellum period and a sustained willingness to allow its cultural productions to surprise and baffle us. For instance, it is obvious to most scholars working in the humanities that the regimes that health reformers prescribe fit comfortably within the bounds of what Michel Foucault in *The Use of Pleasure* (1984) calls "techniques of the self," or "those reflective and voluntary practices by which men not only set themselves rules of conduct, but seek to transform themselves, to change themselves in their singular being, and to make of their life into an *oeuvre* that carries certain aesthetic values and meets certain stylistic criteria."[23] In the Foucauldian view, such techniques enable the workings of governmentality by transforming individuals' daily habits and practices to the point that they become the unwitting tools of power; such an analysis is the approach of literary critics such as Joan Burbick.[24] It would be shortsighted to the point of naiveté to assert that health reformers do not ask individuals to internalize troubling assumptions about health, ability, race, gender, and class. Yet it seems equally shortsighted to assert that there are not some aspects of antebellum health reform that are so particular to their own time and cultural context that they demand an approach that is less totalizing.

Peter Coviello's theoretically rich work on sexuality and biopower in the works of Thoreau demonstrates how an attentiveness to the nuances of language can illuminate irreducible differences between the nineteenth century and our own that might be flattened in less careful accounts. In a recent piece on Thoreau's ambiguous relationship to the concept of wildness, he approaches the ambiguous "love of the wild" Thoreau expresses in *Walden* as "a reminder of all that gets skewed, distorted, or just left out when we view the nineteenth century too much through" our own modern eyes.[25] In a sensitive reading of the restrictions the naturalist placed on himself at Walden Pond, Coviello reminds us not to too quickly dismiss them as mere "post-Protestant asceticism."[26] We might read them, rather, as "an effort to amplify and sensitize the body's receptivity, to shake loose the carnal self from its overcoding."[27] Likewise, the approach this study takes to antebellum ideas about the human body is not only to unearth their ideological force but also to take seriously their claims.

For example, despite what often amounted to male dominance of reformist discourse, women writers found ways to apply the concept of the moldable human body toward ends that we would today call feminist. In Louisa May Alcott's 1875 novel *Eight Cousins, or The Aunt-Hill*, sickly orphan Rose Campbell falls under the care of her physician uncle, Alec. When Rose's aunt

Clara purchases her two corsets—she's "growing stout," Clara worries—Alec threatens to set them on fire.²⁸ Echoing the claims of dress reformers that corseting damages women's health, he warns that putting girls in corsets stunts their lungs and weakens their spines. To shape their malleable bodies in this unnatural way risks their health: "Nature knows how to mould a woman better than any corset-maker, and I won't have her interfered with."²⁹ Thereafter, he gives Rose lectures on physiology in which she learns "how to manage her nerves so that they won't be a curse to her, as many a woman's become through ignorance or want of thought. To make a mystery or terror of these things is a mistake," Alec cautions, "and I mean Rose shall understand and respect her body so well that she won't dare to trifle with it as most women do."³⁰ Although Alec's attitude toward women who "trifle" with their bodies is paternal and condescending, he champions the idea that a woman's body should not be "a mystery or terror" to her; she should know its parts and processes so that she may care for them. His goal is to prepare Rose to manage her body rather than allow it to be deformed by fashion. In Alcott's narrative, this sort of bodily self-management is not so much the sinister manufacturing of a governed subject but rather a way for women, routinely denied access to anatomical and physiological knowledge, to understand their bodies.

Race, Gender, and Health Reform

I do not wish to minimize the fact that with few exceptions, antebellum health reform movements were typically white, male, middle-class enterprises that served white, male, middle-class priorities; the demographics of the authors this book studies reflect that. Indeed, racism was woven into antebellum theories of the nervous system itself. Kyla Schuller offers a compelling reminder of the racist assumptions of early nineteenth-century theories of nervous impressibility, which conceptualized only "white bodies, and the wealthier classes of African Americans, Latinx, and Native Americans, in resistant discourse," as having the sort of impressibility that required them to develop techniques to "discipline their sensory susceptibility."³¹ Schuller contends that one of the functions of antebellum aesthetic sentimentalism was to "intercede in the impressibility of the civilized body by cultivating the ability to respond to sensory stimulations on the basis of emotional reflection, rather than instinctive reflex"; of course, this implied that purportedly uncivilized bodies—and therefore "uncivilized" persons—operated by reflex rather than reflection.³² Invoking Victoria Pitts-Taylor's argument that "'plasticity has been envisioned and enacted through the modification and preemptive governance of individuals and groups'" since its "'earliest modern elaboration,'" Schuller contends that the concept of "agential matter is a central achievement of biopower's racializing effects": "Porosity and vitality are biopolitical tactics of racialization," she argues, "and demand interrogation as such, rather than masquerading as neutral qualities of life that are discovered by science and exist before the political."[33] I agree that concepts of plasticity, including those antebellum concepts this book studies, are products of culture rather than bare facts of life. But we will see that part of the work of literature itself, by which I mean literature's own sculpting of diverse bodies of knowledge, is to call attention to the inequalities that structure many conceptions of the malleable body.

For instance, Alcott's 1873 short story "Transcendental Wild Oats"—a satirical portrait of Fruitlands, the disastrous experiment in communal living her father, Amos Bronson Alcott, undertook in 1843 with the help of journalist Charles Lane—details how the hard work of accommodating the commune's abstentious diet fell to women. The September 2, 1843, issue of the *New York Weekly Tribune* published a letter from Lane describing their "pure and bloodless" diet, which included no animal products: they ate neither "flesh, butter, cheese, eggs nor milk."[34] Dietary reformers such as Sylvester Graham viewed the consumption of animal products as dangerously overstimulating to both stomach and brain, but they rarely considered how to serve palatable food within their strictures. Alcott's communitarians, practicing a principled locavorism, also declined "tea, coffee, molasses, [and] rice," as they were "beyond the bounds" of the "indigenous productions" of Massachusetts.[35] Alcott's short story points up how Sister Hope—a stand-in for her mother, Abby May Alcott—must make do cooking with only "maple sugar, dried peas and beans, barley and hominy, meal of all sorts, potatoes, and dried fruit."[36] "No teapot profaned that sacred stove," Alcott sardonically intones, "no gory steak cried aloud for vengeance from her chaste gridiron; and only a brave woman's taste, time, and temper were sacrificed on that domestic altar."[37] Alcott's narrative investigates the ways that reformers' attempts to revise the American diet required laborious efforts on the women whose kitchens they sought to govern. That Lane hoped that Fruitlands would see "the bringing together of the two sexes in a new relation" only serves to sharpen Alcott's acid depiction of her mother's labor.[38]

Although African Americans were among the groups of Americans most identified with bodies, or *as* bodies and not persons, they were largely excluded from the projects of self-culture that occupied white men such as

Thoreau and Whitman, and indeed, as Tompkins has amply demonstrated and as chapter 2 of this book will explore in detail, the work of health reform reified distinctions such as orderly–disorderly, healthy–unhealthy, and composed–unruly that were always racialized.[39] Yet recent scholarship explores the ways that antebellum black intellectuals incorporated popular scientific and medical concepts into their thought. Andrea Stone writes that in their appeals to black Americans to immigrate to Canada, Mary Ann Shadd and Martin Delany emphasize that political freedom in Canada would refresh and revivify immigrants' bodies; thus, their proposals, she argues, give shape to a "black sense of self at a time when legal, medical, governmental, and economic institutions functioned, at times in conjunction, to divide and subjugate it."[40] In doing so, Stone writes, Shadd and Delany "underscore the health of the black body that is at once physical, intellectual, emotional, and moral."[41] And Britt Rusert's landmark work on what she calls "fugitive science" in early African American culture calls to attention the work of intellectuals who are, as she notes, relatively unknown in literary studies, including Robert Benjamin Lewis, Hosea Easton, James W. C. Pennington, and the educator and abolitionist Sarah Mapps Douglass, whose lectures on physiology and bodily self-care "doubled," in Rusert's words, "as powerfully embodied performances of black women's humanity and intelligence" for her African American audiences.[42] Rusert's work also illustrates the difficulty of finding archival evidence of African American writers' engagement with disciplines such as phrenology; in her chapter on the subject, she uses a methodology that takes "a necessarily creative approach to the archive" by combining analysis of "forms of performance that have left printed traces" with "more speculative readings" of those aspects of performance that leave no record behind.[43]

Despite such modes of reading, the medical training of such writers as Delany and William Wells Brown, and Brown's and Harriet Jacobs's encounters with Thomsonian medicine, antebellum African American writers of slave narratives, poetry, and fiction did not have the same profound investment in health reform discourses as did the white, middle-class authors at whom those discourses are directed, even taking into consideration such forms of print as pamphlets, magazines, and newspapers.[44] This might be due to abolition, not personal or national renewal, being the overwhelming social reform effort championed by African American writers during the antebellum period. And one might speculate that those same writers did not deeply engage with health reform discourses because of their tendency to locate concepts such as health and well-being within ideologies of white racial purity. I can envision a fascinating project on notions of bodily change in nineteenth-century African American literature that might examine narratives of fugitives from slavery "passing" as different genders and races; tales of transformation, such as those published by Charles Chesnutt after the Civil War; and the nascent Afrofuturism of Delany and Pauline Hopkins. But such a project would trace different intellectual and cultural genealogies (conjure, West African folktales, varieties of colorism and racialization) than the ones I highlight here, conceptually founded on Western physiology and disseminated in white, northeastern spaces.

Reforming the Bioplastic Body

The Perfecting of Nature argues that antebellum American writers marshaled concepts of the changeable body to imagine into being new ways of thinking about the potential of the embodied self. In this book, I recover the historical interplay between such seemingly disparate textual genres as novels, poems, exercise manuals, cookbooks, phrenology pamphlets, medical texts, and sermons. In doing so, I read literary texts as doing what literary critic Jane Tompkins calls "cultural work," or as "articulating and proposing solutions for the problems that shape a particular historical moment" and as "providing men and women with a means of ordering the world they inhabited."[45] Literature does not merely reflect the world but acts on it by offering readers ways to think through and be affected by new ways of understanding themselves. In turn, I read scientific and medical texts through literary modes of analysis, such as close reading and interpretation, particularly when seemingly stable ideas such as "health" change as they pass through different disciplinary regimes or as they overlap with other concepts. I am not interested in the question of whether the efforts of antebellum health reform were successful, be it by the standards of the past or those of the present day, nor am I interested in positioning literary authors as partisans of a given set of positions about the human body. I rather wish to recover how the efforts of reformers and writers alike created and moved within the epistemological conditions necessary for Americans to understand themselves as plastic beings.

The book proceeds chronologically, beginning with debates about bioplasticity and reform within transcendentalism and ending with the revolution in biology precipitated by the work of Charles Darwin. I frame the study with two chapters on heredity, questions of which were foundational to debates about the body's ability to change: How are characteristics transmitted from parent to child? How malleable are those characteristics? Does the reform of the body take place over lifetimes or over generations? The book's middle chapters explore literary depictions of dietary management and physical training, practices that were crucial to efforts to manage the flux of bioplasticity. The story that emerges offers an alternative reading of nineteenth-century embodiment that foregrounds how literature made possible ways of understanding the body that were, however paradoxically, both more constrained and more free.

American transcendentalism, the United States' first coherent intellectual movement, inspired countless efforts to reform humankind from the 1830s through the 1850s. Chapter 1, "Transcendental Self-Culture and the Horizons of Bioplasticity," argues that transcendentalists' well-documented differences regarding whether social reform is best reached individually or communally rest partly on oppositional ideas about individuals' ability to guide their physiological processes. The chapter follows Channing's concept of self-culture through two decades of debate among Ralph Waldo Emerson, Margaret Fuller, Henry David Thoreau, and Nathaniel Hawthorne about whether reform occurs at the small scale of the individual body, as illustrated in Thoreau's attempts to master his "slimy, beastly life" through diet, or at the large scale of wholesale social change, as argued by thinkers such as Orestes Brownson. This analysis culminates in a reading of Nathaniel Hawthorne's *The House of the Seven Gables* (1851) that argues that the novel positions reform as occurring over centuries, through the biological mechanisms of hereditary inheritance, rather than quickly and through the refinement of individual bodies. By foregrounding this debate, the chapter emphasizes what was for the transcendentalists the mutual unsettledness of both the human body and the project of reform.

The same year Hawthorne published *The House of the Seven Gables*, his friend Herman Melville published his masterwork *Moby-Dick*, which likewise probes emerging conceptions of the human body. The novel especially engages questions raised by dietary reform, proponents of which conceptualized the brain as susceptible to gastrointestinal disorders, necessitating regimes of dietary management for both protection (from the maddening effects of spices, alcohol, and sugar) and improvement (toward vitality and mental health). Chapter 2, "Governance, Race, and Alimentary Selfhood in Melville," argues that Melville explores the philosophical, theological, and racial implications of the alimentary selfhood envisioned by dietary reformers. The chapter begins by addressing a question posed by Ishmael early in *Moby-Dick*: "I wonder now if this here [chowder] has any effect on the head?"

The question, the chapter argues, points to Melville's engagement with contemporary dietary reformers' efforts to convince individuals to govern themselves by governing their diets. *Moby-Dick* makes visible how these efforts made individuals' choices about how and what they consumed a technology for sculpting the alimentary self. At the same time, the novel centers the absurdity of reformers' ascribing different digestive capacities to different racial groups by depicting both white and nonwhite characters eating in ways characterized in the works of Graham and others as "savage." The novel's depictions of ingestion, digestion, and excretion ultimately explore both the possibilities and the perils of the governed stomach.

The book's second half concerns writers who are altogether more optimistic than Hawthorne and Melville about the reform of the American body. Chapter 3, "Sculpting the Body Electric: Exercise and Self-Fashioning in Walt Whitman," reassesses *Leaves of Grass* in light of Whitman's recently rediscovered exercise and lifestyle series, "Manly Health and Training" (1858). Scholars tend to celebrate Whitman's poetry for its energetic, unruly, and even undisciplined form and scope; it is typical to view his breaking of poetic norms as an act of resistance against ossified norms and institutions. And his poem's joyful, democratic cataloging of bodies and body parts seems to cherish bodies for what they are rather than what they might be. But revisions made to *Leaves of Grass* between the 1856 and the 1860 editions, the period during which he wrote "Manly Health and Training," demonstrate the poet's increasing interest in the trained body. A reading of "A Hand-Mirror," a poem new to the 1860 edition that urges the reader to carefully attend to his body's health, grounds my argument that Whitman's interest in exercise and other forms of bodily intervention continually surface in his poetry from 1860 onward. Exercise disciplines the plastic body to achieve health and longevity; formal techniques that produce poetic repetition and organization play an analogous role in sculpting the contours of Whitman's unruly poetry. If "only health puts you in rapport with the universe," as Whitman writes in *Leaves of Grass*, then part of what lends the poem its enduring vitality is its author's repeated efforts to shape its form.

The book concludes with a return to heredity. Chapter 4, "Tricks of the Blood: Heredity and Repair in Oliver Wendell Holmes Sr.," argues that Holmes's literary efforts in the 1860s were devoted to exploring how individuals' hereditary physical makeup imposes limits to their self-determination. That Holmes, the first American writer to mention Darwin, emphasizes heredity as a central aspect of one's self at first appears to affirm Hawthorne's sense of the tenacity of inherited traits. But Holmes's novels *Elsie Venner*

(1861) and *The Guardian Angel* (1867) depict negative or destructive inherited characteristics as amenable to change through both physiological and social interventions. Holmes's novels ultimately figure the potential of such interventions to render supposedly fixed natural characteristics pliable. The book's conclusion turns to the present day to consider how literature might help us reflect on what Rose and Abi-Rached call "neurological selfhood": a "neurological dimension to our self-understanding" engendered by neuroscientific ideas that emphasize the brain's plasticity.[46]

CHAPTER ONE

Transcendental Self-Culture and the Horizons of Bioplasticity

> A good deal of our politics is physiological.
> —RALPH WALDO EMERSON, "Fate"

What would it mean if much of our politics were "physiological," as Emerson asserts in "Fate," the first piece in *The Conduct of Life* (1860)? In the essay, he uses the question to draw distinctions between English and American forms of progressivism: in England, the rich man who works for "progress" during his "years of health" will often become a conservative "as soon as he begins to die," but the "strong natures" of the United States citizenry yields "inevitable patriots" with the physical vigor necessary to pursue the nation's future. In this way, Emerson connects the progress of nations to the vitality of bodies. In this chapter, I argue that the philosopher's transcendentalist contemporaries, including Margaret Fuller, Henry David Thoreau, and Nathaniel Hawthorne, similarly engage physiology's relationship to politics, specifically in the form of debates about the ability of the body to change in ways that would enable a more just world. The question they addressed, put simply: Can William Ellery Channing's emphasis on self-searching, self-forming, and being responsible for pursuing "the unfolding and perfecting" of one's "nature" create social reform?[1] And if so, to what extent, by what means, and how quickly?

Some transcendentalists felt that the millennium of physical and national renewal was just over the next hill. Our ability to manage our somatic capacities, writes Amos Bronson Alcott in his 1836 treatise on education, *The Doctrine and Discipline of Human Culture*, is key to "the mission of this Age . . . to reproduce Perfect Men."[2] It will, he hopefully asserts, "mould anew our Institutions, our Manners, our Men. It is to restore Nature to its rightful use; purify Life; hallow the functions of the Human Body, and regenerate Philosophy, Literature, Art, Society" altogether.[3] Like Channing, Alcott locates one's knowledge of and cultivation of one's self, the formation of "Perfect Men," as the foundation of reform. In a section of the book titled "Self-Apprehension," he emphasizes scrutiny of the body: "Man's mission is to subdue Nature; to hold dominion over his own Body; and use both these, and the ministries of Life, for the growth, renewal, and perfection of his Being. . . . But before he shall attain this mastery he must apprehend himself. In his Nature is wrapt up the problem of all Power reduced to a simple unity."[4] Understanding and mastering one's body, the "Alphabet of all else," renders the world knowable and amenable to improvement.[5] Similar formulations percolate throughout transcendentalist writing, whether in Emerson's insistence that politics is physiological or Thoreau's that a human is "but a mass of thawing clay."[6] For these thinkers, reform is a project of self-culture grounded in bioplasticity, the ability of the body to change. As understood by advocates of Channing's project of self-culture, the self-searching and self-forming powers he describes enables an understanding of the human body as knowable, plastic, and open to influence from the self and the world. Fuller and Thoreau share this understanding, and in this chapter I read Fuller's *Woman in the Nineteenth Century* (1845) and Thoreau's *Walden* (1854) as epitomizing the transcendentalist tendency to look to bioplasticity as the mechanism of social reform.

Yet this impulse was not shared by all transcendentalist writers; to conclude the chapter, I read Nathaniel Hawthorne's novel *The House of the Seven Gables* (1851) as questioning attempts to reform the human body that do not take the conservative force of heredity into account. In the face of inherited characteristics, passed down through generations and centuries, can bodies change as rapidly and as fully as Fuller and Thoreau suggest? Is reform really possible within one lifetime? As documented in his miserable experiences at the Fourierist commune Brook Farm, his thinly veiled lampooning of those experiences in his novel *The Blithedale Romance* (1852), and his ambivalence about abolition, Hawthorne was skeptical about contemporary reformist efforts and practices.[7] My reading of *The House of the Seven Gables* demonstrates his similar skepticism toward claims about the reformist force of bioplasticity by attending to the novel's depictions of generational and individual change. Taken together, the works of transcendentalist writers propose a question that penetrates, as we will see in chapter 4, at least to the revolution in biology wrought by Charles Darwin: If human nature is perfectible, is it refined within the course of a single lifetime or over generations?

The Mission of This Age

With a few notable exceptions, scholars have tended to neglect the transcendentalists' ideas about the human body.[8] Some of this neglect might be a result of Emerson's own habit of framing the physical world, especially the human body, not as interesting in its own right—as flesh and bone—but as a metaphor for matters of spirit. When he asks "What is a farm but a mute gospel?" in *Nature* (1836), he emphasizes the spiritual truths for which the farm is emblematic rather than the farm itself, despite his sincere interest in the natural sciences. But a farm is many things other than a gospel: an ecosystem, a node in market networks, a producer of food, a home. Recently, a renewed attention to questions of bodies and embodiment among scholars of nineteenth-century American literature has begun to recover how transcendentalists such as Margaret Fuller and Henry David Thoreau situate human physiology in their thought. Responding to this recovery, I argue that both Fuller and Thoreau find in the human body's bioplasticity the basis for an embodied mode of reform. Although the two thinkers are distinctly Emersonian in that they pursue individual-scale reform projects, they move past Emerson's habitual indifference to blood, muscle, and viscera to consider the possibilities afforded by embodiment. To be sure, Fuller and Thoreau pursue different ends: she seeks new ways of thinking through sex and gender, and he hopes to discipline his body into a more pure way of living. Yet understood together, they affirm the role of bodily cultivation in creating a better world.

Recent studies by C. Michael Hurst and Rachel A. Blumenthal make compelling arguments for the importance of the body to Fuller's thought. Hurst argues that her works "include theories of the body as a site of knowledge that begin to undo the mind/body split that functions so powerfully as a mode of women's oppression."[9] Blumenthal claims that "Fuller's ambivalence" toward contemporary medicine "leaves room for alternative models of medicine that treat symptoms rather than diseases and that embrace the positive, rather than negative, effects of a 'sick' condition."[10] Fuller's lifelong susceptibility to nervous diseases, Blumenthal claims, were for her a vital source of intellectual energy rather than a burden. These arguments do much to recover the somatic context of Fuller's thought, but how she thinks through the body's capacity for change remains unexplored. Attending to her ideas about the body and its capacity to fluidly change yields insights into how human physiology itself refuses attempts to categorize it into a given gender: in Fuller's formulation of embodiment, the human body's vital processes, far from determining gender, confound it.

In *Woman in the Nineteenth Century*, a revision of Fuller's 1843 essay "The Great Lawsuit. Man versus Men. Woman versus Women," she describes gender as "the great radical dualism." Far from being mutually exclusive, she writes, male and female "are perpetually passing into one another. Fluid hardens to solid, solid rushes to fluid. There is no wholly masculine man, no purely feminine woman."[11] As Hurst and others argue, Fuller here expresses a "fully androgynous" theory of gender that "establishes a continuum of behavior that contains all possible intermixtures of the masculine and the feminine, making every combination available to both sexes."[12] Surprisingly, what Fuller says about physiological basis of those "intermixtures" has remained unnoticed:

> History jeers at the attempts of physiologists to bind great original laws by the forms which flow from them. They make a rule; they say from observation what can and cannot be. In vain! Nature provides exceptions to every rule. She sends women to battle, and sets Hercules spinning; she enables women to bear immense burdens, cold, and frost; she enables the man, who feels maternal love, to nourish his infant like a mother. Of late she plays still gayer pranks. Not only she deprives organizations, but organs, of a necessary end. She enables people to read with the top of the head, and see with the pit of the stomach. Presently she will make a female Newton, and a male Syren. Man partakes of the feminine in the Apollo, Woman of the masculine as Minerva.[13]

Physiologists' empirical observations of natural phenomena, Fuller says, leaves them unable to understand that "great original laws" cannot be known solely by "the forms which flow through them." Knowing a law by its physical expression as a form, she says, does not reveal everything about it; what physiologists do not see are the natural "exceptions" that baffle their efforts to categorize vital functions. Of such exceptions, she is most concerned with those that concern sex and gender. Women can bear "immense" environmental pressures; men, she hints, might breastfeed or "nourish" their children just as their mothers can. She maintains male and female as categories, but she interweaves them so that one sex "partakes" of the other.

Fuller's ideas about "exceptions to every rule" of physiology ground her theory of gender. Bodies or "forms," she says, do not have "necessary end[s]" that constrict what they can or cannot do. They are plastic, not rigid, and they are not made for any specific purpose. When she writes that "organizations"—a word typically used in antebellum America to describe either nervous systems or individual organisms—have no necessary end, she says nothing with which a forward-thinking nerve physiologist would disagree. As Justine Murison has argued, antebellum Americans considered their nervous systems to be utterly changeable, even unruly parts of their bodies.[14] But Fuller's assertion that organs, hunks of meat that seemingly serve only a certain number of functions, themselves have no set purpose signifies her departure from mainstream physiological theory. Her contemporaries would have recognized the examples she gives of this theory (reading a book set atop one's head or seeing with one's stomach) as common mesmeric feats. British physiologist Herbert Mayo, in his 1849 *Letters on the Truths Contained in Popular Superstitions*, discusses mesmerized subjects as possessing "transposed vision," or the ability to, for example, see objects held behind their heads or read books nestled into their chests.[15] At the same time, Fuller does not import mesmerism wholesale into her theories about the human body; as Blumenthal writes, Fuller looked to mesmerism to articulate a distinct "materialist feminist psychology" that "excises" the male mesmeric "physician-operator," leaving only the female subject sensitized to mesmerism's occult energies.[16] "In excising the (male) magnetizer and refusing the (masculine) cure," Blumenthal argues, "Fuller asserts irreducible feminine difference (nervous sensibility) as the material condition of intellectual activity."[17] To this assertion I add that Fuller's revised mesmeric theory frames fluidity as a natural yet overlooked facet of embodiment. Yet that fluidity demands care; Fuller's vision of bioplasticity requires the sorts of attentive self-cultivation Channing advocates in "Self-Culture." "Only in a strong and clean body," she writes, "can the soul do its message fitly."[18] To achieve that strength and cleanliness, she advocates—in chorus with a host of health reformers, including Amos Bronson Alcott—cold-water bathing, simple dress, and a plain diet.[19]

The same year Fuller published *Woman in the Nineteenth Century*, Henry David Thoreau settled at Walden Pond to pursue similar ascetic practices "alone, in the woods, a mile from any neighbor."[20] Famously, he hoped "to live deliberately" there; any student reading *Walden* in a survey course learns what the deliberate life is (slow, introspective, and contemplative), but what should we be deliberate *about*?[21] I contend that Thoreau's stay at Walden Pond was, among other things, both a study of the self's astonishing capacity for change and an exercise in self-formation. For Thoreau, living deliberately means being deliberate about how one pursues the mundane functions of life. When he praises "the Hindoo lawgiver" for teaching "how to eat, drink, cohabit, void excrement and urine, and the like," he brings into focus how processes fundamental to daily living—ingestion and evacuation—can be performed in a deliberate, mindful, or even reverential manner.[22] He identifies the keeping of such discipline as "elevating the mean" functions of the human body, giving a sacred cast to "the necessary functions of human nature."[23] No function of the body is too "mean" to escape attention and care in Thoreau's conception of Hinduism; rather, they are "regulated by law" and managed by the individual precisely because they are so important.[24] Governing the body is for Thoreau a sort of sacrament—an affirmation of the human body's divine cast. He continues: "Every man is the builder of a temple, called his body, to the god he worships, after a style purely his own, nor can he get off by hammering marble instead. We are all sculptors and painters, and our material is our own flesh and blood and bones."[25] Thoreau here echoes 1 Corinthians 6:19: "What? know ye not that your body is the temple of the Holy Ghost *which is* in you, which ye have of God, and ye are not your own?" But when he writes that every man builds a "temple" in honor of "the god he worships," Thoreau does not necessarily mean the Christian God. A man's body, Thoreau writes, is not a temple "of" God but rather a temple "to" whatever god he worships. Corinthians says that one's body is not one's own, but that runs counter to Thoreau's sense that one commands radical agency over one's body, which one builds in "a style purely his own."[26] Doing so means understanding oneself as a sculptor whose own body is the clay he shapes.

Pushing against critics such as Michael Gilmore and Sacvan Bercovitch, who view Thoreau's exercises in self-discipline as disconnected from broader reform projects, Michelle C. Neely argues that those exercises disclose "political possibilities" informed by "contemporary antebellum debates about consumption of food and other commodities."[27] Attending especially to the theories of dietary reformer Sylvester Graham, Neely identifies a connection between the body of the individual and that of the republic. Historicizing the deliberate manner with which Thoreau approaches consumption, she argues, reveals in *Walden* "a civic project at the heart of the book that depends on Thoreau's vegetarianism."[28] The naturalist's engagement with Graham, she writes, "played a complicated role in consequential debates over capitalism, citizenship, freedom, and the body taking place in the turbulent antebellum United States."[29] His attempts to maintain a vegetarian diet and his ongoing conversations with antebellum dietary reform animates, she writes, both his "decrying his neighbors' and contemporaries' lack of market independence" and his condemnation of ungoverned appetite.[30] She concludes that the "somatic management techniques" Thoreau derives from Grahamian dietetics enable his hope "to revitalize American citizenship."[31] By connecting Thoreau's reform project to the material physiology of the human body, Neely recovers the somatic context of transcendentalist reform. But on the subject of the body, *Walden* draws from still deeper wells: its regenerative vision owes as much to Romantic theories of biological form as it does to Grahamian physiology. These ways of understanding the body, its workings, and its place in the world enable Thoreau to understand his individual actions as reverberating at national and even planetary scales.

A journal entry written sometime after July 16, 1845, just days after Thoreau first settled at Walden Pond, hints at how one person's actions might work in larger contexts. Even an apple, he muses, might serve as an avenue to a bettered cosmos:

> I have carried an apple in my pocket to-night—a sopsivine they call it—till, now that I take my handkerchief out, it has got so fine a fragrance that it really seems like a friendly trick of some pleasant dæmon to entertain me with. It is redolent of sweet-scented orchards, of innocent, teeming harvests. I realize the existence of a goddess Pomona, and that the gods have really intended that men should feed divinely, like themselves, on their own nectar and ambrosia. They have so painted this fruit, and freighted it with such a fragrance, that it satisfies much more than an animal appetite. Grapes, peaches, berries, nuts, etc., are likewise provided for those who will sit at their sideboard. I have felt, when partaking of this inspiring diet, that my appetite was an indifferent consideration; that eating became a sacrament, a method of communion, an ecstatic exercise, a mingling of bloods, and [a] sitting at the communion table of the world; and so have not only quenched my thirst at the spring, but the health of the universe.[32]

The scent of an apple leads Thoreau to draw connections between himself and divinity: its fragrance "seems like a friendly trick of some pleasant dæmon," and he comes to feel "that men should feed divinely" on "nectar and ambrosia." He thinks of a divine diet as "inspiring" in ways that render appetite "an indifferent consideration." Far more than a way to fuel his body, "eating" itself is "a sacrament, a method of communion" that culminates in a vital link between body and world: he simultaneously satisfies his "thirst and the spring" and sees to "the health of the universe." The rest of the entry affirms how if eating "were rightly conducted, its aspects and effects would be wholly changed, and we should receive our daily life and health, Antaeus-like, with an ecstatic delight, and, with upright front, an innocent and graceful behavior, take our strength from day to day."[33] Less than a month into his life at Walden Pond, Thoreau begins to draw the connections between individual and cosmic cultivation that permeate *Walden*.

Key to Thoreau's understanding of the links between the individual and the world is gnomicism, the element of Coleridgean organicism that, as Laura Dassow Walls notes in her study of Emerson's intellectual commitments, posits "an exemplary object that by embodying its own constructive law was utterly self-evident."[34] Gnomicism has three facets: first, "'gnomic' sayings" are "compact to the point of self-evidence"; second, "gnomic figures" grow proportionally, like a nautilus shell; and third, "they are 'nomian' in that they give the law, or 'nomos,' to themselves; hence their self-similarity."[35] Walls argues that gnomicism enables Emerson to think about the correspondence of matter and spirit because a gnomic object, in compacting the whole within the part, "literally embodies in matter the divine idea or formula of its genesis, revealing nothing less than the harmonic proportions that create and govern the universe."[36]

Near the end of "Spring," *Walden*'s penultimate chapter, Thoreau thinks through the shared gnomic structures of both organic and inorganic matter and concludes that the plasticity of the human body reveals the plasticity of the planet itself. Taking a walk, he observes a steep bank left by "a deep cut on the railroad through which I passed" on the way to Concord.[37] He watches as the ground sliced for the railroad tracks—"sand of every degree of fineness . . . commonly mixed with a little clay"—melts and flows down "like lava."[38] The "innumerable streams" of combined water, sand, and clay "overlap and interlace one with another, exhibiting a sort of hybrid product, which obeys half way the law of currents, and half way that of vegetation."[39] "As it flows," he writes, it looks less like water or earth and more like plants or animals: "it takes the forms of sappy leaves or vines, making heaps of pulpy sprays a foot or more in depth, and resembling, as you look down on them, the laciniated, lobed, and imbricated thalluses of some lichens; or you are reminded of coral, of leopard's paws or birds' feet, of brains or lungs or bowels, and excrements of all kinds."[40] The progression of the sentence from earth and water to vines, lichens, feet, organs, and excrement illustrates the shared gnomic structure of diverse natural forms: even something as structurally complex as the brain shares the same elemental form as a lichen. That form even bridges the divide between animate and inanimate matter: the laws of creation impress the same stamp on the whole of the universe.

This profusion of natural forms leads Thoreau to reflect on the shared vitality of the earth and its inhabitants: "I feel as if I were nearer to the vitals of the globe, for this sandy overflow is something such a foliaceous mass as the vitals of the animal body"; animal viscera, he implies, are but gnomic iterations of the very guts of the planet.[41] And those guts themselves echo the forms of leaves. "*Internally*, whether in the globe or animal body," he writes, the leaf form "is a moist thick *lobe*, a word especially applicable to the liver and lungs and the *leaves* of fat . . . ; *externally* a dry thin *leaf*."[42] Not only bodily organs but also "feathers and wings" are foliate: they are "still drier and thinner leaves."[43] To understand the leaf structure is to understand the planet, for "rivers are still vaster leaves whose pulp is intervening earth, and towns and cities are the ova of insects in their axils."[44] At one scale, a stick insect lays its eggs in a leaf axil, setting in motion yet another iteration of the life cycle; at another, a town founded in the crook of a river hums with vibrant activity. For Thoreau, the relationship between an insect egg and a town is not merely analogous. Rather, the two are distinct expressions of the same biological law.

As Thoreau's meditation on structure and form proceeds, it ventures into the human body. Branching streams of flowing sand show "how blood-vessels are formed," and the tips of those streams take the form of "a drop-like point, like the ball of the finger, feeling its way slowly and blindly downward."[45] He asks:

> What is man but a mass of thawing clay? The ball of the human finger is but a drop congealed. The fingers and toes flow to their extent from the thawing mass of the body. Who knows what the human body would expand and flow out to under a more genial heaven? Is not the hand a spreading *palm* leaf with its lobes and veins? The ear may be regarded, fancifully, as a lichen, *Umbilicaria*, on the side of the head, with its lobe or drop. The lip—*labium*, from *labor* (?)—laps or lapses from the sides of the cavernous mouth. The nose is a manifest congealed drop or stalactite. The chin is a still larger drop, the confluent dripping of the face. The cheeks are a slide from the brows into the valley of the face, opposed and diffused by the cheek bones. Each rounded lobe of the vegetable leaf, too, is a thick and now loitering drop, larger or smaller; the lobes are the fingers of the leaf; and as many lobes as it has, in so many directions it tends to flow, and more heat or other genial influences would have caused it to flow yet farther.[46]

For Thoreau, the human form—fingers, toes, lips, ears—drips, congeals, and solidifies like clay. Like clay, it must assume the forms that the laws of nature make it possible to assume. But the question "Who knows what the human body would expand and flow out to under a more genial heaven?" shifts the emphasis from the dominance of natural law to the claylike plasticity of the human body. Bodies might find different forms, different capacities, in a better world. What power we have to shape our bodies lies in creating the sorts of environments—physical and moral—that might shape our clay for the better.

The earth, Thoreau concludes, is "stratum upon stratum" of "living poetry," a font of vital power "compared with whose great central life all animal and vegetable life is merely parasitic."[47] The earth is not the scene of life, an inert mass on which life happens, but rather life itself. Ultimately, "not only it, but the institutions upon it, are plastic like clay in the hands of the potter."[48] Even though the earth is the source of all life, it is moldable. The melting bank teaches Thoreau that everything, even the planet itself, has the capacity for change. His articulation of the earth and "the institutions upon it" as "plastic like play in the hands of the potter" emphasizes his view that change might have elements of intention, craft, and artistry. We can shape, in other words, the sort of world we live in, and not always for the better: the gouged earth and mechanical shrieks that followed the railroad's path through Concord must have made humans' ability to alter the world seem a stark fact.

Thoreau's reminder that both the planet and "the institutions upon it" are plastic translates his characteristically sharp observations of thawing clay into a more directly political language. Elsewhere in *Walden*, when he mentions institutions, he uses the word to describe the post office, the railroad, and the powers of the state. These institutions have in common the power to shape the minds and habits of the people who partake of them. "Have not men improved somewhat in punctuality since the railroad was invented?" he asks. "Do they not talk and think faster in the depot than they did in the stage-office?"[49] The railroad's unprecedented convenience and predictability imprint themselves on the plastic minds of the people, Thoreau suggests, which makes everyone a little bit more like trains themselves. He notes how "the foolishness of that institution," the Concord prison, lies within its treating him "as if I were mere flesh and blood and bones, to be locked up."[50] The state, he implies, not only wishes to imprison his body but to teach him that he is just a body; it does not confront "a man's sense, intellectual or moral, but only his body, his senses," because it lacks "superior wit or honesty."[51] What it has instead is "superior physical strength."[52] For Thoreau, the state is an institution that seeks to form humanity into purely physical forms that it can control through brute force. Because our institutions have such power to shape us, as "Spring" concludes, we ought not forget that we can shape them.

In *Walden*, the work of reform involves moving within an ecology that is at the same time physical, moral, and spiritual. Because every action ripples throughout the cosmos, each individual carries within him- or herself both the ability and the responsibility to lead a better, purer, more simple life and, in so doing, remake the world. At the conclusion of the chapter "Higher Laws," Thoreau imagines a farmer, resting at the end of his day of labor, who suddenly hears a voice: "Why do you stay here and live this mean moiling life, when a glorious existence is possible for you? Those same stars twinkle over other fields than these."[53] "But how to come out of this condition," the farmer wonders, "and actually migrate thither? All that he could think of was to practise some new austerity, to let his mind descend into his body and redeem it, and treat himself with ever increasing respect."[54] Asceticism is here not a refusal of the body but rather the engine of its redemption.

The Limits of Self-Culture

Thoreau contrasts his individualized, somatic approach to social reform with that of single-issue-oriented philanthropists at several points in *Walden*. A philanthropist, he writes, "too often surrounds mankind with the remembrance of his own castoff griefs as an atmosphere, and calls it sympathy. We should impart our courage, and not our despair, our health and ease, and not our disease, and take care that this does not spread by contagion."[55] Philanthropy is a projection of one's own "castoff griefs," one's own troubles and peccadilloes, onto everyone else.[56] Because that projection leads the philanthropist to mistake his own problems for the world's, he construes all social ills as having one cause and one solution:

> If anything ail a man, so that he does not perform his functions, if he have a pain in his bowels even—for that is the seat of sympathy—he forthwith sets about reforming—the world. Being a microcosm himself, he discovers—and it is a true discovery, and he is the man to make it—that the world has been eating green apples; to his eyes, in fact, the globe itself is a great green apple, which there is danger awful to think of that the children of men will nibble before it is ripe; and straightway his drastic philanthropy seeks out the Esquimau and the Patagonian, and embraces the populous Indian and Chinese villages; and thus, by a few years of philanthropic activity, the powers in the meanwhile using him for their own ends, no doubt, he cures himself

of his dyspepsia, the globe acquires a faint blush on one or both of its cheeks, as if it were beginning to be ripe, and life loses its crudity and is once more sweet and wholesome to live.[57]

Philanthropy, for Thoreau, is a perversion of self-culture. His approach views the care and governance of one's own body as the avenue to self-betterment; that of the philanthropist, he asserts, mistakes a person's individual bodily troubles for those of the world. He identifies the philanthropist's disordered sympathy as leaving him unable to distinguish between himself and the rest of humanity.

Yet some of Thoreau's contemporaries viewed individual self-improvement as an inadequate response to the nation's ills. Unitarian minister Orestes Brownson, as Philip Gura writes, "rejected outright" Channing's ideas about self-culture.[58] Surveying the aftermath of the Panic of 1837, he concluded that self-improvement alone "could not abolish inequality nor restore workers' rights"; instead, Gura writes, what he required was "whole-scale changes to the social structure."[59] The disagreement is one of both temporal and social scale. Does reform happen quickly and at the individual scale, or slowly and at the scale of societies? In what follows, I turn to Nathaniel Hawthorne's novel *The House of the Seven Gables* to address questions of bodily reform in terms of the large scale of human physiology: hereditary inheritance. To what extent, the novel asks, can individuals change the characteristics inherited from their ancestors?

As I discuss in greater detail in chapter 4, conceptions of hereditary inheritance were in flux during the early and middle decades of the nineteenth century; for instance, different theorists of hereditary transmission disagreed about the determinative power of inherited characteristics. Thinkers such as Jean-Baptiste Lamarck, an early theorist of evolution, conceptualized hereditary inheritance as relatively plastic and fluid. His 1809 *Philosophie Zoologique* makes the case that an organism transmits to its descendants a tendency to develop phenotypic characteristics it acquired before it reproduces. He famously explains his theory by way of the giraffe's long neck:

> It is interesting to observe the result of habit in the particular shape and size of the giraffe (*Camelo-pardalis*): this animal, the largest of the mammals, is known to live in the interior of Africa in places where the soil is nearly always arid and barren, so that it is obliged to browse on the leaves of trees and to make constant efforts to reach them. From this habit, long maintained in all its race, it has resulted that the

animal's fore-legs have become longer than its hind legs, and that its neck is lengthened to such a degree that the giraffe, without standing up on its hind legs, attains a height of six metres (nearly 20 feet).[60]

For Lamarck, a giraffe's "constant efforts" to reach high leaves forms a "habit" that elongates its neck during its lifetime. *"The frequent use of any organ,"* he explains, *"when confirmed by habit, increases the functions of that organ, leads to its development and endows it with a size and power that it does not possess in animals which exercise it less."*[61] According to this theory, giraffes developed their long necks over many generations of individual animals habitually stretching their necks, resulting in each generation having, on average, a longer neck than the last. What is reproductively transmitted from parent to child, he later explains, is a "tendency of the organs or a state of the viscera adapted" to a given environment.[62] In other words, "it is essential that circumstances should favour the development of this tendency in the new individual; for otherwise the individual would acquire another temperament, inclinations, and characteristics."[63] Because offspring only inherit a *tendency* to develop like their parents, they can only develop in like manner when their environments are the same. A giraffe would have to be born into an environment with high leaves to develop a long neck and to end its life with a neck longer than that of its parents. Otherwise, it would never experience the environmental pressures necessary for it to habitually stretch its neck, and its children's children's children might be very short giraffes indeed. The Lamarckian theory of acquired characteristics thus opens up the possibility of plasticity both within and across generations by situating (postnatal) environmental triggers rather than inherited biological structures as the foundation of hereditary inheritance.

Some theorists of heredity imagined it as something much more limiting. Dominique Auguste Lereboullet, a French physician working at what was then the cutting edge of studies of inheritance, writes in his 1834 *De l'hérédité dans les Maladies* that heredity is an "unshakable law":

> If we direct our gaze to the members of the same family we will find between the children and the parents the most obvious conformity: features of the face, of the stature, the sound of the voice, the color of the skin, the constitution, temperament, habits, character . . . , everything is similar. It is under the influence of this unshakable law, in virtue of which man gives life to beings similar to him, that one can see sometimes that vices of conformation are transmitted from

generation to generation. In such way we inherit the constitution and temperament from our parents; we inherit their physical and moral characters; we inherit their conformational vices.[64]

For Lereboullet, parents and offspring share not only "obvious" similarities, such as facial features and skin color, but also "constitution and temperament" and "physical and moral characters"; in his account, we see the explanatory reach of hereditary transmission ranging beyond physical traits into mental and moral characteristics. His framing of heredity as an "unshakable law" throws into relief his understanding of it as something that limits and confines; indeed, he emphasizes that inherited "conformational vices" ensure that our children have no choice other than to echo our flaws.

It is in light of this tension between bioplasticity and hereditary transmission that I read *The House of the Seven Gables* as an encounter between the transformative power of individual reform and the conservative force of inheritance. My contention is that the novel works out this encounter in ways that render heredity the victor; Hawthorne therefore follows Lereboullet and others in imagining the characteristics passed down from generation to generation as unamenable to attempts to change them, with the notable exception of the daguerreotypist Holgrave. My reading contextualizes the characters Hepzibah and Phoebe within contemporary reformist discourses that envisioned activity itself, whether in service of commerce or domesticity, as transformative. Such transformation never manifests: Hepzibah's efforts to make money operating a cent shop, far from making her fit for the bracing rigors of the market, leave her a sickly automaton, and Phoebe's preternaturally successful domestic efforts are revealed to be the consequence of an inherited knack for housekeeping, not of domestic reform. The failure of these characters to create change in their lives represents a larger failure on the part of self-culture to produce reform that persists across generations.

By focusing on the commercial efforts of Hepzibah and the domestic efforts of Phoebe, my reading joins a rich tradition of scholarship on women's labor in *The House of the Seven Gables* inaugurated by Gillian Brown's contention that the novel encodes, especially in the figure of Phoebe, the dislocation of women from their labor. Phoebe's seemingly effortless housework and the way it allows her aunt Hepzibah "a more secure ladyship," Brown argues, "figures the installation of the domestic ideal as a reenactment of a fantasized prior order. Not only do housekeepers appear as ladies in this romance, but housework appears as leisure."[65] Assessing what she describes as "Phoebe's magical restoration of Hepzibah," she concludes that "under the presiding spirit of domesticity even the ills of the past can be transformed."[66] Likewise, Martha Baldwin, studying Hawthorne's use of the language of ghosts and specters to describe domestic servants, argues that the novel "participates in the cultural work of domestic literature by engaging with nineteenth-century anxieties regarding the ambiguous social status of domestic servants and their employers within a democratic but slave-owning nation."[67] Ultimately, she argues, although he "exposes the oppressed ghosts of servant and slave laborers haunting American domestic spaces," Hawthorne "offers no possibility of a national exorcism."[68] Distinct from these arguments, my reading situates labor in the novel, commercial or domestic, within an antebellum reform culture that posed brisk activity as a tonic for American women enervated by modernity. I contend that the transformative power of labor quails in the face of inherited characteristics, as does, the novel implies, all efforts to effect lasting change.

Nina Baym points out that although it is unclear who, exactly, the protagonist of *The House of the Seven Gables* is, Hepzibah takes up the first four chapters of the twenty-one chapter novel.[69] Yet before the novel introduces her to readers, the author's preface delineates its "moral, — the truth, namely, that the wrong-doing of one generation lives into the successive ones, and, divesting itself of every temporary advantage, becomes a pure and uncontrollable mischief."[70] This sort of language evokes the doctrine of original sin, a subject that haunts such works as "The Birthmark" (1843) and *The Marble Faun* (1860). Yet it also echoes the scientific views of Lereboullet and like thinkers, who emphasize the ways that hereditary transmission preserves ancestors' faults. The narrator of the preface goes on to remark that "the act of the passing generation is the germ which may and must produce good or evil fruit in a far-distant time; that, together with the seed of the merely temporary crop, which mortals term expediency, they inevitably sow the acorns of a more enduring growth, which may darkly overshadow their posterity."[71] The language of agriculture — "passing generation," "fruit," "seed," "crop," "sow" — again evokes specifically biblical formulations of inheritance.[72] What Hawthorne adds is the idea that events that are "temporary" might affect the degree to which moral characteristics, "good or evil," are inherited.[73] In the first passage, "every temporary advantage" garnered by the moral goodness of this or that generation might dissolve over the centuries into an "uncontrollable mischief"; any moral "advantage" is, first and foremost, "temporary."[74] The second passage presents a different view, in which "the merely temporary crop," or "expediency," might meld with the original stock in such a way that produces "a more enduring growth," albeit one that "may darkly overshadow their posterity."[75] The "moral" of *The House of the Seven Gables* is, then, less straightforward than it at first appears. Rather than depicting a definite, predetermined lesson about hereditary inheritance, or putting a pin in a butterfly, the novel works out the question of whether "temporary" events—such as, for instance, the reformist cultivation of the self—might redirect hereditary forces.

The titular house itself compresses into one space the events of centuries— after all, it is the setting of most of the events the novel narrates, both past and present. After Colonel Pyncheon, the rich and politically connected seventeenth-century progenitor of the Pyncheon family, works to have the "obscure" Matthew Maule executed for spurious charges of witchcraft, he builds his house on the ground that had been Maule's. The novel's plot, such as it is—as Baym reminds us, "at times the book seems to lack plot altogether"—begins in the middle of the nineteenth century in the very same house, as Colonel Pyncheon's descendant Hepzibah, near destitution, opens a cent shop.[76] Far from a simple amalgam of wood and stone, the house plays witness to various "act[s] of the passing generation."[77] The ghost of Maule seems to haunt the premises: "His home would include the home of the dead and buried wizard, and would thus afford the ghost of the latter a kind of privilege to haunt its new apartments, and the chambers into which future bridegrooms were to lead their brides, and where children of the Pyncheon blood were to be born. The terror and ugliness of Maule's crime, and the wretchedness of his punishment, would darken the freshly plastered walls, and infect them early with the scent of an old and melancholy house."[78] This is to say that the house is the site of Pyncheon reproduction: it is where "future bridegrooms were to lead their brides," or where new blood might have the chance to mingle with the Pyncheon stock, and it is where "children of the Pyncheon blood" specifically "were to be born."[79] It is where Pyncheon generation—and generations—happens; because the stains of Maule's execution "infect" its very walls, members of the Pyncheon family come into the world with "the scent of an old and melancholy house" in their noses.[80] A mirror reputed to "contain within its depths all the shapes that had ever been reflected there," both "the old Colonel himself, and his many descendants, some in the garb of antique babyhood" and some in youth or middle age," collapses into one space and one moment many generations, thereby symbolizing the essential homogeneity of the Pyncheon bloodline.[81] Later, the narrator affirms that the house's materiality, its "white-oak frame, and its boards, shingles, and crumbling plaster," appear to "constitute only the least and meanest part of its reality."[82] That "so much of mankind's varied experience had passed there" bestows upon it a greater reality, for "so much had been suffered, and something, too, enjoyed, — that the very timbers were oozy, as with the moisture of a heart. It was itself like a great human heart, with a life of its own, and full of rich and sombre reminiscences."[83] Moral stain "infect[s]" the house; its timbers are "oozy," wet and slick; it seems alive.[84] Endowed "with a life of its own," the host of disease and the site of reproduction, the house is itself an organism, or part of one, perhaps more womb than "heart."[85] The question at the center of the novel is whether the house's offspring might be able to diverge not only from their inheritance of property (the house itself) but also from their inheritance of characteristics (the behaviors and attitudes characteristic of Pyncheons).

We first meet one of the house's offspring, Hepzibah, an impoverished "hereditary noble" who has sunk "below [her] order" yet was born "in Pyncheon Street, under the Pyncheon Elm, and in the Pyncheon House," as she stands at the precipice of transformation from "lady" to "woman."[86] She has converted part of her family's home to a cent shop, where she hopes to make a living selling candy, trinkets, and kitchen staples. This would appear to be an affirmation of individuals' ability to be something other than what they were born to be: Hepzibah is shaking off the weight of inherited nobility, and even the house itself has changed in the conversion. Yet the novel consistently frames Hepzibah's activity within the cent shop in the language of nervous reflex action: far from rendering her independent, financially or psychologically, keeping shop makes her a flesh-and-blood automaton. Note her behavior in the moments before she enters the shop for the first time: "After a moment's pause on the threshold, peering towards the window with her near-sighted scowl, as if frowning down some bitter enemy, she suddenly projected herself into the shop. The haste, and, as it were, the galvanic impulse of the movement, were really quite startling."[87] Hepzibah's sudden and "quite startling" lurch into her store is a "galvanic," or electric, "impulse" rather than a smooth, intentional step across the threshold. The word "galvanic" derives from the eighteenth-century Italian physician Luigi Galvani, who discovered the role of electricity in muscular contractions.[88] To demonstrate electricity's role in muscle movement, Galvani electrocuted beheaded frogs into the semblance of twitching life; Hepzibah's entry into her store, then, has more in common with the reflexive hop of an electrocuted frog than with the forceful stride of an entrepreneur.[89]

Once Hepzibah makes her way into the shop, the narrator describes her nervous system itself as besieged by the demands of activity and commerce:

as she arranges toys and treats in the window to attract young customers, she does so "nervously—in a sort of frenzy, we might almost say."[90] Gillian Brown reads Hepzibah's nervousness as a nod to national "nervousness about the risks of commerce," which she argues the novel puts to rest with its "fairy-tale ending."[91] That reading misses the historical and somatic contexts of nineteenth-century nervousness. To be "nervous" in the nineteenth-century context is not merely to be emotionally agitated, as Jane F. Thrailkill and Justine Murison, among others, have argued; rather, it is to be agitated specifically because of the overexcitement of one's nerves. Read in this light, Hepzibah's nervousness as she works in her store appears as a nervous pathology, one that manifests as "a sort of frenzy" of activity.[92] The word "frenzy" itself connotes shades of what Hawthorne's contemporaries would have called "mental derangement"; to be frenzied is not merely to be busy but rather to be crazed. The "instant of time when the patrician lady is to be transformed into the plebeian woman" is therefore also a moment of debility; the transformation is not only of social rank but of bodily health. Being a woman, rather than a lady, threatens to make Hepzibah sick.

Her nerves remain in a state of overexcitement after she opens the shop. The narrator frames the very act of unbarring the shop door in the language of nervous agitation:

> Nothing remained, except to take down the bar from the shop-door, leaving the entrance free—more than free—welcome, as if all were household friends—to every passer-by, whose eyes might be attracted by the commodities at the window. This last act Hepzibah now performed, letting the bar fall with what smote upon her excited nerves as a most astounding clatter. Then—as if the only barrier betwixt herself and the world had been thrown down, and a flood of evil consequences would come tumbling through the gap—she fled into the inner parlor, threw herself into the ancestral elbow-chair, and wept.[93]

Murison has described the ways that popular antebellum conceptions of nerve physiology allowed Americans to understand their bodies as open to and affected by cultural forces: "The senses relayed environmental information along the nerves and, in turn," she writes, "the nerves cued muscles to move the body. When in working order, the nervous system kept the mind in tune with bodily actions and reactions."[94] In Hepzibah's case, unbarring the shop door performs the same openness to the environment: the entrance is "free"—no, "more than free"—flattening distinctions between "household friends" and "every passer-by" who might wish to peek in the window.⁹⁵ The narrator describes her flight into the parlor, "excited nerves" in turmoil, as the result of her feeling that "the only barrier betwixt herself and the world had been thrown down"; when the borders of her home become permeable, so too do her own.

Hepzibah's retreat to the inner recesses of the house figures the sort of retreat a person with a nervously "open" body, as Murison puts it, might hope to make into some inner sanctum to find shelter from the penetrating forces of culture.⁹⁶ But no such sanctum exists for someone who wishes to engage the world in commerce; the tinkling of "a little bell" set above the shop's door alerts her to the arrival of a customer, and she rises out of her chair. The bell "was so contrived as to vibrate by means of a steel spring, and thus convey notice to the inner regions of the house when any customer should cross the threshold"; it is an artificial nerve, connecting and communicating the exterior to the interior.⁹⁷ And just as nerves convey the impulses that trigger muscular reflexes, the vibration of the house's artificial nerve causes Hepzibah's nervous system to resonate in "responsive and tumultuous vibration," making her the bell's "enslaved spirit."⁹⁸ Ultimately, the ringing brings upon her a "crisis," which in the middle of the nineteenth century still connoted, as the *Oxford English Dictionary* defines it, "The point in the progress of a disease when an important development or change takes place which is decisive of recovery or death." The nervous openness metaphorized in the shop's bell constitutes a turning point in Hepzibah's well-being.

Hepzibah's boarder, the reform-minded Holgrave, finds her turn to commerce an unalloyed good. When Hepzibah "piteously" informs him that opening the shop has made her a "woman" rather than a "lady," a role she considers "as past," Holgrave responds that she is "the better without it."⁹⁹ "I speak frankly," he says: "Hitherto, the life-blood has been gradually chilling in your veins as you sat aloof, within your circle of gentility, while the rest of the world was fighting out its battle with one kind of necessity or another."¹⁰⁰ For Holgrave, Hepzibah's pretenses to nobility have rendered her physically inert, causing her blood to chill; its biological circulation is as tepid as is her social circulation outside of her "circle of gentility."¹⁰¹ Those outside that circle struggle with blunt "necessity" itself, which has the effect of warming their blood and energizing their bodies. Being a woman rather than a lady, he asserts, is the healthier course, despite her nervous debility: "You will at least have the sense of healthy and natural effort for a purpose, and of lending your strength be it great or small—to the united struggle of mankind."¹⁰² That Holgrave views the healthiness of Hepzibah's commercial efforts as enabling her to participate in "the united struggle of mankind" highlights his belief that the point of bodily health is to contribute to the renewing work of universal reform—a belief comically at odds with Hepzibah's actual struggle, which is to feed herself. This joke suggests that health reformers' faith in the invigorating power of activity might be misplaced. There might be some bodies, like Hepzibah's, unaccounted for in the universalizing rhetoric of reform, that are better suited to more circumscribed circulations.

The entry of the shop's first customer soon puts Holgrave's assertion to the test, as the tinkling of "the shop-bell, right over her head," causes Hepzibah's heart, which "seemed to be attached to the same steel spring," to jump "in unison with the sound."[103] The boy who enters, Ned Higgins, purchases a gingerbread figure of Jim Crow, the blackface minstrel performer, for one cent; he consumes it immediately.[104] As Brown notes, the novel's description of Hepzibah's acceptance of payment for the gingerbread focuses on Hepzibah's corporeality: "not only is the merchant on display with her goods, her materiality subject to public perusal and indeed a factor in her selling, but she is in touch with each transaction."[105] The narrator lingers over her acceptance of Ned's copper cent, "the first solid result of her commercial enterprise": "It was done! The sordid stain of that copper coin could never be washed away from her palm. The little schoolboy, aided by the impish figure of the negro dancer, had wrought an irreparable ruin. The structure of ancient aristocracy had been demolished by him."[106] The cent seems to "stain" Hepzibah's very skin in a way that can never be cleaned, causing her to view herself as a Cain-like figure, marked for eternity. Further, Ned's purchase destroys the "structure of ancient aristocracy" that sustains Hepzibah's self-image: "What had she to do with ancestry? Nothing; no more than with posterity! No lady, now, but simply Hepzibah Pyncheon, a forlorn old maid, and keeper of a cent-shop!"[107] She experiences the self-sustaining activity of commerce not as a connection to "the united struggle of mankind" but rather as a disconnection from her family.[108]

Yet from Holgrave's perspective, such a disconnection might be part of the point: by some lights, Hepzibah's dislocation from her ancestry is a step toward a happier, healthier, more progressive future. And, after her initial dismay at her new role, she indeed begins to feel "a thrill of almost youthful enjoyment":

> It was the invigorating breath of a fresh outward atmosphere, after the long torpor and monotonous seclusion of her life. So wholesome is

effort! So miraculous the strength that we do not know of! The healthiest glow that Hepzibah had known for years had come now in the dreaded crisis, when, for the first time, she had put forth her hand to help herself. The little circlet of the schoolboy's copper coin—dim and lustreless though it was, with the small services which it had been doing here and there about the world—had proved a talisman, fragrant with good, and deserving to be set in gold and worn next her heart. It was as potent, and perhaps endowed with the same kind of efficacy, as a galvanic ring! Hepzibah, at all events, was indebted to its subtle operation both in body and spirit; so much the more, as it inspired her with energy to get some breakfast, at which, still the better to keep up her courage, she allowed herself an extra spoonful in her infusion of black tea.[109]

Hepzibah's "wholesome" activity within the shop is "miraculous," lending her a "glow" at the precise moment of her "dreaded crisis." Notably, the same magical language that Baym and Brown have argued characterizes Phoebe's domestic activities describes Hepzibah's newfound health, for not only is her strength "miraculous" but Ned's cent is "a talisman," a magic charm "deserving to be set in gold" that Hepzibah presumably cannot afford.[110] The comparison the narrator makes between the talisman and the "galvanic ring," which is "perhaps endowed with the same kind of efficacy" as the cent, suggests another link that connects the energizing effects of commerce to those of electricity. Galvanic rings, as attested by a letter from "A Peripatetic and Cosmopolite" to the editor of the *Boston Medical and Surgical Journal* published on July 8, 1846, were considered by mainstream medicine to be one of many species of quackery.[111] Not only galvanic rings but also "bracelets and belts," reports the sardonic writer, are "greatly in vogue," particularly in New York, as "cures of frightful disease."[112] On September 2, 1848, the British medical periodical the *Lancet* reported that "galvanic ring mania is quite epidemic in New England."[113] The coin having, perhaps, "the same kind of efficacy" of a galvanic ring suggests that we read Hepzibah's spurt of energy with a skeptical eye, "extra spoonful" of tea notwithstanding.

Soon, the shop's "many and serious interruptions" disrupt Hepzibah's "mood of cheerful vigor," indicating that her newfound energy is not so much a transformation as it is a temporary surge, a caffeine rush.[114] It is not long before "the despondency of her whole life" once again looms over her; it is "like the heavy mass of clouds which we may often see obscuring the sky, and making a gray twilight everywhere, until, towards nightfall, it yields temporarily to a glimpse of sunshine. But, always, the envious cloud strives to gather again across the streak of celestial azure."[115] Her mind continually returns to the disconnection she feels from her family's past, crossing "the spaceless boundary betwixt its own region and the actual world" and leaving her body behind "to guide itself as best it may, with little more than the mechanism of animal life."[116] Thereafter, readers find her still responding, albeit "mechanically, to the frequent summons of the shop-bell," but her former energy has waned into a sort of automatism that "is like death, without death's quiet privilege,—its freedom from mortal care."[117] What a reformer like Holgrave does not understand, the novel suggests, is that the weight of the past generally, and of inheritance specifically, cannot be unburdened by cheerful labor; individual efforts do not redirect the accumulated force of history.

Even Hepzibah's country cousin Phoebe, who, as multiple scholars have noted, undertakes transformative domestic labor with the ease of magic, cannot alter the force of inheritance. In fact, the narrator frames her domestic talents not only in the language of magic but in that of hereditary transmission: her "gift of practical arrangement" is not only "a kind of natural magic" and "homely witchcraft" but also, as the narrator comments, an "exclusive patrimony."[118] After she finds success running a sales table at a fancy fair, she tells Hepzibah that her abilities "are not to be learnt"; rather, "they depend upon a knack that comes, I suppose, . . . with one's mother's blood."[119] Gillian Brown argues that the magical language the novel uses to describe Phoebe's effortless labor functions to "disguise" "labor as magic and play," but the other guise Phoebe's labor wears is that of inheritance. Her domestic touch, by which "Phoebe soon grew to be absolutely essential to the daily comfort, if not the daily life," of both Hepzibah and Clifford—her enervated, childlike brother—is "the involuntary effect of a genial temperament" rather than a cultivated sense of how to care for a household.[120]

That Phoebe says that she inherited rather than learned her abilities is surprising, given that she seems ripped from the pages of reformer and educator Catharine Beecher's *A Treatise on Domestic Economy*, a guide for "the use of young ladies at home, and at school," which was, as Kathryn Sklar notes, so popular that it was "reprinted nearly every year from 1841," when it was first published, "to 1856."[121] Beecher's work was the cornerstone of efforts to reform American domestic life by offering women guidance on such subjects as farming, cooking, dusting, and gardening. Much of its contents concern womanly health; in the preface to the third edition of her book, published in 1848, she explains that she wrote it to remedy "the combined influence of poor health, poor domestics, and a defective domestic education" on American women.[122] Phoebe strikingly resembles the sort of healthily active woman to whom Beecher hopes to give form, one in possession of not only, "as of first importance, a strong and healthy constitution" but also "all those rules of thrift and economy that will make domestic duty easy and pleasant."[123] Phoebe is, as Beecher says of the reformed American homemaker, "constantly interested and cheered" in her activities, which lends her efforts their air of blithe ease; likewise, the novel's narrator remarks that her "activity of body, intellect, and heart impelled her continually to perform the ordinary little toils that offered themselves around her."[124] By positioning Phoebe's domestic gifts as the fruits of inheritance rather than of the sort of education that Beecher imparts, the novel suggests the limits of self-culture.

Holgrave retains his sense of the promises of universal reform throughout most of the novel. His "inward prophecy," the narrator states, tells him "that we are not doomed to creep on forever in the old bad way, but that now, this very now, there are the harbingers abroad of a golden era, to be accomplished in his own lifetime."[125] Holgrave, here sounding like the Emerson of *Nature*, echoes transcendentalist rhetoric about the possibilities of a renewal in which the "moss-grown and rotten Past is torn down, and lifeless institutions to be thrust out of the way, and their dead corpses buried and everything to begin anew."[126] Yet the narrator gently chides him for an "error" in his worldview, which "lay in supposing that this age, more than any past or future one, is destined to see the tattered garments of Antiquity exchanged for a new suit, instead of gradually renewing themselves by patchwork."[127] Social betterment happens over long spans of time, "by patchwork," and not necessarily in Holgrave's "own little life-span."[128] And, "more than all," Holgrave's greatest error is "fancying that it mattered anything to the great end in view whether he himself should contend for it or against" reform, for, ultimately, "man's best directed effort accomplishes a kind of dream, while God is the sole worker of realities."[129] The narrator here lays out a vision of gradual reform diametrically opposed to antebellum schemes of social renewal through individual self-culture. It goes without saying that this vision dovetails with Hawthorne's conservative worldview, but because the novel aligns Holgrave with "reformers, temperance lecturers," and other "men with long beards" who "ate no solid food, but lived on the scent of other people's cookery," it is more specifically a comment on the inability of contemporary reform efforts to create lasting change.[130]

What does create lasting change is the inheritance of characteristics, in the novel not a perfectly conservative force but rather a process of physical and spiritual refinement that takes place over generations. Colonel Pyncheon and Judge Pyncheon, for instance, share a strong "similarity, intellectual and moral," and they are the villains of the story, but the differences in climate between England and New England, as Phoebe notes upon first meeting the judge, "must inevitably have wrought important changes in the physical system" over the years.[131] In fact, the narrator notes in the judge "a certain quality of nervousness," one of the effects of which is a "keener vivacity" of countenance "but at the expense of a sturdier something" present in the colonel.[132] This difference might be part of a slow change, the work of "the great system of human progress, which, with every ascending footstep, as it diminishes the necessity for animal force, may be destined gradually to spiritualize us, by refining away our grosser attributes of body."[133] Physiological change does accompany progress, but it has less to do with the efforts of any one person than it does the gradual spiritualization of the human form. We see this slow "system of human progress" at work in the figure of Holgrave, who, when he has the chance, chooses not to mesmerize Phoebe as Matthew Maule mesmerized Colonel Pynchon's daughter Alice centuries before, leaving her at his beck and call. His having the self-control and "reverence for another's individuality" not to follow in the footsteps of his ancestor has less to do with his dabblings in reform than with what the novel posits as the natural tendency of humanity to become more refined over centuries.

Holgrave himself develops shifting views on inheritance. When he first addresses the subject, it is to disparage its conservative force. When he and Phoebe meet in the house's garden, he tells her that the Pyncheon family's troubles are due to Colonel Pynchon's "inordinate desire to plant and endow a family," which he views as "at the bottom of most of the wrong and mischief which men do."[134] At least every fifty years, he tells Phoebe, "a family should be merged into the great, obscure mass of humanity, and forget its ancestors. Human blood, in order to keep its freshness, should run in hidden streams, as the water of an aqueduct is conveyed in subterranean pipes."[135] The novel later reveals that he is a fork of just such a hidden stream: he is a descendant of Matthew Maule, whose lineage had been mired in an "opaque puddle of obscurity" for thirty years before the events of the novel.[136] When Phoebe points out that he is speaking poorly of her family, his response, delivered with "vehemence," is that "the truth is as I say!"[137] The "wretched" traits of Colonel Pyncheon, "his very image, in mind and body," have been echoed in the form of Judge Jaffrey Pyncheon, the novel's antagonist; it would have been better if the Pyncheon blood had run out to parts unknown, diluting the colonel's evil.[138]

Yet by the end of the novel, when Holgrave's marriage to Phoebe puts him in the position of enjoying the Pyncheon family's wealth, he develops an altogether different view. Speaking of Judge Pyncheon's country house, which Hepzibah inherits after his death and in which Holgrave, Phoebe, and her family are to live forever after, he acknowledges that it "is certainly a very fine one, so far as the plan goes."[139] But he wishes that Pyncheon had employed more permanent materials building it: "I wonder that the late Judge—being so opulent, and with a reasonable prospect of transmitting his wealth to descendants of his own—should not have felt the propriety of embodying so excellent a piece of domestic architecture in stone, rather than in wood. Then, every generation of the family might have altered the interior, to suit its own taste and convenience; while the exterior, through the lapse of years, might have been adding venerableness to its original beauty, and thus giving that impression of permanence which I consider essential to the happiness of any one moment."[140] A wooden exterior implies a degree of plasticity with which the artist is uncomfortable. This comment marks the moment that Holgrave, the roguish reformer, becomes a conservative after marrying into inherited wealth—why not build the house out of stone, which would not change throughout the generations? Doing so would give the house "that impression of permanence," which the erstwhile itinerant says is "essential to the happiness of any one moment."[141] Earlier in the novel, he tells Phoebe that each generation should be "expected to build its own houses" and that he doubts whether even "state-houses" and "churches" should "be built of such permanent materials as stone or brick": the rebuilding of such "public edifices" every twenty years would serve "as a hint to the people to examine into and reform the institutions which they symbolize."[142] His wish for a stone exterior and wood interior that changes slowly, generation to generation, is a far cry from his earlier advocacy of universal struggle.

Phoebe keenly remarks this change in perspective, noting, "How wonderfully your ideas are changed! A house of stone, indeed! It is but two or three weeks ago that you seemed to wish people to live in something as fragile and temporary as a bird's-nest!"[143] With "a half-melancholy laugh," Holgrave replies, "You find me a conservative already! Little did I think ever to become one. It is especially unpardonable in this dwelling of so much hereditary misfortune, and under the eye of yonder portrait of a model conservative, who, in that very character, rendered himself so long the evil destiny of his race."[144] The conversion of Holgrave complete, the novel immediately reveals him to be the descendant of Matthew Maule, heir to "the only inheritance that has come down to me from my ancestors": knowledge of the hidden location of Colonel Pyncheon's rumored colonial deed to "the greater part of what is now known as Waldo County, in the state of Maine," worthless in the nineteenth century.[145] In this way, the novel's plot resolves with an affirmation of heredity and inheritance. The hidden stream of Holgrave's Maule blood resurfaces, and its joining with Phoebe's Pyncheon blood promises a new start, free from the evils of the past. Hepzibah and Clifford also seem headed for a new start as they leave the house of the seven gables, "the abode of their forefathers," with nary a glance backward—although they depart for another inherited Pyncheon property.[146]

By depicting human progress as the consequence of generational change rather than the transformative force of individual reform, *The House of the Seven Gables* probes the horizons of bioplasticity. The novel asserts that only the lapse of time can effect lasting change. If Hawthorne is a conservative author, as he is so often characterized, then one of the most important forms his conservatism takes is his antipathy toward contemporary reform schemes. Individual bodies, his novel implies, are not plastic in the ways supposed by many of his contemporaries; rather, what change occurs happens over centuries. As Hawthorne's novel suggests, debates about the means and ends of reform were intimately connected with debates about the capacities of the human body. In surfacing these debates, I wish to emphasize the unsettledness of not only ideas about the human body but of the project of reform itself.

CHAPTER TWO

Governance, Race, and Alimentary Selfhood in Melville

> Thus the habitual manner in which digestion is performed or affected, makes us either sad, gay, taciturn, gossiping[,] morose or melancholy, without our being able to doubt the fact, or to resist it for a moment.
>
> —JEAN ANTHELME BRILLAT-SAVARIN, *The Physiology of Taste; or, Transcendental Gastronomy*

> We resumed business; and while plying our spoons in the bowl, thinks I to myself, I wonder now if this here has any effect on the head?
>
> —HERMAN MELVILLE, *Moby-Dick*

In July 1854, Herman Melville returned to his home in Pittsfield, Massachusetts from Boston with a present for his wife, Elizabeth, in hand.[1] He chose a practical gift: a copy of a new book of domestic advice, Matilda Marian Pullan's *The Modern Housewife's Receipt Book: A Guide to All Matters Connected with Household Economy with Receipts Tested by John Sayer, the Medical and Other Portions of the Work Revised by J. Baxter Langley* (1854).[2] Although Pullan would in time become best known for her books on needlework, *The Modern Housewife's Receipt Book* is, as Wyn Kelley notes, a domestic guide similar in scope to Catharine Beecher's landmark *Treatise on Domestic Economy*.[3] Such guides, immensely popular in the middle decades of the nineteenth century, gave homemakers advice on cooking, child rearing, and mending; they also, as Pullan's title indicates, gave medical advice on such matters as nutrition and treatments for common diseases.[4] An introductory essay by physician J. Baxter Langley asserts the centrality of women's "domestic duties," especially cooking healthy food, to the happiness and health of her family: "We do not believe that the happiness of home depends entirely upon the cuisine, or that WOMAN is never to have higher ambition than to be food-maker to the sterner sex. Not at all. But we do believe that woman's duties are in the domestic sphere, and that some of them refer to the material comforts without which the brain—the organ of the mind—cannot perform its functions."[5]

For Langley, the importance of cooking lies at least partly in its nourishment of the brain, "the organ of the mind." If chowder has any psychological repercussions, as Ishmael wonders, those effects manifest through food's effect on the brain.

Far from anomalous, Langley's emphasis on the centrality of diet to the brain's health ties into a broader system of ideas about the stomach and brain that pertained in antebellum America. Melville might have first encountered these ideas in dietary reformer Sylvester Graham's *A Lecture to Young Men on Chastity* (1834), available in the library of the whaling ship *Charles and Henry*, aboard which he served from November 1842 to April 1843.[6] Readers of the book learn of the anatomical and functional links binding the nervous, digestive, and reproductive systems into a web of "reciprocal influences" whose balance must be maintained through a strict dietary and sexual regimen.[7] Eating the right food, Graham and like reformers believed, makes for a healthy brain; conversely, a stomach irritated by spicy or fatty meals might disorder the brain and corrode the mind. This view was held by a diverse group of writers, including dietary reformers, cookbook authors, and physicians; domestic guides such as Pullan's emphasized the brain's dependence on proper nutrition, drawing on medical works such as Alexander Philip Wilson Philip's *Treatise on Indigestion and Its Consequences, Called Nervous and Bilious Complaints* (1821) and James Johnson's *Essay on Morbid Sensibility of the Stomach and Bowels* (1827). At the same time, popular dietary reform movements such as Grahamism and vegetarianism warned that common digestive troubles could lead to insanity. And earlier in the century, British Romantics such as Percy Bysshe Shelley, author of *A Vindication of Natural Diet* (1813), taught that "all bodily and mental derangements" could be traced to the consumption of meat and alcohol.[8] These and other writings argue that attending to one's digestion by carefully monitoring the circumstances of one's ingestion—specifically, what is ingested and in what manner—is the best way to establish and maintain control of oneself.

Reformers' advocacy of dietary regulation as a tool to govern one's urges brings to light the relationship between food and the self by making food thinkable as an agent for governing one's digestion and thus one's brain and mind. Food was, for dietary reformers and their followers, at once agential (food affects the embodied self) and subject to the eater's agency (the eater, armed with self-knowledge, chooses to eat a certain way). The concept of food as opening the body to modification enables reimagining Nikolas Rose and Joelle M. Abi-Rached's affirmative theories of bioethics in an alimentary rather than a neurological context. Those theories illuminate how dietary management functioned as a technique for self-management in the decades preceding the Civil War. Although antebellum dietary reformers emphasize that the mind-body is susceptible to outside determinants in ways invisible to the scrutiny of consciousness, they also seek to make the individual an expert on both his own physiology and the ways he can alter his mind-body's substance through his diet. Thinking of dietary management in the terms made available by Rose and Abi-Rached adds to the prevailing scholarship on dietary reform the insight that following Graham's dicta was a way for individuals to take responsibility for the very makeup of their selves.[9]

Herman Melville's *Moby-Dick* (1851) figures, through the lens of Ishmael's own dyspeptic narration, dietary reformers' ideas about the connections between the stomach and the brain. The novel's depiction of these connections brings into focus reformers' efforts to enable individuals to view their dietary choices as shaping their selves. Such choices imagine bioplasticity as rendering the self amenable to prudent and reasoned intervention. Political theorist Jane Bennett writes that the philosophical projects of Thoreau and Nietzsche affirm the "productive power intrinsic to foodstuff, which enables edible matter to coarsen or refine the imagination or render a disposition more or less liable to ressentiment, depression, hyperactivity, dull-wittedness, or violence."[10] Digestion is thus "the formation of an assemblage of human and nonhuman elements, all of which bear some agentic capacity."[11] Antebellum Americans' attempts to guide the formation of such assemblages by exercising control of their diets, as *Moby-Dick* makes visible, made their choices about how and what they consumed a technology for sculpting the alimentary self. Ultimately, the novel's depictions of ingestion, digestion, and excretion explore both the possibilities and the perils of alimentary selfhood.

Dyspepsia, the Most Varied of All Diseases

The forty-third chapter of *Moby-Dick*, titled "Hark!," depicts a line of sailors transferring buckets of water hand to hand from one of the *Pequod*'s fresh water butts to the scuttlebutt in the middle of the night.[12] Archy, one of the sailors, insists to his neighbor Cabaco that he hears what sounds like hidden sleepers shifting in the after hold, to which Cabaco retorts, "Caramba! have done, shipmate, will ye? It's the three soaked biscuits ye eat for supper turning over inside ye — nothing else. Look to the bucket!"[13] Echoing Ebenezer Scrooge's dismissal of Jacob Marley's ghost as "an undigested bit of beef," Cabaco assumes that indigestion has disordered Archy's senses. The idea that Archy might mistake the activity of biscuits in his stomach for the activity of sleepers under his feet underscores the ways that midcentury theories of indigestion unsettle clear distinctions between the body's exterior and its interior.

Cabaco's retort to Archy prompts a question: How do biscuits affect the imagination? Or, as Ishmael puts it in one of this chapter's epigraphs, how does chowder affect the head? Historian of science Evelyn L. Forget writes that nervous sympathy, a nineteenth-century medical term that "characterize[s] the unconscious communication between different organs in the human body" via the nerves, structured the relationship between food and the brain in antebellum America.[14] Physiologists used nervous sympathy to conceptualize the organs' communication as a series of reflexive, unconscious feedback loops. If "the nervous system, and nervous function, became the mechanism that coordinated the actions of the human body," Forget writes, then "nervous sympathy was the tool of its communication."[15] The brain was no longer considered to be in charge of the nervous system but rather a part of it.[16] Such an understanding of the brain's place in the nervous system meant that the brain was thought to be vulnerable to the ailments of the organs to which the nerves connected it.

The stomach emerged as among the organs most in sympathy with the brain in the early decades of the nineteenth century. Alexander Philip Wilson Philip, a Scottish physician, was an early proponent of this view. As suggested by the title of his foundational work on indigestion, *A Treatise on Indigestion and Its Consequences, Called Nervous and Bilious Complaints; with Observations on the Organic Diseases in Which They Sometimes Terminate*, first published in 1821 and revised and reprinted until 1842, Philip viewed "nervous" as synonymous with "bilious." In the eighteenth century, William Cullen's contribution to medicine was to view most diseases as nervous in nature; Philip's was to explore the ways that nervous disorders could be understood as either causing or having been caused by indigestion. He writes that the "sympathies of the stomach" are so widespread and potent that "whatever greatly disorders the function of any important organ may be ranked among the causes of Indigestion."[17] The resultant indigestion, in turn, "so re-acts on the digestive organs" as to further sympathetically afflict the originally disordered organ.[18] A disease can thus flow back and forth from the liver to the stomach, for example, feeding on itself and worsening rapidly. Philip writes that in this way disease sometimes leads to death "with a rapidity which at first view appears unaccountable."[19] And because the brain "is one of those parts which are most apt to sympathize with the digestive organs," even slight digestive complaints can swiftly result, if untreated, in impaired mental function.[20]

Because Philip views indigestion as having the potential to damage or even destroy the body's organs, he devotes a large portion of his treatise to a set of complex and exacting guidelines addressing "diet and exercise both of mind and body."[21] Similarly complex dietary rules reappear in the works of physicians, dietary reformers, and cookbook writers throughout the antebellum decades. Of ingestion, he writes that one should "eat moderately and slowly" to ensure the food is "masticated and mixed with saliva" before traveling to the stomach.[22] One ought to avoid "tough, ascescent, and oily articles of food with a large proportion of liquid" because they dilute the gastric juices; "a diet, composed pretty much of animal food," or meat, "and stale bread, is the best" for those suffering mild indigestion.[23] Yet beef is "most apt to excite fever," so game meats are healthier.[24] Because, he says, "meat most mixed with fat" is "most oppressive" to the stomach; thus, fatty meats such as pork, geese, pheasant, and duck are difficult to digest. Turkey (without the skin) and the "lean part of venison" are more digestible.[25] Similar recommendations, each more restrictive than the last, abound in his work.[26]

Philip's characterization of indigestion as "the most varied of all diseases," a disorder that "so undermines every power of the system, that it is difficult to give a view of its symptoms," establishes one of dyspepsia's defining qualities: its protean range and power.[27] "It is," he writes, "an affection of the central part of a most complicated structure [the nervous system], capable of influencing even its remotest parts, and each, through many channels, and in various ways."[28] This model of dyspepsia as affecting and affected by disparate parts of the body "through many channels, and in various ways" enables Philip and those he influenced to construe any ailment as in some way connected to the stomach. When Philip writes that in dyspepsia "the organic affection rarely takes place in the original seat of the disease [the stomach], but in other organs with which the stomach sympathizes, the liver, pancreas, spleen, mesenteric glands, lower bowels, heart, lungs, brain, &c," he makes it possible to view all diseases as varieties of indigestion.[29] His emphasis on the stomach lays the groundwork for digestive reformers to locate it as the site of all the mind-body's problems and therefore the site of all possible cures for those problems.

When Irish physician James Johnson took up Philip's line of research in *An Essay on Morbid Sensibility of the Stomach and Bowels, as the Proximate Cause, or Characteristic Condition of Indigestion, Nervous Irritability, Mental Despondency, Hypochondriasis, &c. &c.* (1827), he sought to limit the extent to which all diseases could be traced to the stomach. "In short," he writes, "while I agree with Dr. Philip, that every part of the body sympathizes readily with the stomach, whether in health or disease, I do contend, from attentive observation and long experience, that these sympathetic affections of distant parts end, comparatively speaking, but rarely, in organic disease."[30] He asserts that Philip's "doctrine is calculated to excite a great deal too much alarm in the mind of the patient, as well as in that of the inexperienced practitioner."[31] Although Johnson downplays Philip's insistence on the stomach's centrality to all disease, he emphasizes the stomach's influence on the brain much more than Philip does. For Johnson, the brain "is the first to sympathise with disorder of the abdominal viscera."[32] Echoing Philip, he asserts that sympathy can volley disease back and forth between the stomach and the brain, "by which the temper is broken and the health impaired."[33] The sympathetic connection is so strong that indigestion can lead to "gusts of passion, fits of despondency, brooding melancholy, permanent irascibility, and still higher grades of intellectual disturbance."[34] Other mental symptoms include "confusion of thought, unsteadiness of the mind, irritability of the temper, defect of the memory, fickleness of disposition, and many other phenomena which are little suspected of corporeal origin."[35] By affecting dyspeptics' moods, symptoms such as "irritability of the temper" and "fickleness of disposition" project disorders of the body's nervous sympathy into the social fabric, thus disrupting interpersonal sympathy. Melville's own dyspeptic tendencies worried others; his friend and neighbor Sarah Morewood reports in a December 1851 letter to George Duyckinck that Melville writes all day and does not "leave his room till quite dark in the evening—when he for the first time during the whole day partakes of solid food—he must therefore write under a state of morbid excitement which will soon injure his health."[36]

Wary of being accused of philosophical materialism, Johnson treads cautiously in his explanation of how gastric disturbances might afflict one's mind. In a section called "Nervous Irritability; Mental Despondency," he writes that he knows nothing of "the intimate nature of *mind*"; he wishes to leave "that department" to "metaphysics."[37] "It is very evident," he says, that "man is a compound being—moral and physical, or mental and corporeal."[38] In a lengthy footnote, he carefully distances himself from materialism; he writes that just as the eye "is the material organ of sight, but it is not the faculty of vision," the brain is "merely that portion of matter which is in most proximate communication with the mind or immaterial principle."[39] The brain is thus "only an *instrument* through which the mind receives impressions from without, and transmits its dictates from within."[40] "But," he writes, "in all intellectual operations, the material organ is as necessary to the mind, as the mind is to the material organ."[41] Although he subscribes to substance dualism, it is a dualism that puts mind and body in close relation, meeting in the brain.

Of indigestion's effects on the brain, Johnson writes that because the "mind can only be manifested, in this world, through the instrumentality of matter, so its faculties and dispositions are pretty regularly influenced by the state or conditions of our corporeal organs."[42] The mind, he says, suffers along with the body:

> Some of our mental faculties, however, are much more under the influence of physical disorder than others: but I much doubt whether any, even the very highest attributes of the mind, can stand completely independent of, and unaffected by, derangement of function or structure in the corporeal fabric. A very slight inflammation of the membranes of the brain, will destroy, for a time, the judgment, the memory, the feelings, the affections, of the greatest philosopher or divine. How, then, can we wonder that various derangements of the body, and especially of those organs with which the brain is closely linked in sympathy, should disturb the subordinate attributes of mind, as, for example, the TEMPER of an individual?[43]

Here, two definitions of the word "ruminate" intersect—a philosopher ruminates on existence; a cow ruminates cud.[44] Nervous sympathy links the two processes together in such a way that one might disorder the other. Johnson goes on to write that "the aids of religion and philosophy are much less available, and much less effectual," as treatments for deranged minds.[45] That he specifies that inflamed brain membranes "will"—not "might"—"destroy" the mental function of even "the greatest philosopher or divine" illustrates the extent to which he understands the mind and brain as the province of physicians, not philosophers and theologians.

If a philosopher's mind were to be destroyed by indigestion, he or she might not know it; Johnson views the stomach's influence on the brain as unconscious. One's temper, he writes, is not altered by the pain of indigestion but rather the sympathetic resonance between stomach and brain: "An individual who would bear . . . a fit of the gout, or the pain of a surgical operation, will be completely changed in his temper, and become waspish, irascible, and captious, by an irritation of the stomach (transmitted sympathetically to the brain), of which he is perfectly unconscious."[46] Because the stomach affects a dyspeptic person's brain unconsciously, he or she may not be aware of the onset of the disorder's mental effects. At the same time, Johnson worries that "connecting irritability of temper with a physical disorder" might "furnish the person thus afflicted, with an excuse for giving way to every impulse of an irritable mind," especially when that person can say that his or her affliction is unconscious.[47] His solution is vigilance: "The moral curb which he should now endeavor to keep on his temper, ought to be more forcibly strained than ever."[48] That vigilance and its attendant practices (self-knowledge and self-control) lie at the heart of Johnson's approach to what he calls the "abstract of all maladies."[49] His insistence on "a more rigorous system of self-control" makes preventing and treating indigestion a matter of willpower rather than the toxic "farrago of tonics and stimulants" advertised in newspapers.[50]

The Sins of Indigestion

In his heavily marked copy of Emerson's *Essays: First Series* (1841), Melville records his humorous reaction to the philosopher's claim in "Spiritual Laws" that "hideous dreams are exaggerations of the sins of the day"; according to Melville, Emerson means, "of course, the sins of indigestion."[51] What Emerson sees as metaphysical reckoning, Melville sees as the result of an upset stomach. The conceptual move Melville makes in his marginal note is to put Emerson's philosophical speculations into conversation with the physiological processes of the human body; the same holds true for *Moby-Dick*. Just as dietary reformers insist that changes within the stomach unconsciously influence the brain and therefore the mind, *Moby-Dick* continually returns to questions about how what individuals think might be affected what they eat.

Melville pushes against the contemporary philosophical tendency, most prominently found in the Goethean strain of American transcendentalism, to imagine philosophy, thought, and emotion as actuated by the disembodied mind. Emerson writes in *Nature* (1836) that "standing on the bare ground," he feels that "all mean egotism vanishes. I become a transparent eye-ball; I am nothing; I see all; the currents of the Universal Being circulate through me; I am part or particle of God. The name of the nearest friend sounds then foreign and accidental."[52] Emerson's famous eyeball, bereft of a body, has no identity ("I am nothing"), no physiological limitations ("I see all"), and no connections that it values over others ("The name of the nearest friend sounds then foreign and accidental"). In other words, it signifies a relationship to the universe in which the body plays no part. But humans have bodies, or *are* bodies; Emerson cannot actually become a transparent eyeball, free of physical needs.

Melville follows this line of thought throughout his literary career. In his poem "Art" (1891), he distinguishes "brave unbodied scheme[s]" speculated upon in "placid hours" from "unlike things" that "must meet and mate," as in digestion, to create "pulsed life," the stuff of art.[53] He makes a similar point when he writes of the limitations of Goethe's optimistic philosophy to his friend Nathaniel Hawthorne in June 1851:

> In reading some of Goethe's sayings, so worshipped by his votaries, I came across this, "*Live in the all.*" That is to say, your separate identity is but a wretched one, — good; but get out of yourself, spread and expand yourself, and bring to yourself the tinglings of life that are felt in the flowers and the woods, that are felt in the planets Saturn and Venus, and the Fixed Stars. What nonsense! Here is a fellow with a raging toothache. "My dear boy," Goethe says to him, "you are sorely afflicted with that tooth; but you must *live in the all*, and then you will be happy!"[54]

Melville makes a sharp point, and it is one that reappears in *Moby-Dick*: contra Goethe and "his votaries," including Emerson, the physical body—its pains, pleasures, and changes—punctures the hope of transcending the bounds of one's self and partaking in universal kinship. Goethe advises us to "get out of yourself," but few things situate us within our bodies like a toothache. In a note at the bottom of his letter, Melville adds that Goethe's "all" feeling is not entirely without truth: one feels it, he writes, "lying in the grass on a warm summer's day."[55] But, Melville adds, "what plays the mischief with the truth is that men will insist upon the universal application of a temporary feeling or opinion."[56] As a dyspeptic would know, part of what makes feelings and opinions temporary is their susceptibility to changes in and to the body; how long can a body that needs to drink, eat, and excrete lie in the grass experiencing transcendence?[57]

If, as Stephanie Browner writes, "Melville preferred to write about the body from the ground level and to immerse his readers in spectacularly somatic worlds," part of what makes *Moby-Dick* so "spectacularly somatic" is its insistence on the influence of digestion, the body's "ground level," or fundament, on thought, emotion, and behavior.[58] Scholars have long recognized that *Moby-Dick* concerns itself with eating, digestion's sister art; Robert T. Tally Jr. says as much when he asserts that the novel "uses culinary rhetoric to establish its analysis of power relations in the nineteenth century."[59] Caleb Crain links the novel's many references to cannibalism to homoeroticism, noting that both instances involve "unusual male-male intimacy."[60] Mark Edelman Boren, surveying the novel's many dining scenes, remarks that "eating and being eaten play such a large role in *Moby-Dick* that even if Ishmael doesn't understand it, he must acknowledge its presence."[61]

But focusing exclusively on eating extracts it from a historical context in which ideas about what, when, and how to eat are inextricable from ideas about digestion. Indeed, for dietary reformers and their adherents, attaining a healthy digestion (and thus one's best self) was the sole end of eating. Literary criticism that focuses on eating tends to construe it as a contained event, but the act of eating is not in and of itself the sum total of a person's relation to food, especially in the antebellum context. Food is ingested and digested; it goes inside the body—and, in the antebellum United States, affects that body in powerful ways. Critics' focus on the act of eating to the neglect of digestion accounts for their tendency to approach the alimentary elements of *Moby-Dick* as sociopolitical concepts whose ideological operations are unearthed by critique. My argument is in distinction to, for instance, Kyla Wazana Tompkins's push toward establishing "critical eating studies," which "seeks to render discursive two kinds of matter toward which so much human appetitive energy is directed: food and flesh."[62] Attending to the ways that food and eating overlap with social and political forces is a necessary project that uncovers the discourses that structure the biopolitics of eating—and Tompkins very successfully accomplishes just that and more—but in what follows I attend to food and flesh not as discourses but as many antebellum Americans encountered them: as agential matter.[63]

Manufacturing Mind and Soul

Dietary reformers in the 1830s, 1840s, and 1850s, the decades of Melville's youth and greatest literary productivity, enshrined three important elements of James Johnson's focus on treating indigestion with "self-control" rather than medicine: self-knowledge, vigilance, and self-management. Self-knowledge promises to make one an expert on the subject of one's own body. The self-knower is aware of his or her mental and bodily processes and is thus cognizant of those deviations that signal the early stages of disease. Vigilance ensures that those deviations will be recognized for what they are. Self-management allows one to master the impulse to gratify the "palate at the expense of the stomach," as Philip writes.[64] And dietary reformers, as they mediated Johnson's work, added their own ingredient to this recipe: the concept of using diet not to prevent madness but to sculpt the self.

In *Fowler's Practical Phrenology* (1840), one of the most popular midcentury phrenological texts, publisher and health reformer Orson Fowler seems to borrow from Philip and Johnson in constructing his own theory of digestion.[65] He effuses about digestion's key role in health:

> By the truly wonderful process of digestion, food and drink are converted into thought and feeling—are manufactured into mind and soul. Is it then unreasonable to suppose that different kinds of food produce different kinds of mind? Reasonable or unreasonable, it is nevertheless the *fact*. . . . Ardent spirits and wine excite the animal organs, located in the base of the brain, more than they do the intellectual or moral faculties. This is unquestionably the fact with every thing heating in its nature; such as condiments, flesh, tea, coffee, and high-seasoned or highly stimulating food of any kind.[66]

He goes on to predict that physiologists will one day discover that "animal food," or meat, excites the animalistic mental organs at the back of the head at the expense of the intellectual organs at the front of the head.[67] He predicts that "vegetable food" will soon be found by physicians to reduce body temperature and thus clear the mind and calm the nerves.[68] In a broad sense, then, Fowler agrees with what physicians such as Philip and Johnson thought about the stomach: that different foods digest differently, and that the conditions of the stomach affect other organs, especially the brain.

But the differences, rather than the similarities, between Fowler and the physicians indicate the ways that reformers adapted medical theories of digestion into their broader ameliorative schemes. In Fowler's case, he grafts digestion onto phrenology, which forms his core structure of beliefs about the human body. Johnson writes of the stomach as influencing the whole of the brain, particularly its enveloping membrane, which suggests that he does not view indigestion as affecting one part of the brain more than another. For Fowler, who takes the phrenological doctrine of cerebral localization as a matter of course, different foods affect different mental faculties. Whereas Philip's dietary guidelines distinguish between more and less healthy meats (turkey without the skin versus fatty beef, for example), Fowler understands all meat as "keeping the body in a highly excited, not to say feverish state," which overwhelms the delicate intellectual organs that sit atop the head, the furthest away from the rest of the body.[69] Those organs require a cool and calm (rather than feverish and irritable) body to function, which necessitates the need for cool, bland food, such as vegetables. That he views vegetables as beneficial is at odds with Philip's and Johnson's advice to avoid them altogether because they ferment in the stomach, but because Fowler understands "cooling" foods as reducing nervous excitation, he construes them as promoting "placidity of mind."[70] This is to say that although Fowler retains the core elements of medical theories of digestion, he modifies those theories so that they fit with phrenology's emphasis on equilibrium and balance. Thus, when he writes that to "distinguish yourself intellectually, you *must* regulate the quantity and quality of your food and drink in accordance with the established laws of physiology, or your wings of fame will be melted in the heat of animal indulgence," he refashions Johnson's prescription of self-control as a cure for dyspepsia into the key to intellectual achievement.[71]

Dietary reformers adapted medical theories of digestion to create extensive, sophisticated, and popular systems of self-improvement. These systems incorporate the core elements of Johnson's therapeutic approach to dyspepsia, but they make refashioning the self their end. They thus see managing one's diet as a way for one to "manufactur[e] mind and soul" according to one's wishes, as Fowler writes.[72] Nikolas Rose and Joelle M. Abi-Rached's work on "neurotechnologies," which they define as techniques that "seem to open ourselves up to new strategies of intervention through the brain," articulates some of the philosophical stakes of self-formation.[73] Although they ground their thinking on neurotechnologies in the specifically neurological modes of selfhood that emerged in the late twentieth and early twenty-first centuries, antebellum dietary reformers saw themselves as sculpting the self by making interventions not through the brain but through the stomach. And they understood themselves to be reforming their entire bodies and not the brain alone. Dietary reformers thus made it possible for nineteenth-century Americans to understand themselves as what Rose elsewhere calls "somatic selves," shaped by their diets but also able to shape those diets.[74]

Sylvester Graham is by far the most influential dietary reformer of the antebellum period, and his work was integral to the structure of antebellum alimentary selfhood. After dropping out of Amherst College and training as a Presbyterian minister, Graham devoured physiologist François J. V. Broussais's *Treatise on Physiology*, published in America in 1826, and other physiological and medical texts.[75] Thereafter, he traveled throughout the Northeast delivering lectures on the virtues of temperance and of learning what he called "the science of human life," or physiology. He rose to prominence in 1832, when, as food historian Andrew F. Smith writes, adherents of his dietary regimen of fruits, vegetables, and water "appeared to thrive" in the wake of a cholera epidemic in New York City.[76] He achieved fame practically overnight, and, no less a publicist than a reformer, he wasted no time publishing the dozens of letters he received from those who believed they had survived cholera because of his diet.

Graham's influence was such that in 1833 Asenath Nicholson, a boardinghouse owner in New York City, instituted his dietary regimen in what was afterwards known as a "Graham boardinghouse."[77] Other Graham boardinghouses soon arose in Boston and other northern states.[78] In an appendix to *A Lecture on Epidemic Diseases Generally* (1833), Graham includes a three-page-long copy of the "Rules and Regulations of the Graham Boarding House," the contents of which comprise exacting rules for when and how to wake, sleep, eat, bathe, and exercise.[79] Boarders, a group that included such luminaries as Horace Greeley and William Lloyd Garrison, were to rise between four and five each morning, depending on the season; eat breakfast at seven, lunch at one, and dinner at a mutually agreed-on time.[80] They were to drink no alcohol, coffee, or tea, and ideally eat no meat, but if meat were served it should be done so simply, without spices or condiments.[81] Graham also recommended that boarders take cold sponge baths daily and immerse themselves wholly in water at least weekly.[82] Grahamian health reform is not a change of diet but of lifestyle.

The Grahamian system is not so much a deviation from what antebellum Americans described as "regular" medicine as it is an elaboration of medical theories of the stomach-brain connection. In *A Lecture to Young Men on Chastity*, first published in 1834, Graham emphasizes the interconnectedness of every organ of the human body, which he says form a "grand web of organic life."[83] He writes that a disturbance in any part of this web resonates throughout the whole, which does not differ significantly from Johnson's thought; but Graham's shift is to dramatically widen the range of what could be considered a disturbance. His use of a web as a metaphor for the nerves is fitting, for he understands them as fragile in the extreme: "All extraordinary and undue excitements," he writes, "whether caused by mental, moral or physical stimuli, increase the excitability and unhealthy activity of the nerves of normal life; and tend to bring on, and establish in them, a state of diseased irritability and sensibility; which is more or less diffused over the whole domain."[84] In Graham's view, any nervous excitement whatsoever can be pathological: a caffeine rush would court death. And because in that view nervous excitement can be caused by any "mental, moral or physical stimuli," not just poorly digested food, avoiding such excitement requires adhering to a controlled regimen such as that found in Graham boardinghouses.

A Lecture to Young Men on Chastity, like Graham's other early writings, focuses on the perils of lust, masturbation, and sex. He writes that genital nerves "partake, in common with those of other organs, of this general debility and diseased excitability, and become exceedingly susceptible of irritation; — sympathizing powerfully with all the disturbances of the system, and especially of the brain and alimentary canal."[85] Graham thus adds the genitals to the brain-stomach connection, thereby extending his emphasis on dietary asceticism to sexuality. He recommends shunning "stimulating and heating substances, high-seasoned food, rich dishes, the free use of flesh, and even the excess of aliment, for they "increase the concupiscent excitability and sensibility of the genital organs," which in turn slows digestion, obstructs the lungs, and floods the organs with large amounts of quickly-circulating blood.[86] In this view, even nocturnal emissions are hazardous; sufferers, Graham says, would be best served avoiding all stimulating foods, rising early, exercising often, sleeping on a hard bed, and taking cold baths.[87]

Mary Peabody Mann, wife of reformer Horace Mann and sister of Sophia Hawthorne, published a cookbook, *Christianity in the Kitchen: A Physiological Cook-Book* (1858), that extends Graham's logic to assess both the physiological and the religious value of food. She writes that foods such as "wedding cake, suet plum-puddings, and rich turtle soup, are masses of indigestible material, which should never find their way to any Christian table"; she grieves to see such food eaten at weddings, for "a book of reckoning is kept for the offences of the stomach, as well as for those of the heart, and this is one of the deeds done in the body, for which the doer will be called to account."[88] She terms such indigestible food "unchristian" because "health is one of the indispensable conditions of the highest morality and beneficence."[89] In her view and that of many of her contemporaries, eating healthily is a personal and a moral responsibility, because to mistreat one's stomach is to mistreat one's temperament, making one a less moral person.[90] "It is a good omen," she writes, "that practical physiologists, even now, begin to feel ashamed of ill health, and feel bound to apologize for it."[91] In a footnote, she remarks that Graham "published an apology in the newspapers for having been sick."[92] She hopes for a future that sees medical expertise in women's hands: "every mother will be a physiologist, and all nurses [nursing women] will be physicians."[93]

Nikolas Rose and Joelle Abi-Rached's work on neuroscience, the self, and society in the twenty-first century highlights the potential of the alimentary selves that emerge from the writings of Graham and other dietary reformers. They identify the brain as Westerners understand it today as the focus of "an emerging style of thought" that locates brain disorders as "encompass[ing] everything from anxiety to Alzheimer's disease," even "includ[ing] both addictions and obesity—all, it seems, have their origin in the brain."[94] This new style of thought asks us to think of ourselves as "somatic selves" equipped with a "neurobiological dimension to our self-understanding and our practices of self-management."[95] Identifying the brain as the seat of disorders previously conceptualized primarily as moral or social issues (addiction and obesity) echoes the ways that the stomach came to be understood as the site of all disease, and dyspepsia, the "abstract of all maladies."[96] And just as in the early nineteenth century the stomach became a site of treatment for a variety of ills, in the twenty-first century the brain is thought of as open to a range of treatments and interventions, or "neurotechnologies," which include tailored pharmaceuticals, gene therapy, and transcranial magnetic stimulation.

Rather than attempt to depict such neurotechnologies as the horsemen of the reductionist apocalypse, as is the tendency of many humanists and social scientists, Rose and Abi-Rached "seek to trace out some directions for a more affirmative relation to the new sciences of brain and mind."[97] They argue that neurotechnology construes brains as "open for intervention and improvement, malleable and plastic" rather than as destined to be or to work a certain way.[98] Although brains being "open for intervention and improvement" means that they are made available to government and corporate influence, brains also "become open to action by each individual themselves. . . . The plastic brain becomes a site of choice, prudence, and responsibility for each individual."[99] In this formulation, "our selves are shaped by our brains but can also shape those brains."[100] Individuals thus understand themselves as subject to unconscious influences; at the same time, their awareness of those influences and their access to the means by which to affect them (interventions such as drugs and mindfulness) mean that they can exercise "choice, prudence, and responsibility" with respect to their brains.[101] Rose and Abi-Rached note that "each of us is now urged to develop a reflexive understanding of the powers of these nonconscious determinants of our choices, our affections, our commitments: in doing so, we will no longer be passive subjects of those determinants, but learn the techniques to act on them in order to live a responsible life."[102] In other words, twenty-first-century somatic selves are encouraged to develop self-knowledge, particularly of those unconscious processes that affect their mental lives, so that they can manage those processes. Thinking of oneself as corporeal is thus not a capitulation to biological determinism but an opportunity to exercise choice about how to navigate the claims of biology.

The same commitment to shaping oneself through self-knowledge and the management of unconscious bodily processes propels Grahamian dietetics. Graham's binding of the digestive and the reproductive systems has received most of the scholarly attention directed toward him. But his later writings, such as *Lectures on the Science of Human Life* (1849), show Graham extending the benefits of his regimen to improved longevity, beauty, agility, stamina, resistance to disease, mental clarity, "cerebral development," and moral sentiments.[103] *Lectures*, written for the "unlearned reader," includes a glossary of medical terms such as "hepatic" and "renal," a feature that indicates the degree to which he takes the book's epigraph, "Know thyself," seriously.[104] It also indicates that he seeks to make individuals experts on their selves. Arranged in the style of Euclid's *Elements of Geometry* to refer "continually to previously ascertained principles, or established facts and conclusions," it begins with Graham's understanding of the basics of physiology and builds logically to his dietary regimen.[105] Graham writes it so that "every individual of suitable age and ordinary intelligence, by a proper degree of application," can understand his or her body and maintain it.[106] The underlying ethos of the *Lectures* is that the human body, being part of the natural world, is subject to fixed laws and principles, including "relations between human organic life, and the animal, vegetable, and inorganic world around us; relationships which not only greatly affect the body, but, in the present state of being, modify mind and morals and religion to an extent which cannot safely be disregarded."[107] Because "mind and morals and religion" are subject to the human body's conditions, only knowing oneself well enough to manage those conditions can keep them under control. The care one takes of oneself becomes ethically and theologically salient.

When literary scholars focus exclusively on the politics of dietary reform, they do so at the expense of its medical context and its therapeutic aims. Specifically, they miss the ways that dietary management offered nineteenth-century Americans opportunities to govern bodily processes otherwise out of their control even as they ceded control of their appetites to reformers. Although other nineteenth-century popular sciences such as craniometry and physiognomy assume the permanence of mental ability or temperament, dietary reformers envisioned the stomach as a site of change. Individuals were able to understand their dietary choices as choices about themselves—choices that provided the opportunity to exercise responsibility in the care of their bodies. Despite its emphasis on the stomach's influence over the brain, dietary reform is not a science of determination but of the possibilities afforded by embodiment.

Regulating the Circulation

Melville "seems to be familiar" with contemporary dietary reformers' ideas, as Ralph James Savarese writes; further, he elaborates those theories in his fiction.[108] Nippers of "Bartleby, the Scrivener" (1853), after all, is a "victim" of "indigestion," a condition that—Melville writes in chorus with physicians and reformers—is "betokened in an occasional nervous testiness and grinning irritability."[109] A moment in *Pierre; or, The Ambiguities* (1852) indicates that Melville was familiar with (and skeptical toward) the Grahamian model of dietetics. The young Pierre Glendinning lives in New York City with a group of Grahamists and philosophers known as the Apostles, who partake of seemingly every reform movement the city has to offer and live "huskily muttering the Kantian Categories through teeth and lips dry and dusty as any miller's, with the crumbs of Graham crackers."[110] They keep, in fact, "a bushel of Graham crackers" as some of their "only convivials."[111] Melville's narrator inveighs against the attention they give to their diets with a specificity that indicates the author's familiarity with not only Grahamism but also like movements: "Nor shall all thy Pythagorean and Shellian dietings on apple-parings, dried prunes, and crumbs of oat-meal cracker, ever fit thy body for heaven."[112] Melville was not a passive recipient of others' theories of digestion, then, but someone who shaped the structure of their cultural reception.

Moby-Dick addresses the governed body in its first paragraph, in which Ishmael, who finds himself growing restless with life on land, decides to "sail about a little and see the watery part of the world" as a way of "driving off the spleen, and regulating the circulation."[113] Melville thus makes bodily regulation the cause of Ishmael's adventures. The young man views sailing as restorative to his health: "Whenever I find myself growing grim about the mouth; whenever it is a damp, drizzly November in my soul; whenever I find myself involuntarily pausing before coffin warehouses, and bringing up the rear of every funeral I meet; and especially whenever my hypos get such an upper hand of me, that it requires a strong moral principle to prevent me from deliberately stepping into the street, and methodically knocking people's hats off—then, I account it high time to get to sea as soon as I can."[114] When a grim, splenetic view of the world begins to overtake Ishmael, he goes to sea. This is especially so when his "hypos" threaten to rule his actions. In the antebellum United States, a hypo attack meant hypochondriasis, a commonly self-diagnosed condition with symptoms equal in nebulousness to those of late-century nervous diseases such as neurasthenia and hysteria. Ishmael's use of the shorthand term "hypos" presumes that he and his reader have a shared language for the disorder, which indicates its prevalence in antebellum culture. James Emmett Ryan, in an incisive study of illness and healing in *Moby-Dick*, argues that Ishmael is a hypochondriac, noting that his hypos "figure as commonplace symptoms within nineteenth-century medical theory."[115] Justine Murison characterizes hypochondriasis as causing a person to believe him- or herself an animal or an inanimate object.[116] But hypochondriasis was not a singular stable epistemic category; rather, it was a mélange of symptoms, the causes and cures of which were topics of vigorous debate in the mid-nineteenth century.[117] For James Johnson, hypochondriasis was a "curse of civilization," arising when "the mind has been cultivated at the expense of the body."[118] He writes that "mental anxiety, too much exercise of the intellect, and too little exercise of the body" are the chief causes of the disease and recommends that sufferers "narrowly watch" fluctuations in their "natural temper or feelings" to alert themselves to its influence.[119] Some hypochondriacs, he writes, "conscious of the danger they ran, by the slightest collision or contradiction from even the nearest relations," shunned company until their attacks wore away.[120] Ishmael does much the same thing: he takes responsibility for his body by monitoring his moods and relying on his "strong moral principle" to stay violence.[121] When he feels the "damp, drizzly November" in his soul, he goes to sea as soon as he can, not only because he relishes "*being paid*" for his labor but also "because of the wholesome exercise and pure air of the forecastle deck" that can reverse the adverse effects of hypochondriasis.[122] The passage thus illuminates the cultural aspects of hypochondriasis, which are predicated, for both Ishmael and Johnson, on regimes of self-observation and self-restraint.

Going to sea, for Ishmael, is an attempt to cure a disorder both corporeal and moral in nature. Benjamin Rush writes that although hypochondriasis is "seated in the mind," it "is as much the effect of corporeal causes as a pleurisy, or a bilious fever."[123] Ishmael's wish to "regulat[e] the circulation" as a way of curing his hypos suggests that he believes as much. But he also sees hypochondriasis as a moral disorder: when his hypos are strongest, "it requires a strong moral principle to prevent me from deliberately stepping into the street, and methodically knocking people's hats off."[124] When his body is not fully under conscious control, it causes him to wish to act in ways that are morally dubious—here, knocking others' hats off. This echoes Mann's emphasis on maintaining health as a way of maintaining one's good temperament: moral agency requires a healthy, properly regulated body. Ishmael goes to sea not only for his health but also for his soul; further, he takes care of his soul precisely by taking care of his health. Yet whether his time on the *Pequod* alleviates his indigestion is an open question, for his narration wavers between dyspeptic—irritable, mutable, reactive—and possessed of the sort of iron stomach he attributes to hyenas: "He [the hyena-like man] bolts down all events, all creeds, and beliefs, and persuasions, all hard things visible and invisible, never mind how knobby; as an ostrich of potent digestion gobbles down bullets and gun flints. And as for small difficulties and worryings, prospects of sudden disaster, peril of life and limb; all these, and death itself, seem to him only sly, good-natured hits, and jolly punches in the side bestowed by the unseen and unaccountable old joker."[125] Ishmael here makes the connection between cognition and digestion clear: both are ways of understanding one's relation to the environment. To have the digestion of a hyena or an ostrich is to be able to maintain one's equanimity in the face of "small difficulties and . . . peril of life and limb" alike. His avid narration, like the ostrich, attempts to "bolt down all events, all creeds, and beliefs, and persuasions, all hard things visible and invisible," but ultimately he can only stomach so much: his acidic, ulcerative digressions mark the consequent dyspepsia.

The Try Pots, where Ishmael and Queequeg lodge before their journey on the *Pequod*, is the site of much of the novel's early engagement with food and digestion. The famous chowder scene figures food's agency by invoking its power to affect whatever ingests it. The sentence describing the clam chowder served to Ishmael and Queequeg at the Try Pots emphasizes its deliciousness: "It was made of small juicy clams, scarcely bigger than hazel nuts, mixed with pounded ship biscuits, and salted pork cut up into little flakes; the whole enriched with butter, and plentifully seasoned with pepper and salt."[126] The friends consume their supper "with great expedition," and soon Ishmael orders a round of chowder made with cod rather than clams.[127] It is while attending to this second bowl that Ishmael wonders whether chowder might affect his head. His question indicates an awareness that contemporary physicians and dietary reformers would balk at the rapid consumption of a great quantity of rich, hot food; thus, Melville structures the chowder scene as a site of engagement with dietary reform. Sylvester Graham inveighs against soups in general; they are "altogether too complicated to be healthy."[128]

He writes that "a dish of salted or smoked fish, broiled and perfectly saturated with butter, and perhaps also dressed with mustard and pepper," a dish much like chowder, "is enough to give a hyena a fit of dyspepsy."[129] Ishmael narrating his meal in a way that makes it sound irresistible—"Oh, sweet friends! hearken to me," he says before describing it—brings to attention the tension inherent in dietary reform between what is healthy and what tastes good. And though Philip warns against pleasing the "palate at the expense of the stomach," Ishmael has a second bowl of chowder.[130]

Ishmael might look to the structure and surroundings of the Try Pots itself, the "fishiest of all fishy places," for evidence of food's potency:

> Chowder for breakfast, and chowder for dinner, and chowder for supper, till you began to look for fish-bones coming through your clothes. The area before the house was paved with clam-shells. Mrs. Hussey wore a polished necklace of codfish vertebra; and Hosea Hussey had his account books bound in superior old shark-skin. There was a fishy flavor to the milk, too, which I could not at all account for, till one morning happening to take a stroll along the beach among some fishermen's boats, I saw Hosea's brindled cow feeding on fish remnants, and marching along the sand with each foot in a cod's decapitated head, looking very slipshod, I assure ye.[131]

In this passage, the Try Pots's kitchen, which continuously transforms fish into chowder, acts as the stomach of its environs, spreading fishiness to human, animal, and object alike. Eating fish for every meal makes one fishy, as Hosea's cow demonstrates, literalizing epicure Jean Anthelme Brillat-Savarin's mantra, "Tell me what you eat, and I will tell you what you are." The passage thus dramatizes dietary reformers' dismantling of the ontological distinction between eaten and eater (a distinction absent from Queequeg's cannibalistic dietary practices). That is why Ishmael imagines fish bones poking through his clothing: because he eats chowder for every meal, his body itself becomes fishy. And because food's psychological effects are coterminous with its effects on the eater's body, Ishmael's (or is it Fishmael's?) question of whether the chowder has affected his head is bound to the question of whether it has changed his body.

Ishmael and Queequeg's relationship, forged while searching for a whaling ship in Nantucket, is marked by Ishmael's anthropological interest in Queequeg's cultural differences from white New Englanders. Those differences extend to habits and beliefs regarding food. Queequeg "never consorted at all, or but very little," with other sailors; instead, to Ishmael's eye exhibiting a "Socratic wisdom," the harpooner "seemed entirely at his ease; preserving the utmost serenity; content with his own companionship; always equal to himself."[132] "Surely," Ishmael asserts, "this was a touch of fine philosophy; though no doubt he had never heard there was such a thing as that."[133] Ishmael thinks of Queequeg, who seems to live philosophically without being trained for it, as a born philosopher. He finds this far preferable to the typical philosopher, of whom "I conclude that, like the dyspeptic old woman, he must have 'broken his digester.'"[134] For Ishmael, philosophy as it is typically practiced is a product of poor digestion; it follows that Queequeg, whose mind is impervious to the debilitating effects of dyspepsia, is a different type of philosopher, one not "conscious of so [philosophically] living."[135] Early on, then, Melville takes care to align digestion (or rather, indigestion) not only with what Ishmael sees as Queequeg's personal philosophy but also with philosophy in general: Queequeg's healthful digestion makes him a harpoon-flinging Socrates, while the common breed of philosophers must have disordered stomachs. As Melville's responses to Goethe and Emerson suggest, he meditates on the body's ability to challenge philosophical perspectives that neglect its role in thought and knowledge. To call philosophy the result of a "broken digester" is to subordinate it and its traditional practitioners not to rational argumentation but to the body's vagaries.

Ishmael's characterization of Queequeg as a natural-born philosopher hints at civilized–uncivilized differences in digestion, a subject that I will address in detail later in the chapter. Here, Ishmael's conception of differences in digestion inheres in the differences between his dyspeptic mood swings and morbid introspections and what appears to him to be Queequeg's calm self-assurance. Johnson wrote that indigestion is a "curse of civilization" that can arise from overexertion of the mind at the cost of the body, which explains why philosophers have "broken digesters"; if Ishmael goes to sea to treat his dyspepsia, part of what he seeks from his journey is a shift away from the sort of mental taxation that, per Johnson, burdens intellectuals with indigestion.[136] Ishmael thinks that Queequeg, who lives rather than thinks philosophically, is not subject to the "curse of civilization" because, in the young man's view, he is not civilized. Queequeg, for Ishmael, is a member of a natural aristocracy whose very lack of civilization equips him with the cool-headedness and equanimity that dietary reformers sought to attain.

Ishmael construes not only philosophy but also religion as subject to the influence of digestion. After a day spent searching for work, Ishmael returns to his and Queequeg's shared room to find the harpooner silently sitting with a carven idol, Yojo, on his head.[137] To his roommate's alarm, he holds the position for a full day. At the end of Queequeg's religious observance, Ishmael takes it upon himself to educate him on the history of religion, "beginning with the rise and progress of the primitive religions, and coming down to the various religions of the present time, during which time I labored to show Queequeg that all these Lents, Ramadans, and prolonged ham-squattings in cold, cheerless rooms were stark nonsense."[138] These practices are "bad for the health; useless for the soul; opposed, in short, to the obvious laws of Hygiene and common sense."[139] Fasting is central to Lent and Ramadan, and Queequeg takes no food during his worship, so it is most likely fasting that is "bad for the health" and "opposed . . . to the obvious laws of Hygiene." Ishmael then delivers to Queequeg an extended monologue on fasting and religion: "Besides, argued I, fasting makes the body cave in; hence the spirit caves in; and all thoughts born of a fast must necessarily be half-starved. This is the reason why most dyspeptic religionists cherish such melancholy notions about their hereafters. In one word, Queequeg, said I, rather digressively; hell is an idea first born on an undigested apple-dumpling; and since then perpetuated through the hereditary dyspepsias nurtured by Ramadans."[140] Here, Ishmael explicitly binds body to spirit: if "fasting makes the body cave in," then it necessarily does the same to the spirit. And if, as Fowler asserts, the process of digestion transforms food into mind and soul, then it is unsurprising that "all thoughts born of a fast must necessarily be half-starved." Ishmael thus understands religious belief as something intrinsically tied to adherents' digestion (or, in the case of fasting, lack thereof): hell is not the punishment of a just God but the product of the dyspeptic's disordered mind.

Ishmael's monologue reflects his own indigestion. It is rude and presumptuous, if not ill-tempered; it is the philosophizing of someone with a broken digester, which means that we should not ourselves swallow what Ishmael says before seasoning it with a skeptical grain of salt. When he finishes his lecture, he asks Queequeg about his digestion, to which the harpooner responds that his only episode of dyspepsia was after a feast of fifty of his kingdom's enemies.[141] His friend declines to hear any more. Melville's writing of Queequeg so that he makes this joke suggests that we not take Ishmael's professed views on digestion to be the same as Melville's. But, as Samuel Otter writes, Melville "does not reject the idea of the body as meaningful," even though his work at times critiques contemporary American culture's obsession with phrenology, physiognomy, and other modes of reading the body.[142] Indeed, the early chapters of *Moby-Dick* engage digestion in ways informed by contemporary physicians and dietary reformers. What Melville adds is an exploration of digestion's effects: the early chapters of *Moby-Dick* consider how both philosophy and religion are inflected by the stomachs (and thus the psychological states) of thinkers and believers.

Sharks Well Governed

Queequeg's gustatory boast foregrounds the connections between purported cannibals—the feared and exoticized South Sea Islanders whom the whaling trade and Melville himself brought to the national consciousness—and dietary reform. Ishmael himself ponders this relationship, asserting that his friend's "royal," "excellent" blood was "sadly vitiated, I fear, by the cannibal propensity he nourished in his untutored youth."[143] Ishmael's play on "nourished" emphasizes the degree to which the cultural practice of cannibalism might translate biologically into a "vitiated" body deprived of healthy and morally sound food. Like Ishmael and Queequeg's friendship, the relationship of cannibalism and dietary reform indexes questions of racial and national difference, distinctions between purportedly civilized and uncivilized digestive systems, and the possibilities of a shared biological humanity. Kyla Wazana Tompkins has amply demonstrated that food, eating, and digestion were central to how white nineteenth-century Americans viewed, in particular, black bodies. The "performative production" of race, she writes, depended on an alimentary dialectic that was in turn predicated on the notion of racial differences in eating and digestion.[144] On the one hand, black bodies were commonly construed not just as commodities but as edible commodities—recall, for example, the Jim Crow–shaped sweets Hepzibah sells in her shop in Hawthorne's *The House of the Seven Gables*. On the other hand, black bodies were also construed as prodigiously appetitive, as pervasive stereotypes about their purportedly insatiable appetite for watermelons and sweets attest. Tompkins concludes that in Graham's dietetics, "correct eating, like correct sexual behavior, is understood as a performative act of national identification and formation. In eating as national subjects flesh is called into social being through a model that understands race as anchored" to digestion.[145] The claim that "correct eating" is an act of "national identification and formation" rests on the argument that Sylvester Graham characterizes "foods that constitute a threat to the body" as "'foreign' and 'exotic' to the United States (spices, coffee, sugar, tea, and wine)," which is not wholly accurate, for he inveighs equally against such domestic products as whiskey, meat, and butter.[146] *Moby-Dick*, by highlighting the appetites of the cannibal harpooners, calls attention to dietary reform in an international context in which "not one in two of the many thousand men before the mast employed in the American whale fishery, are Americans born, though pretty nearly all the officers are."[147] I contend that the novel's depiction of nonwhite, purportedly cannibal appetites is only nominally distinct from its depiction of the white crews' civilized appetites; through the nervous figure of the steward Dough-Boy, it portrays whites' anxieties about the harpooners' consumption as expressions of facile credulousness, and it portrays the white officers' civilized consumption as a mask for ravenous desires. The novel collapses distinctions of race and nationality into the singular figure of the shark, whose mindless killing and consumption can only be restrained, as the ship's cook Fleece says, by self-governance: "For all angel is not'ing more dan de shark well goberned."[148] And the inevitable failure of sharks to govern themselves suggests Melville's ultimately skeptical stance toward projects of alimentary self-fashioning.

Chapter 34, "The Cabin-Table," depicts two dining scenes: the officers' dinner and the harpooners' dinner. Every aspect of the officers' dinner is choreographed and restrained. They depart from the deck to the cabin in order of rank: first Ahab descends, then Starbuck, then Stubb, and then Flask. Ishmael notes that the absolute deference given to the ship's captain at mealtimes is linked to the "unchallenged power" of "he who in the rightly regal and intelligent spirit presides over his own private dinner-table of invited guests." "Who has but once dined his friends," Ishmael declares, "has tasted what it is to be Caesar."[149] The officers are served by Ahab in total silence according to rank: Starbuck "received his meat as though receiving alms; and cut it tenderly; and a little started if, perchance, the knife grazed against the plate; and chewed it noiselessly; and swallowed it, not without circumspection."[150]

Although all the officers observe the table's traditional silence, one seems to find it stifling: "What a relief it was to choking Stubb, when a rat made a sudden racket in the hold below."[151] Why does Stubb choke when Starbuck, in harmony with both *Pequod* tradition and contemporary dietary discourse, swallows his food carefully, "not without circumspection"?[152] Put another way, what is it that Stubb has trouble swallowing? The readiest answer, of course, is that he chokes on the parching salted beef served by Dough-Boy. Stubb's being so relieved at the sound of a stowaway rat leads me to propose a different answer: he chokes on the cabin's restrained—and restraining—quiet, for it cannot accommodate his capacious appetite. He might be more comfortable dining with the harpooners, who dine in lively "contrast to the hardly tolerable constraint and nameless invisible domineerings of the captain's table."[153] Their table is characterized by "almost frantic democracy" and "entire care-free license and ease": "While their masters, the mates, seemed afraid of the sound of the hinges of their own jaws, the harpooneers chewed their food with such a relish that there was a report to it. They dined like lords; they filled their bellies like Indian ships all day loading with spices. Such portentous appetites had Queequeg and Tashtego, that to fill out the vacancies made by the previous repast, often the pale Dough-Boy was fain to bring on a great baron of salt-junk, seemingly quarried out of the solid ox."[154] The harpooners here seem to break every dietary rule that reformers set. They eat so loudly that the noise echoes, and, contrary to prevailing medical ideas about digestion, they stuff themselves with "relish." The simile Melville uses to describe their hunger—"they filled their bellies like Indian ships all day loading with spices"—playfully points to the dangers associated with spiced foods in general, but especially with the fiery Indian foods that were popular with sailors in the nineteenth century. In *Lectures on the Science of Human Life*, Sylvester Graham praises "Hindostan and India generally" for their vegetarian diets; he condemns, however, their taste for "curry powder—a composition made of cayenne pepper, black pepper, ginger, mustard, and several other ingredients of a very heating and irritating character, calculated to produce the worst disorders of the alimentary canal."[155]

Here, the harpooners, not "Indian ships," are the harbingers of dyspepsia. Contemporary physicians and dietary reformers might have thought that eating with such speed and immoderation would lead to nervous debility, but as Ishmael discovers early in his friendship with Queequeg, dyspepsia is not a universal complaint. In fact, the only one whose nervous system seems affected by the harpooners' dinner is Dough-Boy, worried that he himself might be eaten: "[Dough-Boy] was naturally a very nervous, shuddering sort of little fellow, this bread-faced steward; the progeny of a bankrupt baker and a hospital nurse. And what with the standing spectacle of the black terrific Ahab, and the periodical tumultuous visitations of these three savages, Dough-Boy's whole life was one continual lip-quiver. Commonly, after seeing the harpooneers furnished with all things they demanded, he would escape from their clutches into his little pantry adjoining, and fearfully peep out at them through the blinds of its door, till all was over."[156] If the harpooners are ships loaded with spices, then Dough-Boy is just what his name suggests: soft, impressible bread dough. Ishmael's description of him as both "bread-faced" and perpetually nervous—his "whole life was one continual lip-quiver"—marks his role as the living intersection of food and health as surely as does his heritage as "the progeny of a bankrupt baker and a hospital nurse." When the harpooners eat in ways considered hazardous by prevailing medical thought, only the glutinous Dough-Boy suffers.

The novel's depiction of Dough-Boy's abject nervousness and terror over the harpooners' purported cannibal tendencies satirizes white anxieties about cannibalism. As he hears Queequeg's "moral, barbaric smack of the lip in eating," he cowers, "trembling" and looking "to see whether any marks of teeth lurked in his own lean arms."[157] His fear of being eaten causes him to mistake the salted beef on the table for his own flesh; in his mind, he is both Dough-Boy and a dough boy, a server who might be served as a dish. The harpooners, aware of his terror, make a joke out of it when he does not serve them quickly enough: "And once Daggoo, seized with a sudden humor, assisted Dough-Boy's memory by snatching him up bodily, and thrusting his head into a great empty wooden trencher, while Tashtego, knife in hand, began laying out the circle preliminary to scalping him."[158] This joke and the harpooners' other jests—at one point Tashtego calls to him "to produce himself, that his bones might be picked"—cause Dough-Boy yet further nervousness, afflicting the "simple-witted steward" with "sudden fits of the palsy."[159] Yet the novel depicts his fears as unfounded; it is precisely because his ears are "credulous, fable-mongering" that he swallows whole stereotypes and anxieties about the harpooners' appetites. As they depart the dining room, he imagines "all their martial bones jingling in them at every step, like Moorish scimetars in scabbards."[160] The novel's depiction of Dough-Boy's association of the harpooners with the Moors emphasizes the degree to which his anxieties about cannibalism reflect anxieties about nonwhite aggression.

The stark differences between the quiet and restraint of the officers' meal and the "frantic democracy" of the harpooners' meal seem to reinforce Ishmael's ideas about racial differences in digestion: whites' digestive systems are suited for eating in moderation, while other races' systems drive them to ravenous consumption. But that reading overlooks the ways that the diners act contrary to this idea. Although Stubb is third in command, he seems as if he would be happier eating with the harpooners than with the officers. And Daggoo, the "great negro" harpooner, runs counter to stereotypes about black bodies by taking considered, "dainty" bites of his food, seeming to Ishmael to subsist mostly on air alone.[161] These details indicate the failure of racialized ideas about eating and digestion.

After Stubb kills a whale, the crew fastens it to the ship's side so that its oil can be harvested. Stubb, "flushed with conquest," demands that a steak be cut from the whale's "small," or "the tapering extremity of the body," for, being "a high liver," he is "somewhat intemperately fond of the whale as a flavorish thing to his palate."[162] The word "intemperately" invokes the all-important dietary concept of temperance—"simplicity and temperance in diet," Graham writes, is paramount—a concept that high-living Stubb rejects.[163] As he settles "at the capstan-head, as if that capstan were a sideboard," to eat, "thousands on thousands of sharks" join him in his meal, "mingling their mumblings with his own mastications" in a fractious feast that mirrors not only Stubb's eating but also the harpooners' own "frenzied democracy" at table.[164] The rest of the chapter returns to the linked images of Stubb's and the sharks' consumption repeatedly. He is not aware of their similarities at first, ignoring "the mumblings of the banquet that was going on so nigh him, no more than the sharks heeded the smacking of his own epicurean lips."[165] But when he castigates the ship's cook Fleece for the steak being too cooked and tender, he draws the connection. A good whale steak "must be tough," he says; "those sharks now over the side, don't you see they prefer it tough and rare?"[166] He seems to align himself with the sharks because of their shared taste for tough, rare whale meat. But then he tells Fleece to "tell 'em they are welcome to help themselves civilly, and in moderation, but they must keep quiet."[167] "Go," he says, "and preach to 'em!"[168] That he couches the advice to eat "civilly, and in moderation"—something he struggles to do—as preaching suggests that he views dietary reformers as evangelical; and, as he makes clear, he does not care for their message. Telling Fleece to preach to the sharks is a way of sarcastically telling him to proselytize them into the digestive fold, an absurd and impossible task that in its absurdity and impossibility indicates Stubb's frustration with dietary reform.

Fleece sardonically takes the injunction to "preach" literally and, addressing the bloody waters below, sermonizes the sharks in terms that recall Sylvester Graham's fiercest moralizing: "Your woraciousness, fellow-critters, I don't blame ye so much for; dat is natur, and can't be helped; but to gobern dat wicked natur, dat is de pint. You is sharks, sartin; but if you gobern de shark in you, why den you be angel; for all angel is not'ing more dan de shark well goberned. Now, look here, bred'ren, just try wonst to be cibil, a helping yourselbs from dat whale."[169] The sharks cannot help their sharkishness, for "dat is natur, and can't be helped." The point, Fleece emphasizes, is to govern one's own nature and so govern one's voraciousness. That is, by now, a familiar theme: the call to govern one's appetite, to eat moderately, is the central doctrine of midcentury dietary reform. Just as Graham and his adherents found virtue, freedom, and agency by managing their diets, Fleece's sermon represents the belief that controlling one's appetite leads to the moral and spiritual purity of the angels. Throughout the sermon, though, Stubb "help[s] himself freely" to his steak, a signal that he does not take the message seriously, and the sharks continue to gnaw the whale and each other.[170] Fleece soon grows tired of sermonizing a congregation deaf to his ministry: "No use goin' on; de dam villains will keep a scougin' and slappin' each oder, Massa Stubb; dey don't hear one word."[171] Stubb does not appear to hear, either; as he turns to excoriate Fleece for cooking his steak too much, he does so while "rapidly bolting" whale meat into his mouth.[172] At the end of the chapter, Fleece concludes that he is "more of shark dan Massa Shark hisself."[173] This is a sentiment that Tommo, the narrator of *Typee* (1846), echoes: "The fiendlike skill we display in the invention of all manner of death-dealing engines, the vindictiveness with which we carry on our wars, and the misery and desolation that follow in their train, are enough of themselves to distinguish the white civilized man as the most ferocious animal on the face of the earth."[174]

After Stubb finishes his dinner, Queequeg and another sailor use long spears to kill the sharks swarming around the whale carcass.[175] They seek to strike the sharks' heads, "seemingly their only vital part," but in the churning chaos their weapons instead tear holes in the sharks' sides, unspooling their vitals.[176] The sharks, whose frantic ingestion invokes both the harpooners' dinner and Stubb's taste for raw whale meat, turn cannibal, biting "not only at each other's disembowelments, but like flexible bows, bent round, and bit their own; till those entrails seemed swallowed over and over again by the same mouth, to be oppositely voided by the gaping wound."[177] The figure of the self-consuming shark links cannibalism to mindless consumption and unrestrained hunger: to restrain that hunger, to govern one's wicked nature, as Fleece says, is the point.

Although the harpooners' and officers' dining scenes appear at first to posit racial differences in eating and digestion, the bottomless hunger characteristic of sharks crosses racial lines. What is at stake in humanity's mutual sharkishness is not so much race as self-governance. Yet careful attention to one's intake is not without its difficulties; just as asking sharks to practice temperance and eat "civilly, and in moderation" is absurd, it is absurd to ask Stubb, Queequeg, and Tashtego to adhere to Grahamian dietary rules. Captain Peleg says before the voyage that "pious harpooners never make good voyagers — it takes the shark out of 'em; no harpooner is worth a straw who ain't pretty sharkish."[178] His fear is that they will become too concerned for their souls to risk their lives hunting whales, a fear that is to some extent borne out in Starbuck, the well-governed shark who considers derailing

Ahab's hunt for Moby Dick. Ultimately, though, the business of the *Pequod* and the whale fishery more generally depends on the ferocity of men like Stubb and Queequeg; to expect them to sit and dine as if they were at Sylvester Graham's table is as absurd as preaching to swarming sharks. Ultimately, *Moby-Dick*'s depiction of the links between race, cannibalism, hunger, and dietary reform expresses skepticism about the moral project of manufacturing angels through self-governance.

Vengeance on a Dumb Brute

Much like Stubb and the sharks, Moby Dick is characterized by his consumption. When Ishmael signs up to work on the *Pequod*, he soon learns that the white whale "devoured, chewed up, crunched" Ahab's leg on his last voyage.[179] Especially irksome to Ahab is what appears to be "the White Whale's infernal aforethought of ferocity"; for those who hunt him, "every dismembering or death that he caused, was not wholly regarded as having been inflicted by an unintelligent agent."[180] Ahab hates Moby Dick not because he ate his leg but because he perceives the animal as doing so purposefully. For him, the whale is either a moral agent himself or an instrument of another agent, be it fate or divinity. This means that the loss of his leg appears to him not an accident but a crime; this distinction provides moral justification for his quest for revenge. Starbuck, Ahab's Quaker first mate, recoils from thinking of the whale as an agent: "Vengeance on a dumb brute!" he cries, "that simply smote thee from blindest instinct! Madness! To be enraged with a dumb thing, Captain Ahab, seems blasphemous."[181] Starbuck understands Moby Dick as an animal that acts from "blindest instinct" rather than from deliberation, so it cannot be a moral agent or, consequently, a target of revenge.

Attending to digestion in *Moby-Dick* leads, perhaps surprisingly, to a question not frequently asked: What drives the whale? I contend that the novel poses indigestion as one potential cause of Moby Dick's "inscrutable malice."[182] Ishmael portrays whales' indigestion as a double-edged sword. One edge is its economic value: Ishmael tells us that ambergris, the most commercially valuable substance produced by a whale's body, "is supposed by some to be the cause, and by others the effect," of cetacean dyspepsia.[183] "Who would think," he crows, "that such fine ladies and gentlemen should regale themselves with an essence found in the inglorious bowels of a sick whale!"[184] Laxatives were a common mode of relieving dyspepsia in the mid-nineteenth century; Ishmael therefore proposes, as a way of curing whales' dyspepsia, ramming "three or four" boatloads of laxatives down their throats, "and then running out of harm's way, as laborers do in blasting rocks."[185] Melville draws this striking image from Henry Theodore Cheever, who remarks that ambergris is formed from "that state of the system which calls for a cathartic."[186] "A peck of Morrison's or Brandreth's pills," Cheever writes, naming common laxatives, "would probably remove obstructions in the creature's abdominal viscera."[187] Though Ishmael obviously delights in his scatological humor, he cautions against turning up our noses at ambergris because of its intestinal origins: "Bethink thee of that saying of St. Paul in Corinthians, about corruption and incorruption; how that we are sown in dishonor, but raised in glory."[188] Ishmael aligns the Pauline relationship between corruption and incorruption with that between sweet ambergris and indigestion. Dietary reformers such as William Andrus Alcott understood regulating one's excretion to be as important as regulating one's diet: in *Lectures on Life and Health* (1853), he urges readers to make evacuation "an almost sacred principle to obey promptly the laws of Nature, and at a regular hour of the day."[189]

But the novel also depicts a darker, more dangerous effect of whales' dyspepsia: indigestion produces not only ambergris but also rage and violence. When the *Pequod* meets the *Samuel Enderby*—an English whaling ship— readers meet Captain Boomer, who lost his arm to Moby Dick the previous whaling season (though the whale did not swallow it, he injured it enough to require amputation).[190] Unlike Ahab, Boomer seems to bear the whale no ill will ("he's best let alone") and maintains a cheerful perspective on life.[191] Present during Boomer and Ahab's conversation is the *Samuel Enderby*'s straight-laced surgeon, Dr. Bunger, whom Boomer ribs for his "dietetically severe" course of treatment after being wounded in the struggle with Moby Dick.[192] Bunger, not only a physician but also "late of the reverend clergy," draws on a mixture of science and religion to explain the white whale's violence: "'Well, then,' interrupted Bunger, 'give him your left arm for bait to get the right. Do you know, gentlemen'—very gravely and mathematically bowing to each Captain in succession—'Do you know, gentlemen, that the digestive organs of the whale are so inscrutably constructed by Divine Providence, that it is quite impossible for him to completely digest even a man's arm? And he knows it too. So that what you take for the White Whale's malice is only his awkwardness. For he never means to swallow a single limb; he only thinks to terrify by feints.'"[193] The physician, whose interest in regulating his captain's diet echoes that of physicians such as Philip and Johnson, holds that whales' divinely constructed digestive systems are such that they cannot digest human limbs. This physiological premise leads him to contradict

Ahab's conception of the whale as a moral agent acting with malice; in his view, far from being malicious, the whale suffers from indigestion.[194] And whereas humans can treat their dyspepsia, whales must take the preventive route: they rely on their knowledge (says Bunger) that they cannot digest human limbs to avoid dyspepsia. Moby Dick, to whom the culture of dietary reform is not accessible, cannot exercise the sort of agency-creating self-regulation that Ishmael practices.[195]

The novel teeters on rendering Bunger's explanation ridiculous by immediately following it with the doctor's tale of "the old juggling fellow . . . that making believe swallow jack-knives, once upon a time let one drop into him in good earnest, and there it stayed for a twelvemonth or more; when I gave him an emetic, and he heaved it up in small tacks."[196] This story implies that Bunger is a less than honest or a less than competent physician, which means that his ideas about Moby Dick's digestion might be just humbug. But answering the question of whether the white whale has indigestion is less important than the question itself. Echoing Melville's comic reduction of Emerson's "sins of the day" to "the sins of indigestion," the gam on the *Enderby* poses an encounter between the novel's grandest concepts—fate, God, madness, vengeance—and a whale's upset stomach.

Indigestion is not the only road the novel takes into the whale's interior, as Ishmael's attempts to read his body phrenologically and physiognomically attest. Though these attempts ultimately fail to provide the answers Ishmael seeks, rather than declare the task impossible he challenges others to try their hand: "I but put that brow before you. Read it if you can."[197] Samuel Otter notes that Ishmael's efforts at knowing the whale delve ever deeper into its body, from the skin-deep sciences of dermatology and physiognomy to the depth of the spine.[198] Looking to the depths of the stomach as one among many avenues that provide partial, imperfect views of the whale's mind, with the aid of Bunger's diagnosis, brings the opening chapters' evident interest in the ties between digestion, philosophy, and religion full circle. If the whale's violence is due to dyspepsia, then Ahab's "blasphemous" desire for revenge seems even more heretical: he wishes to hunt not just an unreasoning animal but an animal that acts as he does because of sickness. And a dyspeptic Moby Dick would be much like Ishmael himself; afflicted with illness, the whale would be driven to enact the cetacean equivalent of "deliberately stepping into the street, and methodically knocking people's hats off" by wreaking terrific violence on the ships that hunt him.[199] Unlike Ishmael, however, he would have no "strong moral principle" to ward off the urge to do violence.[200] Finally, if the whale is dyspeptic, then *Moby-Dick* would be a story not just about the fatal consequences of Ahab's cosmic insanity—itself a bodily madness, given that it is the blending of "his torn body and gashed soul" that "made him mad"—but also about the consequences of the whale's illness.[201] True to form, though, the novel refuses to allow this conclusion to stand on unshakable ground; Bunger's explanation is, at best, a guess.

A Very Long Night's Digestion

Early reviewers of *Moby-Dick* found the novel a riotously spiced, hard-to-digest dish. A November 1851 review says that it "is having oil, mustard, vinegar, and pepper served up as a dish, in place of being scientifically administered sauce-wise."[202] The reviewer imagines the greasy, piquant combination of fatty and fiery ingredients as being served by themselves, like a sort of stomach-roiling soup. It would be better, the reviewer implies, to turn to science to find ways to dull its sharp flavors and serve it as a sauce instead. Another review from November 1851 notes that some might enjoy the novel's spice: "There are people who delight in mulligatawny. They love curry at its warmest point. Ginger can not be too hot in the mouth for them. Such people, we should think, constitute the admirers of Herman Melville. He spices up his narrative with uncommon courage, and works up a story amazingly. If you love heroics and horrors he is your man. Sit down with him on a winter's eve, and you'll find yourself calling for candles before the night sets in. . . . You will have supper for a very long night's digestion."[203] A mulligatawny is a spicy English soup derived from an Indian sauce; thus, the reviewer perceives the appeal of *Moby-Dick*'s ecumenical makeup and sharp, pungent flavors. What the novel conjures depends on the reader's own digestion.

CHAPTER THREE

Sculpting the Body Electric
Exercise and Self-Fashioning in Walt Whitman

> A perfect man is the result of urged cultivation.
> —WALT WHITMAN, "Manly Health and Training, with Off-Hand Hints toward their Conditions"

When journalist Walt Whitman sat in the examining chair at the Manhattan office of Orson and Lorenzo Fowler on July 16, 1849, he had recently turned thirty. What was on his mind as he reclined is a mystery, but what was on his head is not. Lorenzo, after carefully measuring and assigning a score to forty-nine different areas of Whitman's skull, wrote in his report of the examination that Whitman's brain size scored a 6, or "large," according to Orson's book *Fowler's Practical Phrenology* (1840); that the cranial bump corresponding to secretiveness scored a 3, or "moderate"; and that another bump, corresponding to self-esteem, scored a "6 to 7," somewhere between "large" and "very large." These and other results mean, Lorenzo concludes with uncanny accuracy, that Whitman is "one of the most friendly men in the world" and has "a good command of language especially if excited." Whitman was so delighted by Fowler's complimentary reading that he included his bumps' scores in the anonymous review of *Leaves of Grass* he published in the *Brooklyn Daily Times*.[1] The report describes Whitman's personality at length, lingering over psychological details and personal quirks that, were they true, Whitman himself surely must have been aware of. Yet what might be the purpose of an analysis that merely tells you about yourself?

Surprisingly, the object of phrenological reports like the one Lorenzo provided Whitman was not simply to tell subjects about who they were but to suggest who they might become, for the Fowlers' reformist brand of phrenology, discussed in chapter 2, assumed that the mental faculties they measured could be changed. An undersized "organ," or portion of the brain devoted to a given faculty, Orson asserts in *Fowler's Practical Phrenology*, can be increased "by exercise."[2] If Whitman wished to pump up his faculty of secretiveness from its relatively puny score of 3 to a 4, for example, he might have devised a systematic schedule of secret-keeping. For the Fowlers and their followers, Whitman among them, the brain is like any other "corporeal organ": use it or lose it.³

In what follows, I argue that attending to Whitman's recently recovered health and exercise series, "Manly Health and Training, with Off-Hand Hints toward their Conditions" (1858), and the 1860 edition of *Leaves of Grass* in light of reformist ideas about bodily exercise yields a new understanding of the poet as celebrating a concept that conjures up the grimmest images of ideological power for many literary critics: discipline. Far from an anomaly, "Manly Health," written and published during a year of Whitman's life when he experienced a "sun-stroke," his first significant health issue, provides a framework through which to understand Whitman's depictions of health in his poetry; because "Manly Health" presents bodily discipline as the prerequisite of well-being, it is an important component of Whitmanian health. I read the changes Whitman made between the 1856 and 1860 editions of *Leaves of Grass*, which include numbering the poems and organizing them for the first time into what Whitman calls "clusters," as a form of discipline the poet enacted upon the form, or the body, of his work. Taking seriously what Whitman says about the benefits of bodily discipline in both "Manly Health" and in his poetry means moving beyond the reflexive suspicion with which we, as literary scholars, tend to regard projects of self-fashioning so that we might attune ourselves to the poet's sense that the body's full capacities for change, affection, and pleasure can be achieved only through discipline and training. The portrait of *Leaves of Grass* that emerges from this analysis is of a poem that embodies the human body's own tensions between sickness and health, growth and decay, stasis and change, freedom and governance.

In his exploration of the interplay between discipline and freedom—both somatic and textual—Whitman moves beyond Grahamian regimes of self-denial to a regime of training meant to enhance the body's capacities. Another way to describe Whitman's contribution is to say that he moves away from the prevailing reformist logic of subtraction (cease this sort of behavior, remove this sort of food from your diet) and toward a logic of addition (train yourself to increase your capabilities, eat what you like so long as you maintain physical activity). Instead of counseling asceticism or avoidance or stressing the modern world's dangers to bodily purity, Whitman advocates a hopeful and deeply engaged encounter with one's environment: "always substance and increase," he sings in "Walt Whitman," the poem that begins the 1860 edition of *Leaves of Grass*.⁴ "Manly Health" and the third edition of

Leaves of Grass thus mark a turning point from the ascetic reform schemes of the antebellum decades to the hearty optimism of Progressive Era physiological reform.

A Nation of Supple and Athletic Minds

Scholars tend to think of Whitman as a writer with an obvious interest in the human body but without much knowledge about it. Part of that conception may be due to the poet's many references to phrenology and other forms of popular science that literary scholars typically find to be disreputable. As Harold Aspiz has convincingly argued, phrenology and other mid-nineteenth-century reformist disciplines do form the basis of Whitman's understanding of the human body. Because of this, Aspiz notes that Whitman would not be considered a medical expert today: "His newspaper pieces devoted to medical and health topics—many of them hardly more than the digests or 'scissorings' of nontechnical writings—reveal no great expertise. . . . Some of his medical ideas now appear to have been forward-looking. . . . He advocated fresh air, adequate exercise, the full and rounded development of the physical and mental self, and the treatment of patients in terms of their total personality and organic being."[5] Yet whether Whitman had "great expertise" in medicine or whether his ideas were "forward-looking" is beside the point in an antebellum context devoid of consensus on what constitutes "real" medicine. (The American Medical Association was only founded in 1847, and medicine was not professionalized until the end of the century.) Whitman himself writes in "Manly Health" that he is "no physician—but one who, by observation and study, has come to view the theme of health as oftentimes able to be better treated, for popular use, by an outsider, than a medical man."[6] To assess the ideas in which Whitman steeped himself on the basis of whether they still have cachet today is, of course, ahistorical; perhaps worse, it also ignores what functions those ideas served in their historical context.

The same holds for blanket assessments of phrenology as racist, essentialist, or biologically determinist. There is no doubt that scientific racists marshaled phrenological, craniometric, and evolutionary ideas to provide scientific cover for their views, especially in the latter half of the nineteenth century. But at the same time, phrenology enabled Frederick Douglass, in his 1854 Western Reserve College commencement address, to discuss how one human species could contain many variations of form and color. In the speech, titled "The Claims of the Negro, Ethnologically Considered,"

Douglass makes reference to phrenologist George Combe's "great work" *The Constitution of Man*, first published in 1828, in his argument against polygenism.[7] In doing so, as cultural historian Britt Rusert argues, he draws on phrenology's emphasis on the brain's ability to change as a way to think through "ways that the individual's power for self-transformation might expand into larger political transformations."[8] When God created humanity, Douglass says, "the Almighty, within certain limits, endowed mankind with organizations capable of countless variations in form, feature and color," which is why, he says, it is wrong to think that it is "necessary to begin a new creation," or a new species, "for every new variety."[9] Douglass's engagement with phrenological styles of thinking makes it possible for him to envision bioplasticity, not only of "form" and "feature" but also of "color," as a "powerful argument in favor of the oneness of the human family."[10] Diversity of color, he concludes, "does not disprove a common nature, nor does it disprove a common destiny."[11] Douglass's example shows the ways that phrenology's emphasis on plasticity made it not only a potent tool for racists, as it proved to be, but also a potentially powerful argument against racial essentialism.

In the first half of the nineteenth century, phrenology offered a biological explanation for mental phenomena that was influential in both Europe and the United States. Though many today dismiss phrenology as being at odds with professional science, the discipline is an important precursor to a variety of developments in modern neurology, especially the concept of neural localization.[12] Austrian neuroanatomist Franz Joseph Gall published one of the foundational texts of phrenology, *Discours d'ouverture, lu par M. le Dr Gall à la première séance de son cours public sur la physiologie du cerveau*, a lecture given during a public course on neurophysiology, in 1808.[13] In it he makes the seminal claim that discrete mental faculties are located within specific areas of the brain and that the skull's structure can offer clues to the relative strengths and weaknesses of these mental faculties in any given person. This connection between cranial morphology and the "mental organs" they index is phrenology's foundational concept.[14]

In the early decades of the nineteenth century, Gall's ideas about the brain spread throughout Europe and the United States, propelled by the immensely popular writings of George Combe and Gall's former assistant Johann Spurzheim; and as they spread, individual thinkers refashioned them to fit their own ends. For example, the works of Orson Fowler, as I discuss in chapter 2, translate phrenological ideas about the materiality of the mind into the meliorist language of antebellum physiological reform. Fowler maintains Gall's emphasis on the connection between brain and mind; as he asserts in

Fowler's Practical Phrenology, phrenology "points out those connexions and relations which exist between *the conditions and developments of the* BRAIN, *and the manifestations of the* MIND, discovering each from an observation of the other."[15] Its central tenant is "that each class of mental function is manifested by means of a given portion of the brain, called an organ, the size of which is the measure of the power of function."[16] And because those organs push against the skull, the topography of an individual's head reveals the size of his or her mental organs. What makes the Fowler brothers' phrenological theory different from that of someone like Gall is their framing of the mental organs as subject to change and deliberate management. In *Fowler's Practical Phrenology*, Orson writes that the "fundamental principle of phrenology" is that the size of the various mental organs might change depending on "the physiology, or the *organization and condition of the body*, which embraces the temperament, the parentage, health, physical habits, diet, exercise, excitement, education, sleep, &c."[17] It follows, he asserts, that to act upon one of these aspects of one's physiology is to act upon one's brain. For example, he advises individuals whose "mental apparatus" has become overused at the expense of their muscles to "suspend business; remove care and anxiety; take things easily; take much physical exercise."[18]

Even individual mental organs might be targeted for improvement. An organ might be *"increased in size* by constant activity," Fowler affirms, a physiological law that "is in perfect accordance with the whole process of nature."[19] Indeed, he continues, "It is a universal *principle of nature*, that *every* 'organ is increased in size by constant activity,' and the increase of the *brain* can be determined just as well as that of any other corporeal organ"; that is, he says, why hatters have noticed "that literary men generally require larger hats than labouring men, even though their *bodies* are smaller."[20] It follows that the same holds for those who exercise individual organs. A man in England, for example, had a cast of his head taken every year for five years, in the meantime exercising "some of the phrenological faculties, and avoiding exercising others"; each cast showed relative increases and decreases in the size of those organs.[21] At the end of five years, he writes, the first and the last casts differed so much that they might have been taken from different people. He takes this example among others as proof that *"the exercise of particular mental faculties, causes the exercise, and consequent enlargement, of corresponding portions of the brain*, and, of course, an increase of the *scull* above them."[22] "This," he concludes, "I conceive to be not only one of the least explored, but one of the most important, departments of this invaluable science."[23]

Fowler's ideas about the mutability of the mental organs remains to this day "one of the least explored" aspects of his phrenological theory, but it is "one of the most important" with regard to health reform. The phrenological subjectivity constructed by the Fowler brothers invites individuals to reshape their brains through mental exercise. Much like Grahamian dietetics, it combines scrutiny of the somatic self with a set of techniques that can mold that self. As is the case with dietary reform, being free to manage one's body means being responsible for doing so; being sick is a consequence of "violat[ing] nature's laws," and humans "have no more right to be sick than to commit suicide, and sick persons are to be *blamed*, not pitied."[24] But whereas Graham focuses on forming the body by governing what goes into it, Fowler in *Practical Phrenology* direct his adherents to harness their bodies' own generative powers.

The primary technique Fowler gives for increasing the size and power of a given mental organ is "exercise," which is a concept that *Practical Phrenology* only sketches. Subsequent publications, such as his *Fowler on Memory* (1842) and *Self-Culture, and Perfection of Character* (1847), flesh out how "the exercise of any *phrenological* organ, causes the blood to flow to *that organ* in proportion as it is exercised, and this blood contains matter for enlarging these parts, which it does in proportion to its abundance."[25] This capability is for Fowler "the greatest discovery of this age or any other—the means of improving the MIND and perfecting the SOUL . . . man is NOT compelled to carry all his faults, excesses, and defects to his grave."[26] He defines "exercise" as "the vigorous and continuous ACTION of any given faculty": "ACTION," he asserts, "is the great means of strengthening every power of our nature."[27] This means that to increase one's faculty of reverence, one should exercise it with "thoughts of God"; those who desire greater mirthfulness should seek "the laughable or ridiculous."[28]

Fowler's strategy of pointing to the physical effects of muscular exercise as analogic proof that mental exercise enlarges mental organs suggests the degree to which notions of physical training inform his vision of physiological reform. Historian Jan Todd's study of nineteenth-century women's exercise regimes charts how what she calls "purposive exercise," or exercise undertaken as training rather than as relaxation or competition, "is about change—about creating a new vision of the body."[29] It is "undertaken to meet specific physiological and philosophical goals," and even in the nineteenth century, Todd argues, it "encouraged women to have a new relationship to their bodies—to view them as trainable and, more importantly, controllable."[30]

In the same vein, the notion of mental exercise was, for the Fowlers and their readers, a way to conceptualize the brain itself as "trainable" and therefore "controllable."

In the years following his phrenological reading in 1849, Whitman retained ties to the Fowlers. After Whitman published the first edition of *Leaves of Grass* in 1855, the Fowler's publishing company, Fowler and Wells (after the Fowlers' brother-in-law, Samuel R. Wells), placed an advertisement in the *New York Tribune* giving notice that it was for sale at their Broadway phrenological cabinet.[31] The next year, Fowler and Wells itself published the expanded second edition of *Leaves of Grass*, which was, perhaps due to the inclusion of sexually charged poems such as his "Poem of Procreation," a financial failure.[32] It was not long after this blow that Whitman tried his hand at health reform. Between September and December 1858, Whitman published "Manly Health and Training" in the *New York Atlas* under the pen name Mose Velsor. (Velsor is Whitman's mother's birth name.) The document, only recently rediscovered by Zachary Turpin and published in its entirety in a special double issue of the *Walt Whitman Quarterly Review* in 2016, eludes easy characterization. Turpin notes that it is difficult even to assign it a genre: "It is part guest editorial, part self-help column, published in the *New York Atlas*. At first, it reads as a fairly straightforward diet-and-exercise guide for men, yet, over its course, the series accretes additional genres."[33] As Whitman published more sections of the essay throughout the autumn of 1858, he came to address, as Turpin writes, "physical beauty, manly comradeship, sex and reproduction, socialization, race, eugenics, war, climate, longevity, bathing, prizefighting, gymnastics, baseball, footwear, facial hair, depression, alcohol, and prostitution," a range of topics that is, as Turpin intimates, broad in scope.[34] But such a range might be found in many of the Fowlers' own publications. It would not be unusual for Orson Fowler, for example, to champion the soul-redeeming power of friendship on one page, the virtues of bathing the next, and the wisdom of choosing a mate with complementary phrenological bumps the next. If antebellum health reformers agreed on anything, it was that the disparate systems of the body are interconnected in such a way that to act on the part is to act on the whole; from this perspective, it makes perfect sense for Whitman to view these body-oriented topics as similarly interconnected.

The influence of contemporary physiological reform generally, and of the Fowlerian school of reform specifically, on "Manly Health" cannot be overstated. The essay, as Turpin discovered, includes a number of "quotations cribbed" from the *Water-Cure Journal*, published by Fowler and Wells, among other contemporary health reform periodicals and books, including Orson Fowler's *American Phrenological Journal and Miscellany* and John William Orr's *Book of Swimming*, making it "quite likely his most plagiarized work."³⁵ Yet Turpin also counsels us to note "that, regardless of source, most installments of 'Manly Health and Training' are almost entirely in Whitman's own words. Only in a few of them does Whitman brazenly plagiarize."³⁶ How, then, to read this work—perhaps as a convenient way to make ends meet? That is Turpin's point of view; he asserts that because the 1855 and 1856 editions of *Leaves of Grass* sold poorly and because Whitman faced "a lawsuit for loan default," the essay "is thus probably best categorized as a side project, one of several freelance jobs Whitman took on during this period, anonymously or pseudonymously, for extra cash."³⁷

But what if we were to read "Manly Health and Training" as Whitman presents it: a "presentation in a collected and connected form, for popular use," on "the subject of developing a perfect and manly physique"?³⁸ Taking the essay seriously as Whitman's contribution to antebellum health reform allows us to understand it as both a catalog of contemporary health reform efforts and an arrangement—a disciplining—of those ideas into an original vision. That vision examines the dynamic tension between, on the one hand, the freedom afforded by conceptions of the body as plastic and, on the other, the discipline necessary to take charge of a body in flux. In "Manly Health," Whitman explores how discipline paradoxically forms the foundation of freedom and well-being in the context of antebellum health reform. In doing so, he troubles easy distinctions between freedom and governance.

Even as Whitman flits from topic to topic in "Manly Health," he maintains steady focus on a few recurrent themes: training and other forms of "cultivation"; bodily form, expressed by the term "physique"; and social attachments to both men and women. Rigorous self-discipline binds these themes, and for good reason: as David S. Reynolds remarks, Whitman's notebooks from his middle age reveal an intense personal struggle to establish not only bodily control but also bodily perfection.³⁹ In 1861, he penned the following entry in his journal: "I have resolv'd to inaugurate for myself a pure perfect sweet, cleanblooded robust body by ignoring all drinks but water and pure milk—and all fat meats later suppers—a great body—a purged, cleansed, spiritualised and invigorated body—."⁴⁰ Reynolds asserts that this entry reflects Whitman's commitment to "straightforward Fowlerian self-control," but the poet's reference to "a pure perfect sweet, cleanblooded robust body," one that is "purged, cleansed, spiritualised and invigorated," much more resembles the language Whitman uses himself in "Manly Health" and in his poetry than it does anything published by Fowler and Wells.[41] By the end of the 1850s, Whitman had developed his own language of health, at once rooted in concepts drawn from popular cultures of reform and expressive of a "spiritualised" vision of Whitman's own devising.

The foundational concept of Whitman's essay is training, defined as "intellect applied to the bettering of the form, the blood, the strength, the life, of man" and as "*the entire science of manly excellence, education, beauty, and vigor.*"[42] Whitman cautions that it "does not consist in mere exercise": "Equally important," he writes, are "the diet, drink, habits, sleep, &c. Bathing, the breathing of good air, and certain other requisites, are also not to be overlooked."[43] By "training," he means taking a reasoned, deliberate, and systematic approach to one's daily activities (food, sleep, bathing, and so on) so that one's whole body might reach its potential. Focusing on the whole body, as Whitman notes, puts him out of step with someone like Sylvester Graham, whose system of dietetics centers on the stomach's signal role in bodily and mental health. "The true theory of health," Whitman writes, "is multiform, and does not consist of one or two rules alone": "The vegetarian, for instance, insists on the total salvation of the human race, if they would only abstain from animal food! This is ridiculous. Others have their hobbies—some of one kind, some of a different. But it is often to be noticed that, in the same person, habits exist that mutually contradict each other, and are parts of opposite theories."[44] Whitman here echoes Thoreau's mocking depiction of the philanthropist as someone who, upon suffering dyspepsia after eating a green apple, "forthwith sets about reforming . . . the world" by making sure that no one else will eat a green apple.[45] For Whitman as for Thoreau, reform cannot be so simple: "A system of health, in order to be worth following, ought to be consistent in all its parts, and complete besides; and then followed faithfully for a long time. It is too much to expect any great immediate results; it is quite enough if they come in the course of a few months."[46] What Whitman advocates is the adherence to a process of careful self-reflection and decisive action that can, not over days but over months or years, renew the self—both physically and spiritually.

Like Sylvester Graham, Catharine Beecher, Mary Peabody Mann, and virtually every other antebellum health reformer, Whitman emphasizes control of the diet as the most important form of bodily care and intervention. He frets that "modern taste and ingenuity have contrived not a hundred, but hundreds of solid and liquid stimulants, artificial tastes, condiments" that have ruined both America's palate and its stomach, echoing Graham's concerns about mustard and other vibrantly flavored condiments.[47] Whitman peppers the whole of "Manly Health" with dietary advice, but he arranges most of it in a section breathlessly titled "The Great American Evil — Indigestion."[48] The idea that (white, male, middle-class) Americans specifically were subject to dyspepsia animates much antebellum discourse about diet, and Whitman is no different; poor digestion is where "four-fifths of the weaknesses, breakings-down, and premature deaths, of American [sic] begin."[49] Only "thorough and regular digestion" can supply "manly and muscular vigor to the system," and the body withers without it.[50] He cannot overstress its significance to his program: "All other rules and requisites may be attended to, but if the stomach be out of order, and allowed to remain so for any length of time, all will be of no avail."[51] To drive home his point, he asserts that "eternal vigilance is the price of — digestion!"[52] In altering the phrase "eternal vigilance is the price of liberty" — which is, as he writes, "one of the stereotyped sayings of the politicians" — to speak to the importance of digestion, Whitman makes "liberty" itself interchangeable with "digestion." To do so is to locate "vigilance," a watchful and wary self-regard, as the guarantor of both national liberty and a healthy stomach. At the same time, the poet hints at healthy digestion itself being a prerequisite of the healthy-bodied, bold liberty he imagines "Manly Health" as making possible. Ultimately, the maintenance of liberty is a matter of both somatic and political well-being.

Although Whitman does agree with other reformers about the centrality of digestion to overall bodily health, he seeks to diverge from their signature alarmism. In a seeming rebuke to Grahamian dietary restrictions, Whitman comments on the "monstrous and enfeebling school" that has lately "obtained considerable foothold in the United States, especially in New England": "We have been flooded in America, during the last fifteen or twenty years, with vast numbers of doctors, books, theories, publications, &c., whose general drift, with respect to diet, had been to make people live altogether on dry bread, stewed apples, or similar interesting stuff."[53] His reference to New Englanders living on "dry bread" and "stewed apples," even if not a direct rebuke to Grahamism specifically, nonetheless pushes against dietary reformers' insistence on radically limiting the American diet. Whitman comments that "there is such a thing as taking too minute and morbid care of the health," a practice that results in "losing it as effectually as by taking no care at all."[54] He reassures his readers that so long as "other things make up for it sufficiently, almost any article of food may be eaten with impunity."[55] For example, although sailors live on a diet of "salt beef, sea-biscuit and strong coffee" — recall the diets of the *Pequod*'s harpooners — they suffer no dietary ill effects because they spend their lives working in the fresh air.⁵⁶ In fact, he writes, "a certain degree of abandon is necessary to the processes of perfect health and a muscular tone of the system."⁵⁷ In this formulation, Whitman returns to the interplay of discipline, perfection, and freedom, or "abandon." That "perfect health" requires "abandon," but only "a certain degree" of it, indicates a tension between freedom and discipline that informs much of "Manly Health." Attaining a perfect body prepared for the rigors of freedom paradoxically requires one to voluntarily limit one's freedom by following Whitman's program. Yet this is a productive tension in that it shows how easy distinctions between discipline and freedom elide their essentially dialectic nature, which is of both a conceptual and a fleshly nature.

"Manly Health" connects physical fitness to other aspects of masculine well-being, from one's intellect to one's complexion to one's struggle to achieve "an ever-happy soul."⁵⁸ The man reformed by Whitman's advice gains not only "herculean strength" and muscular "suppleness" but also "a laughing voice, a merry song morn and night, [and] a sparkling eye!"⁵⁹ Physical training imparts physical health and, consequently, a boisterous happiness. In addition, Whitman claims that this training molds men into more respectable, morally upstanding citizens, despite what he calls the "mutual recoil between the pure moralist and the teacher of healthy bodily exercises and games": as the ancient Greeks believed, a physically healthy man is "more apt to become good, upright, friendly, and self-respected."⁶⁰ And as suggested by his insistence that "one of the greatest benefits of training, exercise, simple food, early hours, &c., is that, under them, the sexual passions are far less morbid," adherents' public and private virtues will see improvement under his plan.⁶¹ Training is not only about making better bodies; it is also about making better men.

Whitman's ideas about what makes a man better than he was before—moral righteousness, a dampened sex drive—align with those of Graham and the Fowlers. Yet he diverges from prevailing reformist thought when he speaks, as he does throughout "Manly Health," of physical fitness as the prerequisite of what he calls "real manly beauty."⁶² He realizes that by focusing on male beauty—and even by implying that men might wish to make themselves more beautiful at all—he moves beyond prevailing ideas about masculinity. But, he says, it is only "pretended to be considered, that personal beauty is something not proper for the attention of men, but must be left for the other sex."⁶³ A man taking pride in his looks is an "instinct" that "can never be eradicated" and "is always more or less operative," despite cultural pressure not to appear vain.⁶⁴ Whitman devotes an entire section of the essay to "Manly Beauty—The True Ambition," in which he emphasizes that the price of beauty is sustained physical discipline: "[I] would here place before our readers, especially the youth, the thought that nothing is more worthy their ambition, and will surely repay the effort and resolution to follow them, than a steady pursuit of the regulations, laws, self-denials, and daily habitudes that lead to the sound condition and beautiful appearance of the body, the manly form—this wondrous and beautiful structure that never wearies the mind in contemplating its inward and outward mysteries."[65] The "steady pursuit" of self-regulation bestows both a "sound condition" and a "beautiful appearance"; later, Whitman adds that "whatever position of wealth or education you may be," personal beauty "is a germ, implanted by nature, that you should make grow."[66] Once attained, manly beauty will "make life sweet" by forming "a main part of that reception of friendship, admiration and good will which all desire."[67]

Although it is tempting to read "Manly Health and Training" as a way to make money after the financial failure of the 1855 edition of *Leaves of Grass* or even as an amateurish imitation of the Fowler and Wells school of popular medicine, attending to its guidelines for exercise, diet, and personal beauty reveals its surprisingly original vision of masculine embodiment. Its focus on training instead of self-deprivation as the mechanism of self-improvement resonates with Whitman's insistence in his poetry for more: more lovers, more cities, more futures. Training brings into focus how care of the bioplastic body means cultivating its capacities through disciplined effort: the embodied subject Whitman imagines in "Manly Health" becomes more free the more he trains his body. This vision of freedom through bodily discipline is something Whitman would continue to develop in his poetry, particularly in the third edition of *Leaves of Grass*, published two years after "Manly Health."

Training, Exercise, and the 1860 *Leaves of Grass*

The 1860 edition of *Leaves of Grass*, the first Whitman published after the conclusion of "Manly Health and Training," includes a number of new poems that take up the essay's themes of bodily care and governance. One such is "A Hand-Mirror":

> HOLD it up sternly! See this it sends back! (Who is it? Is it you?)
> Outside fair costume—within, ashes and filth,
> No more a flashing eye—no more a sonorous voice or springy step,

> Now some slave's eye, voice, hands, step,
> A drunkard's breath, unwholesome eater's face, venerealee's flesh,
> Lungs rotting away piecemeal, stomach sour and cankerous,
> Joints rheumatic, bowels clogged with abomination,
> Blood circulating dark and poisonous streams,
> Words babble, hearing and touch callous,
> No brain, no heart left—no magnetism of sex;
> Such, from one look in this looking-glass ere you go hence,
> Such a result so soon—and from such a beginning![68]

These lines give poetic form to a number of ideas Whitman explores in "Manly Health." A handheld mirror figures the sort of watchful self-regard that animates the essay's prescriptions for physical well-being. In "A Hand-Mirror," the speaker commands the reader to hold up the mirror "sternly," without any attempt to shy away from the image it reflects. At best, such self-regard reveals that one is healthy; here, in a sort of perverse blazon, the mirror displays little less than the walking dead. A "fair" exterior conceals a rotten core of "ashes and filth," rotting lungs, and poisonous blood.

Yet the ravages of the beholder's propensity for alcohol, unhealthy food, and sexual excess have more than physical consequences. Hard living takes one's very freedom away, leaving one with "some slave's eye, voice, hands, step." Here the speaker implies the paradoxical claim that a certain sort of free living, framed as following one's appetitive wants and sexual urges, is in fact a type of enslavement. That enslavement makes one's organs, limbs, and abilities not one's own; the poem's "you" has become "some slave." Whitman does not make clear what sort of slave the beholder has become, or to what or whom he is enslaved. The transformation might rest on the perception of the slave's body as beaten, malnourished, and mistreated or on the racist belief that the bodies of people of African descent are inferior to white bodies. The transformation might also refer to the beholder's voluntary subjugation to his appetites. "Manly Health" supports the final interpretation, for the essay references the travails of young men who have become "slaves of habits they know to be bad" or "slave[s] of custom."[69]

That Whitman leaves the meaning of slavery unclear in "A Hand-Mirror" implies a troubling equivalence among freedom, whiteness, and health that haunts much of his thinking on health and healthy bodies, much as the question of race haunts the vision of the United States he expresses in his poetry.[70] Turpin notes that in "Manly Health," Whitman illustrates his assertion that "some of the most rugged and unfavorable climates turn out the noblest specimens of men" with mentions of Scandinavia, northern Europe, and "chilly and sterile Germania," but not of Africa; it is not a stretch to say that Whitman is most interested in white, male bodies.[71] Yet the slave is just one of many selves the hand-mirror displays: there is also the "drunkard," the "unwholesome eater," and the "venerealee." Ultimately, the poem suggests, to lose control of oneself is to lose one's self entirely.

Although "A Hand-Mirror" is new to the 1860 edition of *Leaves of Grass*, earlier editions also demonstrate Whitman's interest in the human body.[72] Take, for instance, untitled lines from the 1855 edition that would later be part of the poem titled "Song of Myself": "Welcome is every organ and attribute of me, and of any man hearty and clean, / Not an inch nor a particle of an inch is vile, and none shall be less familiar than the rest."[73] Similarly, in the 1856 edition, Whitman titles what he would call in the 1867 edition "I Sing the Body Electric" a "Poem of The Body": "Was it doubted if those who corrupt their own live bodies conceal themselves? / And if those who defile the living are as bad as they who defile the dead?"[74] By welcoming "every organ" of himself, singing the praises of "hearty and clean" men, and referencing "those who corrupt their own live / bodies," Whitman touches on many of the themes that he explores in later poems, such as "A Hand-Mirror." The question is this: Did Whitman's understanding of the human body and its capacities change because of his deep engagement with health reform in the late fifties? If so, to what degree? My contention is that his understanding changed substantially and in ways that led him to emphasize didactic images of the body's nourishment and discipline after 1858. In the first two editions of *Leaves of Grass*, these images are comparatively fleeting; for example, readers in 1855 know that the poet's persona welcomes any "hearty and clean" man, but they do not learn, as readers in 1860 do, what constitutes heartiness or how to achieve cleanliness. In 1860 and afterward, as I argue in the following pages, Whitman pursues images of bodily health in ways that suggest not just how to celebrate it but also how to attain it. And the path to attaining health, he asserts throughout the 1860 edition, begins with exercising control of the body.

Indeed, as scholars such as Gregory Eiselein and Harold Aspiz have remarked, the 1860 edition of *Leaves of Grass* as a whole demonstrates Whitman's "increased attentiveness" to control (here, of the textual body of his poetry) in the form of "organization and structure": for the first time he placed many poems into what he called "clusters," including the "Calamus" sequence, and numbered many poems and stanzas.[75] Eiselein notes that this edition has a clear beginning and end: it "begins with 'Proto-Leaf' (later called

'Starting from Paumanok'), a prefatory poem that announces the poet's intentions and major themes, a poem that deliberately marks the beginning of the book, just as '*So long!*' concludes the book."[76] Aspiz notes that the second edition of *Leaves of Grass*, published in 1856, is the first edition to bear the conceptual imprint of "the Fowler and Wells style" and "their spirit of republican reformism," but I contend that it is in the third edition that the lines of this imprint are at their deepest and most discernible.[77] The changes Whitman made to *Leaves of Grass*—to structure, mold, categorize, and otherwise discipline his poetry—links the 1860 edition to "Manly Health and Training" at not only the thematic level, as demonstrated by poems such as "A Hand-Mirror," but also the formal level. In my reading, Whitman marshals discipline to bestow the same health, virility, and grace to *Leaves of Grass* as it does to the male body. This argument asks us to revise how we think of the relationship between "Manly Health" and *Leaves of Grass*. "Manly Health" becomes something that is not separate from Whitman's poetic production; instead, it provides a conceptual framework for thinking through Whitman's process of textual revision. *Leaves of Grass* itself becomes something like the male body: a plastic living thing whose power and freedom might best be realized by imposing upon it regimes of discipline and management. And Whitman's lifetime of revision becomes an exercise in bioplasticity in its careful, self-oriented modulation of form and content. He intervenes in the body of his masterwork again and again, putting into practice what he advocates in "Manly Health": "a generative and altogether physical cure, involving years of time, and revolution of habits."[78]

It is a sad irony that when Whitman wrote both "Manly Health" and the 1860 edition of *Leaves of Grass*, he was himself in unusually poor health. Aspiz writes that despite "the myth of his quenchless vigor," in 1858 Whitman experienced his first "sun-stroke," an attack difficult to parse today; physician Philip Marshall Dale identifies it as "a small cerebral hemorrhage."[79] In the middle of the nineteenth century, "sun-stroke," or "*coup de soleil*," was "almost universally conceded to be a sudden and intense congestion of the brain sufficiently severe to cause immediate death," notes physician Sanford B. Hunt in "Observations on the Cause of the Disease Known as Sun-Stroke," published in the *New Hampshire Journal of Medicine* in 1855.[80] David S. Reynolds speculates that Whitman's condition was "probably associated with hypertension" and that he was troubled by its aftereffects "periodically during the Civil War and after."[81] Aspiz notes that Whitman's concern about his health bled into other aspects of his life, especially his journalistic work: "Many of his newspaper articles in the *Brooklyn Daily Times*, 1857–59, demonstrated an interest in consumption and in the methods used to effect its cure; others dealt with the care of the sick and injured, the availability of healthful food and pure water, and the need for exercise. Moreover, his frequent visits to patients in the New York hospitals and his careful observation of medical care showed a sympathy with physical suffering which could have stemmed from an apprehension of his own imperfect health."[82] Only two years prior to his illness, in 1856, Whitman had asked in the second edition of *Leaves of Grass*: "How dare a sick man, or an obedient man, write poems for These States?"[83] Suddenly, Whitman found himself "a sick man" who nevertheless dared to write poetry. Whitman's poor health in the late 1850s suggests that his concurrent turn to Fowlerian health reform in both "Manly Health" and the 1860 *Leaves of Grass* was not merely a matter of expediency, financial or otherwise, but rather a reflection of genuine concern for his health. His interest in "healthful food and pure water, and the need for exercise," present in the first two editions of *Leaves of Grass* but much more so in subsequent editions, could well be understood as a response to the health issues that arose in his middle age. And by disciplining his masterwork-in-progress with clusters and numbers, he asserted upon it an orderliness that his own body lacked.

Whitman came to think later in his life that if a poem could be trained, so too could its readers. In his long essay *Democratic Vistas* (1871), Whitman looks to the future of a post–Civil War America and imagines literature as helping to mold new generations of citizens. In it he asserts that the nation's "sole course," if it is to survive, is "a new theory of literary composition for imaginative works of the very first class, and especially for highest poems."[84] Reading is itself a type of training, "a gymnast's struggle":

> Books are to be call'd for, and supplied, on the assumption that the process of reading is not a half-sleep, but, in highest sense, an exercise, a gymnast's struggle; that the reader is to do something for himself, must be on the alert, must himself or herself construct indeed the poem, argument, history, metaphysical essay—the text furnishing the hints, the clue, the start or frame-work. Not the book needs so much to be the complete thing, but the reader of the book does. That were to make a nation of supple and athletic minds, well-train'd, intuitive, used to depend on themselves, and not on a few coteries of writers.[85]

Far from dozing in "a half-sleep," readers of imaginative literature "must be on the alert": faced with nothing else than ink on a page, he or she must strive to create meaning from "the hints, the clue, the start or frame-work" the text provides. Ed Folsom argues that Whitman here articulates an "erotics of reading" in which "words were the seeds, but the womb in which the seed would grow and form was the reader's mind. . . . The poet's job was to cajole, seduce the reader until the seminal ideas could flow into a receptive mind and join with the reader to construct a future unexpected and strong."[86] Yet this interpretation risks characterizing Whitman's reader as the "seduce[d]" recipient of the poet's ideas rather than as an agent who "himself or herself construct[s]" not only interpretive meaning but the "text" or "book" itself. Although Whitman does wish to combine text and reader to create a more vital future for the country, he emphasizes the ways that readers themselves participate in their own transformations.

By metaphorizing "the process of reading" as "an exercise, a gymnast's struggle," and characterizing the reader's mind as "supple and athletic," Whitman draws direct connections between readerly and physical training. The phrase "gymnast's struggle" frames reading as an exertive rather than a passive activity. In *The Illustrated Family Gymnasium*, published in 1857 by Fowler and Wells, Russell Thacher Trall remarks that practicing gymnastics "give[s] energy and precision to muscular movements" by training athletes' bodies with Indian clubs, wooden horses, and climbing ropes.[87] In the same way, Whitman imagines readers' minds gaining ever more "energy" and "precision" as they struggle, as he writes, to "construct indeed the poem, argument, history, metaphysical essay." The goal of this struggle is to produce minds supple enough to navigate the gulf between "democracy's convictions, aspirations, and the people's crudeness, vice, caprices," the central issue the essay addresses.[88] Readers' experiences forming narratives within themselves, the poet writes, will free them from relying "on a few coteries of writers" to supply their thoughts; instead, they will think for themselves and perform the hard work of democratic self-governance. Eventually, he hopes, the government of the United States will render its citizenry, even "the ignorant, the credulous, the unfit and uncouth," more available to reformist interventions; the ultimate role of government is "to develop, to open up to cultivation, to encourage the possibilities of all beneficent and manly outcroppage."[89]

Literature, and especially the composition of the "highest poems," is an important part of Whitman's vision for the nation's future because it simultaneously serves as equipment in the collective mental gymnasium and as an expression of national identity. Indeed, he identifies "imaginative literature, especially poetry, the stock of all," as the "main bearing" of *Democratic*

Vistas.⁹⁰ Most of all, the nation's literature should be altogether new: "America demands a poetry that is bold, modern, and all-surrounding and kosmical, as she is herself. . . . Like America, it must extricate itself from even the greatest models of the past, and, while courteous to them, must have entire faith in itself, and the products of its own democratic spirit only."⁹¹ An essential aspect of American poetry's break from "even the greatest models of the past" and what inspires it with the "democratic spirit" is its use as a tool for a project of national cultivation. Precisely because poetry, more than prose, concerns itself with and is made up of imaginative "hints, the clue, the start or frame-work," it possesses the sort of incompleteness that provides readers the opportunity to sharpen their minds: "Not the book needs so much to be the complete thing, but the reader of the book does."⁹² The concept of training, then, informs Whitman's understanding of both poetic composition and poetic reading. The freedom of both writing and reading—Whitman's oracular spurts, his reader's pleasurable struggle to make sense of them—operates within a greater disciplinary logic.

Both mental and physical training are processual and require time, discipline, and applied effort to effect change. In both "Manly Health and Training" and the 1860 edition of *Leaves of Grass*, Whitman advises his reader to consider the text a companion so that its lessons will remain, at some points literally, close to the heart. The opening sentence of the "Manly Health" series expresses Whitman's desire that the reader who is "arrested by the above headlines" will be "a companion to the end of our series," which frames "Manly Health" as a particularly fit friend who is kindly giving the reader advice on diet, exercise, and clean living. Likewise, the 1860 edition of *Leaves of Grass* includes several references in the newly added "Calamus" cluster that encourage the reader to consider it not only a text but an incarnated friend. In the cluster's third poem, the speaker addresses "WHOEVER you are holding me now in hand"; and in the fifth, the speaker further identifies himself with the physical text of *Leaves of Grass*:

> Or, if you will, thrusting me beneath your clothing,
> Where I may feel the throbs of your heart, or rest upon your hip,
> Carry me when you go forth over land or sea.⁹³

As Folsom notes, lines such as these are "part of the physicality of the book for Whitman: it had a body, a spine, a face, folds, and it received a reader's actual physical touch, just as the reader was touched by the book (in physical and emotional ways)."⁹⁴ That the contents of the book's third edition are organized, named, and numbered to the individual stanza means that it is something like the ideal man of "Manly Health," whose personal beauty wins him the affections of companions and lovers.

Whitman sings the praises of companionship throughout "Calamus"; in the cluster's first poem, he wastes no time in asserting that "the Soul of the man I speak for, feeds, rejoices only in comrades."[95] The phrase "feeds, rejoices" locates male affection as the soul's "only" source of both nourishment and enjoyment. In the same poem, the speaker "resolve[s] to sing no songs to-day but those of manly attachment," for such attachments offer, among other things, the "types of athletic love" that render the affections powerful and supple.[96] In the cluster's eleventh poem, Whitman further explores athletic love, as his speaker rises "at dawn from the bed of perfect health" and bathes in "cool waters" on the beach; he feels a surge of happiness thinking of "how my dear friend, my lover, was on his way coming . . . and all that day my food nourished me more."[97] The poem paints a portrait of a man whose adherence to Fowlerian doctrine—early rising, daily bathing in "cool waters"—interlaces with his "athletic love" for his "dear friend, my lover."[98] In "Manly Health," Whitman asserts that merely the physical presence of a healthy person is healing: "We have even sometimes fancied that there was *a wonderful medicinal effect in the mere personal presence of a man who was perfectly well!*"[99] He imagines this effect as a natural aspect of embodiment. "Let a young man endeavor to realise of his body," he writes, "that, among other things, it is a machine calculated to produce force, an outpouring of subtle force, the same in moving among his fellow men as the orbs in space have in revolving through their orbits."[100] A man's "curious attraction of gravitation," he continues, "is one of the most amazing and delightful of natural results."[101] Just as he encourages readers to think of both "Manly Health" and the third edition of *Leaves of Grass* as companions, Whitman emphasizes in the "Calamus" cluster the pleasurable, "delightful" attractiveness of bodies both biological and textual.

That this edition of *Leaves of Grass* is the first to so insistently conceptualize itself as embodied suggests that Whitman thought about how poetry might function similarly to the healthy body—by affecting those around it, by being affected in return, and by exemplifying the outgoing vitality he celebrates in "Manly Health."[102] Aspiz writes that some nineteenth-century readers actually did feel the healing power of what he calls the poem's "beneficial emanations": he gives the example of John Addington Symonds, an English poet and biographer and one of Whitman's correspondents, who "testified that simply by reading *Leaves of Grass* in the 1860s he had been cured of his former physical debility."[103] Michael Warner writes that Symonds first encountered Whitman's poetry in 1865, when his friend Fredric Myers read to him from the "Calamus" cluster; because the next edition of *Leaves of Grass* would not be published until 1867, he could have only read the 1860 edition.[104] It is perhaps not happenstance that Symonds felt the invigorating effects of Whitman's poetry in this edition in particular; because it embodies the cheerful, affectionate healthiness of *Manly Health*, the 1860 *Leaves of Grass* partakes of the healthy man's ability to transfer his own well-being to others.

Not only the form but also the content of the 1860 *Leaves of Grass* is deeply concerned with exploring the ramifications of the human body's capacity for change. The cluster "Says," comprising eight short numbered poems new to this edition, considers how the plasticity of individual human bodies might become the plasticity of the United States itself. In doing so, it affirms both the sacredness of the body and the reformist potential of biological change. The first poem is only one line: "I SAY whatever tastes sweet to the most perfect person, that is finally right."[105] The phrase "I say," repeated throughout all eight of the cluster's poems, affirms Whitman's poetic persona as self-consciously prescriptive, much as Mose Velsor is. The poem establishes personal perfection, bodily action (the act of tasting), and the search for what is "finally right" as the cluster's themes. It also binds together what is "right" not with aesthetic taste but with gustatory taste, positioning the "perfect" body and its perceptive powers as the arbiter of morality.

The second poem is two lines: "I SAY nourish a great intellect, a great brain; / If I have said anything to the contrary, I hereby retract it."[106] The first line's injunction to "nourish" both "a great intellect" and "a great brain" assumes that one can indeed nourish, or cultivate, those attributes, which echoes the Fowlers' phrenological doctrine of neural plasticity. Crucially, Whitman is never content merely to be a mouthpiece for others' thoughts; the second line toys with how plasticity enables an Emersonian disregard for consistency. The persona simply "retract[s]" "anything to the contrary"; because its advice is always subject to change and revision, it distances itself from the Fowlers' self-sure certainty about human health. Further, that the line begins with "If I have said anything to the contrary" suggests that the speaker is unconcerned with remembering its previous utterances, perhaps those it spoke in previous editions of *Leaves of Grass*. The past, the persona insists, no longer matters. What is at stake is the flow of the present, a process of continuous flux.

The third poem of "Says" is also two lines: "I SAY man shall not hold property in man; / I say the least developed person on earth is just as important and sacred to himself or herself, as the most developed person is to himself or herself."[107]

The persona pushes back against the idea, implicit in Fowlerian health reform, that those who have undertaken regimes of self-management are of greater worth than those who have not. The poem connects this egalitarian approach to development with slavery, particularly as an answer to the practice of justifying slavery as the benevolent care of the more capable race for the less capable. The fourth poem in the cluster maintains the focus on slavery and bodies: "I SAY where liberty draws not the blood out of slavery, there slavery draws the blood out of liberty, / I say the word of the good old cause in These States, and resound it hence over the world."[108] Slavery and liberty are figured as having blood, almost as if they are organisms rather than political constructs. Moreover, these organisms can and do battle or even prey upon each other. Taken together, these two poems extend questions evoked by regimes of bodily development—particularly those that concern the value of purportedly more developed bodies in relation to less developed bodies—into debates about slavery.

The second half of "Says" features significantly longer poems that turn more fully to the prospects of the physiological body politic. The longest of these poems is the cluster's fifth:

> I SAY the human shape or face is so great, it must never be made
>   ridiculous;
> I say for ornaments nothing outre can be allowed,
> And that anything is most beautiful without ornament,
>   And that exaggerations will be sternly revenged in your own
>   physiology, and in other persons' physiology also;
>   And I say that clean-shaped children can be jetted and conceived only
>   where natural forms prevail in public, and the human face and
>   form are never caricatured;
> And I say that genius need never more be turned to romances,
> (For facts properly told, how mean appear all romances.)[109]

The poem defends the materiality of the human body from artistic exaggerations of it, be they "ridiculous" caricatures or "romances" unable to compete with "facts properly told." The speaker advocates taking the human body seriously, especially two aspects of it discussed at length in "Manly Health and Training": its shape, or the form it takes, and the quest to produce a "clean-shaped" citizenry by harnessing the reproductive process. In "Manly Health," Whitman refers to "manly form" as "the sound condition and beautiful appearance of the body . . . this wonderful and beautiful structure."[110] In the poem, "form" or "shape" mean something similar: both physical health and aesthetic beauty. In all of Whitman's poetry, of course, health and personal beauty are coterminous if not synonymous, but this poem emphasizes how "exaggerations," or deviations from moderate living, have the power to change "your own physiology" for the worse. The phrase "sternly revenged" echoes Sylvester Graham's assertion that the somatic repercussions of "exaggerations" are moral as well as biological. Yet in this poem, as in the Fowlers' writing, the moral responsibilities of reproduction involve not only one's own body but those of one's children, the "other[s]" referenced in the fourth line.

The fifth line makes the connection between one's own body and those of one's children clearer: "clean-shaped children," those who are both healthy and beautiful, can be "jetted," or ejaculated, "and conceived only where natural forms prevail in public." The poem's emphasis on ejaculation in addition to conception highlights its assumption that children's forms depend as much on the health of the father at the moment of his orgasm as the health of the mother during her pregnancy. Because it is "children," not "fatherstuff"—a synonym for semen Whitman uses elsewhere in the 1860 *Leaves of Grass*— that the father ejaculates, the poem even suggests that the father's health is more important than the mother's. And the word "jetted," with its connotations of male forcefulness, vigor, and virility, further emphasizes the father's role. As we will see in chapter 4, it was not uncommon for models of heredity prior to Charles Darwin to suppose that the mental and physical conditions of the parents at the moment of conception determined their child's character to some degree. As Daniel Harrison Jacques remarks in *Hints Toward Physical Perfection* (1859), published by the Fowlers, "What is temporary in the parent becomes permanent in the child."[111] "Both the maternal germ and the vitalizing fluid which is destined to impregnate it," he writes, "in common with the other secretions, must necessarily be modified by every condition of body or mind to which the individuals in whom they are prepared may be subjected during the process."[112] The moment of conception is paramount, for "*especially must the condition of body and soul existing at the moment in which the generative act is consummated impress itself upon the germ thereby vitalized.*"[113] For Jacques and others, the future condition of America's children depends on the present condition of their parents. Just as important is that children are conceived, as Whitman asserts, "only where natural forms prevail in public, and the human face and form are never caricatured."

The poem advocates for not only personal but national health, for it is not enough that a child's parents are healthy; the public itself must teem with "natural forms." The speaker suggests that such advocacy—for national health, for more vigorous children—is a more proper role for literary expression than the flights of fancy entertained by "romances."

The sixth poem develops the cluster's focus on projects of national reform more explicitly, announcing that "innovators" will provide "salvation for These States":

> I SAY the word of lands fearing nothing—I will have no other land;
> I say discuss all and expose all—I am for every topic openly;
> I say there can be no salvation for These States without innovators—
>   without free tongues, and ears willing to hear the tongues;
> And I announce as a glory of These States, that they respectfully listen
>   to propositions, reforms, fresh views and doctrines, from
>   successions of men and women,
> Each age with its own growth.[114]

The speaker's injunction to "discuss all and expose all," no matter whether others are willing to discuss it "openly," resonates with Thoreau's paean to "the Hindoo lawgiver," for whom nothing is too "trivial" or "offensive" to discuss and regulate.[115] The United States, a country "fearing nothing," must similarly, Whitman's speaker says, "respectfully listen" to reformers' "fresh views and doctrines." That innovators with "free tongues" will supply the "salvation" and "glory of These States" implies that free, open discussion of reformers' schemes will save both the nation's bodies and its souls.

The seventh poem of "Says," true to Whitman's mercurial and contradictory spirit, apparently retracts the previous poems' affirmations of the body:

> I HAVE said many times that materials and the Soul are great, and that
>   all depends on physique;
> Now I reverse what I said, and affirm that all depends on the æsthetic
>   or intellectual,
> And that criticism is great—and that refinement is greatest of all;
> And I affirm now that the mind governs—and that all depends on
>   the mind.[116]

The first two lines' shift of emphasis from "physique" to "the æsthetic or intellectual" appears to negate what the rest of the cluster has to say about bodily form. Yet that conclusion rests on the assumption that Whitman entertains a Cartesian view of the mind and body as separate substances. To the contrary, Whitman imbibes from midcentury health reform and midcentury physiological theory more generally a sense of the mind and body as interconnected and mutually affecting. In "Manly Health and Training," Whitman critiques the idea that *"true intellectual development"* and *"a noble physique"* are mutually exclusive.[117] So long as the intellect is *"not overstrained and morbid,"* he writes, it *"is highly favorable to long life."*[118] The poem echoes much of what Orson Fowler asserts in the second edition of *Education and Self-Improvement* (1844)—that the first object of self-improvement is the mind: "What part of man constitutes the highest department of *his* nature? Mind. Which is the king, which the subject, in his nature?—which that part for whose special service all others were created? *Mind.*"[119] He identifies "obtaining a knowledge of the laws of mind, and putting this knowledge in *practice*," as "the highest objects that can possibly engage the attention of man."[120] Similarly, the poem's focus on the mind as that which "governs" points up its role in focusing mere action into training. The contradiction that the seventh poem constructs is not so much a contradiction as a way of approaching "refinement" from a different angle.

The eighth and final poem of "Says" draws the cluster to a close by contrasting the first poem's elevation of "the most perfect person" with a focus on "the lowest" person:

> WITH one man or woman—(no matter which one—I even pick out the lowest,)
> With him or her I now illustrate the whole law;
> I say that every right, in politics or what-not, shall be eligible to that one man or woman, on the same terms as any.[121]

What is "the whole law," and how can any "one man or woman" be used to "illustrate" it? Early in the 1860 edition of *Leaves of Grass*, Whitman refers to a law that connects human and animal: "The brood of the turkey-hen, and she with her half-spread wings, / I see in them and myself the same old law."[122] The law that Whitman's speaker, a turkey, and "the lowest" man or woman all demonstrate is the law of life itself—or, more specifically, the shared vital structure of all living things. Whitman here invokes the gnomic concept, beloved by the transcendentalists and discussed in chapter 1, that a part of something contains the whole of it; for example, Goethe's *urpflanze* (ur-leaf) shows how the midrib and veins of a leaf mirror the trunk and branches of a tree. Any "one man or woman," no matter his or her lack of development, demonstrates the law of life—just as the first poem's "perfect person" does.

Taken together, the poems of the "Says" cluster offer an example of how the 1860 *Leaves of Grass* develops the concept of the trainable body as it is understood in "Manly Health and Training." In most cases, the poetry and the exercise guide speak with one voice on such matters as the responsibilities one has to care for one's body and the glories of physical training. Yet in poetry, Whitman gives a fuller voice to the complexities inherent in those issues; freed from the generic impetus to express full confidence in one's prescriptions, he identifies the ways that reformers' quest for human perfection, despite their purportedly egalitarian ethos, risks valuing some bodies more than others. As Whitman was well aware, adherents of the Fowlers' health reform schemes were overwhelmingly white and male; by championing the dignity and divinity of those who do not participate in those schemes, Whitman asserts the primacy of "the whole law," which guarantees "every right" to any "man or woman, on the same terms as any." His contribution to the concept of the trainable body specifically and the bioplastic body generally is to foreground those bodies habitually left behind in reformers' visions of the United States' physiological future. In doing so, his poetry speaks to the prospect of reforming health reform itself.

Later editions of *Leaves of Grass* reflect the goings-on of Whitman's last decades: the Civil War, reunification, and old age. Yet he would continue to ponder health, training, and the sculpting of bodily form after 1860. The 1867 edition was published, as Luke Mancuso writes, "as four separately paginated books stitched together between two covers," which, along with its reordering of the clusters established in 1860, makes it the "most chaotic of all six editions of *Leaves*."[123] That chaos reflects, Mancuso argues, "not only the fracturing of the North from the South" but also "the same stress marks as the contentious rhetoric across America concerned with reinstating rebel states and racial differences between whites and newly-emancipated slaves."[124] He concludes that although this edition is "always on the verge of dissolution in its disarray," it still points up "the productivity of reconstructive solidarity."[125] James Perrin Warren likewise argues that Whitman's arrangement of poems in 1867 brings unity to what in 1860 had perhaps been too well delineated and discrete clusters: in the later edition, these distinctions "are not so wide."[126] To these insights I would add that for Whitman, the pursuit of bodily perfection, whether biological or textual, depends on the ability of bodies to be changed. This is to say that his editions of *Leaves of Grass* are never truly chaotic; rather, they are in the process of being disciplined and of receiving form.

Sons and Daughters Fit for These States

Throughout "Manly Health and Training" and the 1860 *Leaves of Grass*, Whitman affirms both that the individual human body is plastic and thus amendable through training and that the physical condition of children depends on that of their parents. The idea is that by improving oneself, one improves one's children. From the first edition of *Leaves of Grass* onward, Whitman's poetic persona asserts the virile potency of his health: "On women fit for conception I start bigger and nimbler babes," he brags in 1855. "This day I am jetting the stuff of far more arrogant republics."[127] He develops this interest in procreation over time. In the 1856 edition, he adds the following lines, from the poem titled "Poem of Procreation," later collected as one of the third edition's "Enfans d'Adam" cluster:

> I pour the stuff to start sons and daughters fit for These States—I press with slow rude muscle,
> I brace myself effectually—I listen to no entreaties,
> I dare not withdraw till I deposit what has so long accumulated within me.
> Through you I drain the pent-up rivers of myself,
> In you I wrap a thousand onward years,
> On you I graft the grafts of the best-beloved of me and of America,
> The drops I distil upon you are drops of fierce and athletic girls, and of new artists, musicians, singers,
> The babes I beget upon you are to beget babes in their turn,
> I shall demand perfect men and women out of my love-spendings.[128]

By likening his semen as "the stuff to start sons and daughters fit for These States" and as the "love-spendings" that purchase "perfect men and women," Whitman's persona locates the production of "fierce and athletic" children as perhaps the signal expression of a man's health. But such assertions leave unaddressed the relationship of bioplasticity to inherited characteristics. Is a girl born "fierce and athletic" to remain so throughout her life? If so, whence her malleability? Will she be able to mold herself into something else, or is she somehow condemned to remain a fierce athlete? Whitman's work leaves the question unresolved.

Debates surrounding Charles Darwin's *On the Origin of Species*, published in 1859, would set the question of heredity at the center of physiological reform in the coming decades. Much as Whitman envisioned a new generation of Americans whose healthy parentage would prepare them for the strenuous work of democracy, social theorists such as Darwin's half-cousin Francis Galton would soon apply new ideas about heredity to social problems. It goes without saying that Galton and those like him created the intellectual structure on which the eugenic fantasies of the Progressive Era were built—and, indeed, Galton coined the term "eugenics" in *Inquiries into Human Faculty and Its Development* (1883). One way to understand Whitman's contradictory portrayal of the relationship between one's freedom to mold one's body and the freedom of one's children to do the same is as a meeting point between the blue-sky bioplasticity of the 1850s and the hereditary determinism of the 1880s. Although Whitman does not think through whether a child born with certain inherited characteristics might be able to change them, that question would soon be addressed in the novels of Dr. Oliver Wendell Holmes.

CHAPTER FOUR

Tricks of the Blood
Heredity and Repair in Oliver Wendell Holmes Sr.

> Well, we doctors see so much of families, how the tricks of the blood keep breaking out, just as much in character as they do in looks, that we can't help feeling as if a great many people hadn't a fair chance to be what is called "good," and that there isn't a text in the Bible better worth keeping always in mind than that one, "Judge not, that ye be not judged."
> —OLIVER WENDELL HOLMES SR., *Elsie Venner: A Romance of Destiny*

Jonathan Edwards was born to be a theologian. His pious ancestors, writes Oliver Wendell Holmes Sr. in his 1880 essay on the eighteenth-century minister, "fed on sermons so long that he must have been born with Scriptural texts lying latent in his embryonic thinking-marrow, like the undeveloped picture in a film of collodion."[1] Holmes, a physician, poet, novelist, and lifelong skeptic of Calvinist doctrine in general and that of Edwards in particular, suggests that Edwards could not have chosen otherwise than to become a minister, for the scripture had been transcribed in the physical jelly of his brain before birth; all it needed to emerge was time. In this provocative image, Holmes binds theological doctrine to the mechanisms of hereditary inheritance. Later in the essay, he notes of contemporary ideas about hereditary determinism that Americans "are getting to be predestinarians as much as Edwards or Calvin was, only instead of universal corruption of nature derived from Adam, we recognize inherited congenital tendencies, —some good, some bad."[2] The difference, he writes, is that late nineteenth-century Americans recognize that "the subject" of inherited tendencies "is in no means responsible" for them.[3] Holmes suggests that both Calvinist theology and cutting-edge theories of heredity embrace some version of determinism: for the former, Adam's original sin forever corrupted human nature, inclining us all toward depravity; for the latter, "inherited congenital tendencies" incline us toward behaviors determined by our ancestry. Holmes's many essays and three novels consistently return to the philosophical and theological questions raised by the twin determinisms of original sin and heredity: To what extent are inheritors of criminal, violent, or other tendencies deemed socially or morally undesirable—"moral monsters," he calls them in his essay "Crime and Automatism" (1875)—culpable for their behavior?[4] How should legal, theological, and moral codes change to accommodate them? Is immorality better thought of as a congenital disorder? If so, how might such moral disorders be treated?

This chapter argues that Holmes's first two novels, *Elsie Venner: A Romance of Destiny* (1861) and *The Guardian Angel* (1867) offer a vision of inherited characteristics that is more plastic, more open to change, than that offered by either the Calvinist theology of his childhood or the hereditary determinism of his scientific contemporaries. These novels, published at the dawn of the Darwinian revolution (in biology, in heredity, in society), attempt to address how "congenital inheritances" might be amenable to positive change. Both novels conceptualize criminal or socially destructive inherited tendencies as chronic or "congenital" conditions to be managed by treatment, not condemned as the wages of original sin or dismissed as biologically unalterable. Yet they both show that the project of treating a person's hereditary tendencies is ethically fraught, for they depict how such a project invokes questions of identity, agency, and social control that are difficult to resolve. For instance, thinking of a person's inherited qualities as something to be treated or otherwise changed opens the door to imagining inheritors of less desirable traits as best managed by a supposed hereditary elite.

It goes without saying that the late nineteenth century indeed saw the rise of a set of reform movements predicated on the existence of just such an elite; our catchall term for those movements is "eugenics," coined by Darwin's half cousin Francis Galton in 1883. Here, I am interested in how Holmes's first two novels work through notions of governing, manipulating, and cultivating what one might call "the inherited self" in the decade between the 1859 publication of *The Origin of Species* and the 1869 publication of Galton's *Hereditary Genius*, in which he lays the conceptual groundwork for much of his later thinking on eugenics. This is not to say that I think that Holmes "anticipates" or otherwise presages Galton but rather that he published *Elsie Venner* and *The Guardian Angel* during a period of particular intellectual upheaval on the subject of heredity. Situated between Darwin and Galton, Holmes's novels invoke enduring questions about harnessing bioplasticity for reformist ends: What constitutes a behavior that should be changed? Who gets to decide? What say does an individual have in the operations of her own physiology? Is she still the same person in the wake of her body's reformation? At what point does melioration, reform, treatment, or repair become control? By giving narrative form to characters whose inherited tendencies become subject to attempts at intervention and reform, Holmes's novels sound the depths of what philosopher Catherine Malabou calls "destructive plasticity," or the ability of the brain to change itself for the worse. In Holmes's novels, attempts to reform the inherited self similarly carry as much risk as they do reward.

Holmes's vision of malleable heredity clashes with what I argue in chapter 1 is Nathaniel Hawthorne's sense of heredity's determinative force. I do not take this distinction as a Whiggish sign that the scientific culture of the United States, or the United States' citizenry itself, developed a newly enlightened perspective toward heredity in the decade separating the publication of *The House of the Seven Gables* and *Elsie Venner*. I take it instead, as I take the novels' situation between key works of Darwin and Galton, as indicative of the contested status of heredity as a biological concept in mid-nineteenth-century America and, indeed, of the intellectual foment that characterized antebellum reform culture generally. It is within this context — richly, productively in flux — that Holmes offers an intervention into both scientific and theological discourse. In doing so, he suggests that determinative views such as Hawthorne's not only miss the mark on the mechanisms of inheritance but are dismissive of individuals' ability to change their bodies and, ultimately, themselves, for better or for worse.

Estranged from the Womb

Perhaps surprisingly, Holmes's approach to heredity as a biological concept emerges from the strenuous religious training he received in his youth. However, Charles Boewe argues that "the scientific element" of Holmes's writing should receive more attention than the theological element, claiming that science provides the foundation for his arguments against original sin.[5] Much of the recent work on Holmes, which sheds merited light on one of the most understudied figures in nineteenth-century American literature, similarly focuses on the medical aspects of his writing.[6] Yet Holmes's arguments about heredity and moral responsibility are founded equally on his sophisticated understanding of Calvinist theology, in which he was steeped as a child. Holmes made a literary career of decrying the doctrine of original sin; it is the one subject to which he returns continually throughout his life. He found the idea that a child of Adam is damned for his sins cruel, unfair, and unfitting of a loving God. He chafed at the idea that the child can do nothing to alleviate the weight of the ancestor's sin. Despite his distaste for original sin, Holmes read deeply in predestinarian theology, as his essay on Edwards demonstrates, and perceived at its core a barbaric, pessimistic determinism. He also received extensive religious education as a boy at the feet of his father, a minister, and like many other "Boston Brahmins" (a term he coined in *Elsie Venner*), he was schooled in a strain of New England Calvinism devoted to preserving the austere doctrines of centuries past. His father, Abiel, was a pastor at Cambridge's First Congregational Church and was trained at Yale University, at the time a fortress of orthodox Calvinism.[7] Abiel maintained that orthodoxy throughout his life; in the 1820s and 1830s, he became involved in a schism between liberal and conservative Congregationalists that resulted in his association with Lyman Beecher, the conservative pastor of the Hanover Street Church in Boston.[8] He also ceased his practice of exchanging places with liberal, Unitarian, and Unitarian-leaning pastors on Sundays, favoring instead Beecher and other conservatives.[9] Sundays in the Holmes household were strictly reserved for Sabbath activities, which required, as Holmes's biographer Eleanor Tilton writes, "a decorum, a silence, an inactivity very trying to a nervous and talkative boy."[10] Even if Holmes wished to pass the time with a book, his family's library tended toward theological texts; its only secular offering was a volume of Dryden's poems.[11] More representative books included Bunyan's *Pilgrim's Progress* and the *New England Primer*.[12]

Like most other children raised in Calvinist households in New England, Holmes learned from the *Primer* the Westminster Shorter Catechism, including the two pithy verses that summarize the doctrine of original sin: "In Adam's Fall / We sinned all."[13] Put another way, the Fall—the original sin—was committed by Adam, but we, his posterity, bear the weight of sin along with him. The Westminster Shorter Catechism elaborates the Fall and its consequences: "The covenant being made with Adam, not only for himself, but for his posterity, all mankind descending from him by ordinary generation, sinned in him and fell with him in his first transgression."[14] To be fallen, the catechism continues, is to be in "a state of sin and misery," two distinct concepts that bear some unpacking.[15] Humanity's sinful state is threefold: it "consists in the guilt of Adam's first sin, the want of original righteousness, and the corruption of his whole nature, which is commonly called original sin, together with all actual transgressions which proceed from it."[16] In other words, humans are sinful in that they are (1) guilty of Adam's sin, being descended from Adam; (2) stripped of the righteousness enjoyed by Adam and Eve in their innocence; and (3) of a nature forever corrupted by their loss of innocence. And all these punishments are preserved and passed on from Adam by "ordinary generation," or reproduction, which is why another term for the doctrine of original sin is "total hereditary depravity." Because sinfulness is inherited, even newborns are responsible for Adam's sin: "The wicked are estranged from the womb," so goes Psalm 58:3; "they go astray as soon as they be born, speaking lies." Heredity, understood here as the means by which the substance of human nature is communicated from parents to children, is thus the vehicle of original sin.

Charles Hodge, onetime president of Princeton University, elaborates on hereditary guilt and corruption in his magisterial *Systematic Theology* (1870), the nineteenth century's most comprehensive statement of Calvinist theology. His disagreements with predecessor Jonathan Edwards's conception of inherited guilt are few but significant. Hodge writes, correctly, that Edwards explains our inheritance of Adam's guilt as due to God's perception of Adam and his descendants as being ontologically one.[17] For Edwards, whose theology is as metaphysically complex as it is devout, all substance is God, and reality exists because of His continued willingness for it to do so. Because all substance is Himself, and past, present, and future are equally knowable, Adam and his posterity are in God's eyes one in the way we think of a seed and the tree it becomes as one. It would thus not make sense to think of Adam and his descendants as separate agents. Hodge recoils from this theory, writing that "if God is the only substance He is the only agent in the universe . . . therefore there can be no free agency, no sin, no responsibility, no individual existence. The universe is only the self-manifestation of God. This doctrine, therefore, in its consequences, is essentially pantheistic."[18]

In contrast to Edwards, Hodge favors what he views as more intuitive, commonsense distinctions between substances and persons. His articulation of original sin more closely follows the Westminster Shorter Catechism: Adam's descendants bear his guilt, want of righteousness, and corruption through a compromised nature inherited through "ordinary generation."[19] The original sin changed human nature such that our corrupted dispositions incline us toward evil. Hodge does not accept the argument that one cannot be held responsible for inherited depravity: he opposes "the doctrine which admits a hereditary depravity of nature, and makes it consist in an inclination to sin, but denies that it is itself sinful."[20] Some theologians, he writes, make "a distinction between *vitium* [hereditary sinfulness] and *peccatum* [actual sin]," but Hodge finds that distinction flimsy: hereditary sinfulness *is* actual sin.[21] A depraved nature inclines a person toward sin, but that one's nature is so inclined makes one's sins no less sinful, contra Holmes. "Depravity, or inherent hereditary corruption," he writes, "has always been designated *peccatum*, and therefore to say that it is not *peccatum*, but merely *vitium*,

Tricks of the Blood 105

produces confusion and leads to error. . . . It is contrary to Scripture for the Bible undeniably designates indwelling or hereditary corruption, or *vitium*, as ἁμαρτία [*hamartia*, sin]."[22] Despite their differences, Edwards and Hodge agree on one crucial concept: we, as Adam's children, bear the guilt of his sins as surely as he did.

From an early age, Holmes met his father's attempts to educate him in Calvinist theological orthodoxy with, at best, apathy. John T. Morse includes in his *Life and Letters of Oliver Wendell Holmes* (1896), a collection of Holmes's scattered autobiographical reflections, a fragment titled "Religious and Literary Education," in which Holmes writes of Abiel's expectation that he and his siblings would recite to their mother the Westminster Shorter Catechism. She "sat down to hear us recite of 'justification,' 'adoption,' and 'sanctification,' and the rest of the programme," he writes, naming the steps the faithful must take to receive divine grace. "We learned nominally that we were a set of little fallen wretches, exposed to the wrath of God by the fact of that existence which we could not help."[23] "I do not think," he continues, "we believed a word of it, or even understood much of its phraseology."[24] His mind "early revolted from the teachings of the Catechism and the books which followed out its dogmas," and he directs special ire at hereditary depravity, which he calls a particularly "New England doctrine."[25] It asserts, Holmes writes, "that a child must repent of, and be punished for, not only his own sins but those of his first parent. This was the foundation of the condemnation of unborn and unbaptized children, as taught in the *Day of Doom*, the celebrated and most popular poem of Michael Wigglesworth."[26] This doctrine, "held up to scorn in the fable of the 'Wolf and the Lamb,' was accepted by the church as in perfect harmony with the human reason and the divine character."[27] He was left caught between two worlds: the orthodox Calvinism of his home and the liberal "Unitarian atmosphere" of Boston's colleges.[28]

In 1857, well into middle age, Holmes put these tensions into print when he began writing as the "Autocrat at the Breakfast-Table" for the *Atlantic Monthly*, a publication he named and helped bring into being.[29] The first installation of the Autocrat's chatter on "mathematics, mutual admiration societies, puns, the naturalness of conceit, and self-made men" was published in the same issue as Emerson's polytheistic poem "Brahma."[30] The Autocrat pieces, which feature an endlessly chattering Holmesian figure holding court at his landlady's breakfast table, are Holmes at his most charming and affable. Still, the Autocrat insists on needling the Divinity Student, another boarder, on theological matters—Why do so few pastors listen to each other's sermons? he impishly asks—which netted the *Atlantic Monthly* outraged condemnation from the religious press.[31] In the meantime, Holmes delivered a Boston Lyceum lecture on "The Chief End of Man" (1858), suggesting that the chief end of humankind might be found in earthly works rather than in the glorification of God, as dictated by the Westminster Shorter Catechism.[32] In response, a Calvinist periodical, the *Congregationalist*, demanded that Holmes be removed from the Lyceum lecture circuit.[33] Delighting in shocking the religious press, Holmes cut out the *Congregationalist* piece and placed it in a scrapbook.[34] Despite (or perhaps because of) this criticism, the Autocrat pieces were a tremendous success.

With the publication of the first piece of "Professor at the Breakfast-Table" in January 1859, Holmes began a bolder attack on Calvinist theology. The Professor is a far more pointed and critical figure than the urbane, avuncular Autocrat; at one point, he hisses that Jonathan Edwards is "a man with a brain as nicely adjusted for certain mechanical processes as Babbage's calculating machine."[35] In this formulation, Edwards is a computer that assimilates theological concepts in ways that are logically coherent but that are fundamentally removed from and indifferent to human experience. The Professor also mocks ministers who think the earth is four thousand years old and wishfully predicts that a hundred years' time will see an end to the nineteenth century's religious "barbarisms."[36] In one entry, "The Professor Finds a Fly in His Teacup," his gleeful response to Calvinist readers' complaints is declaring that he "didn't know that Truth was such an invalid" that it cannot be subjected to scrutiny; this sally drew exasperated protests from the *Boston Recorder* and the *New York Courier*.[37] By this time, the identity of the breakfast-table writer was Boston's worst-kept secret, and Holmes had ample opportunity to add to his scrapbook.[38]

Holmes's lifelong aversion to Calvinist doctrines of predestination and original sin was rooted in his sense that they figured individuals as unchangeably depraved, with no chance to take action to change themselves. Examining Holmes's engagement with these doctrines demonstrates his commitment to pushing against the idea that people can be damned or otherwise held responsible for something they cannot help. Neglecting the structure of theological beliefs to which Holmes addresses himself—as most scholars writing about Holmes do—risks ignoring the nuances he brings to his critique. Historically, few have taken him seriously at all, preferring instead to characterize him as the Saturday Club's class clown, a whimsical dilettante whose literary contributions happen almost by accident. But attending to Holmes's engagement with Calvinist conceptions of heredity illuminates how he attempts to reckon with what he regards as a rigid theological determinism that hobbles individuals' capacity for freedom.

A Palpable Outside Agency

Near the end of *Elsie Venner*, published serially in the *Atlantic Monthly* from 1859 to 1860, Holmes stages a confrontation between Calvinist doctrine and his ideas about responsibility and freedom in the form of an encounter between Dr. Kittredge, a grizzled country doctor, and Rev. Dr. Honeywood, a local minister whose heart, Holmes writes, is more humane than the doctrines he expounds on Sunday mornings. The two men are invited to the same dinner party, and each takes an armchair and sits "squared off against each other" to converse.[39] The two soon touch on the topic of free will, at which point Kittredge asks Honeywood if he would like to know his views on the subject; the pastor assents. Kittredge, a mouthpiece for Holmes, asserts that theologians "work out the machinery of responsibility in an abstract kind of way; they have a sort of algebra of human nature, in which *friction* and *strength* (or *weakness*) *of material* are left out."[40] Responsibility, Kittredge suggests, is not so abstract as mathematics; human nature, being enmeshed in the material of the body, is such that we ought rather to think of responsibility the way we do mechanical engineering. A wheelbarrow made of wood and one made of iron might perform the same task, but under the same conditions, one will crack while the other bends; exposed to rain, one will swell while the other rusts. By figuring responsibility as a product of machinery and human nature as subject to the same physical forces as any other material, Holmes calls attention to the ways that the will can be damaged by the dents, cracks, and corrosions that affect all machinery, including the human body, in time. The algebraic model of responsibility, in contrast, figures each individual as disembodied and abstracted, and therefore equal in moral agency, so that any given moral calculation is uniformly applicable.

Ministers, Kittredge continues, think of the will as totally unconstrained, "as if it stood on a high look-out, with plenty of light, and elbow-room reaching to the horizon."[41] But physicians see "how it [the will] is tied up by inferior organization, by disease, by all sorts of crowding interferences" imposed by the human body.[42] Monomania and other mental illnesses, he says, teach us that one need not be totally deranged to be insane and thus that we should "recognize all sorts of queer tendencies in minds supposed to be sane, so that we have nothing but compassion for a large class of persons condemned as sinners by theologians, but considered by us as invalids."[43] As we learn more of the ways that a variety of automatic, unconscious bodily processes affect our behavior, Holmes suggests, what used to be a spiritual wickedness looks more like a bodily disorder.

For Kittredge, inherited tendencies, too, should inspire pity rather than condemnation: physicians, who "have constant reasons for noticing the transmission of qualities from parents to offspring," do not condemn a child for behaviors it could not help inheriting. They "find it hard to hold a child accountable in any moral point of view for inherited bad temper or tendency to drunkenness, —as hard as we should to blame him for inheriting gout or asthma."[44] Kittredge's goal is to point out the absurdity of a God who blames Adam's children for inheriting his sinful nature. If sin is passed down through ordinary generation, then it is no different from "gout or asthma," chronic conditions that can never be wholly cured but that whose symptoms can be managed. *Elsie Venner* asks, then, what it would mean to treat original sin as a sort of congenital disease rather than a spiritual defect.

The novel's plot explores the idea that people's inherited tendencies—in theological terms, their inherited sin—cannot be helped and so should be excused, just as insane persons are excused. In a letter to Harriet Beecher Stowe dated September 13, 1860, Holmes elaborates on his assertion, made in the first preface of *Elsie Venner*, that "a grave scientific doctrine may be detected" beneath its charming New England village setting and its melodramatic plot:

> You see exactly what I wish to do: to write a story with enough of interest in its characters and incidents to attract a certain amount of popular attention. Under cover of this to *stir* that mighty question of automatic agency in its relation to self-determination. To do this by means of a palpable outside agency, predetermining certain traits of character and certain apparently voluntary acts, such as the common judgment of mankind and the tribunals of law and theology have been in the habit of recognizing as sin and crime. Not exactly insanity, either general or partial, in its common sense, but rather an unconscious intuitive tendency, dating from a powerful ante-natal influence, which modifies the whole organization.[45]

Holmes seeks, in other words, to wrap his speculations about "automatic agency" as it relates to common judgment, the law, and theology in an interesting story. And, indeed, Holmes's novel does just that: Bernard Langdon, who pauses his medical studies to make money as a teacher, finds in his classroom Elsie Venner, a "strange, wild-looking girl" who moves with serpentine grace, basks in the sun, and dances "wild Moorish fandangos" with rattling castanets.[46] In time, Langdon discovers that Venner's pregnant mother was bitten by a snake, which affects the young woman's bodily organization in such a way that she exhibits snakelike tendencies: she has small, cold, glittering eyes; is rumored to have poisoned a governess; and behaves, at times, with a maliciousness that her community finds unbecoming a wellbred young woman.[47] The novel's first preface announces that in "calling this narrative a 'romance,' the Author wishes to make sure of being indulged in the common privileges of the poetic license"; although "a grave scientific doctrine may be detected lying beneath some of the delineations of character," he does not "pledg(e) his absolute belief in it."[48] "It was adopted," he writes, "as a convenient medium of truth rather than as an accepted scientific conclusion."[49]

What Holmes seeks to evoke in *Elsie Venner* is the idea that from the infant's or the irrevocably insane person's total lack of moral agency, "the scale mounts upwards by slight gradations" to a fully responsible person, as he writes in "The Autocrat at the Breakfast-Table."[50] Holmes's interest is in individuals such as Venner, who fall somewhere on that scale. Such individuals call for a more fine-grained way to reckon their legal, ethical, and theological obligations to God and humankind. A scene in *Elsie Venner* in which Honeywood writes a new sermon, "On the Obligations of an Infinite Creator to a Finite Creature," after considering Venner's situation dramatizes how Holmes imagines theologians might incorporate the idea of limited responsibility into their theology:

> He did not believe in the responsibility of idiots. He did not believe a new-born infant was morally answerable for other people's acts. He thought a man with a crooked spine would never be called to account for not walking erect. He thought if the crook was in his brain, instead of his back, he could not fairly be blamed for any consequence of this natural defect, whatever lawyers or divines might call it. He argued, that, if a person inherited a perfect mind, body, and disposition, and had perfect teaching from infancy, that person could do nothing more than keep the moral law perfectly. But supposing that the Creator allows a person to be born with an hereditary or ingrafted organic tendency, and then puts this person into the hands of teachers incompetent or positively bad, is not what is called sin or transgression of the law necessarily involved in the premises? Is not a Creator

bound to guard his children against the ruin which inherited ignorance might entail on them? Would it be fair for a parent to put into a child's hands the title-deeds to all its future possessions, and a bunch of matches? And are not men children, nay, babes, in the eye of Omniscience?[51]

In Honeywood's sermon, Holmes suggests how attending to the lessons of biology might lead to doctrinal shifts; the theological conclusions Honeywood draws arise from the "logic which had carried him to certain conclusions with reference to human nature."[52] The minister begins by articulating the Holmesian argument that a crook in the brain, just like a crook in the back, is a "natural defect" that lessens culpability. Here, though, the pastor puts biology into contact with doctrine: the crook in the brain could be part of a "hereditary or ingrafted organic tendency" toward sin rather than a total lack of mental function. Honeywood argues that God is obligated to protect humanity, who are not only children but babies compared to divinity, "against the ruin" wrought by inheritance. This sermon, Holmes writes, "was really much more respectful to his Maker" than the usual "Oriental hyperboles of self-abasement."[53] Treating those with inherited tendencies toward sin humanely thus begins with better understanding human biology.

After Langdon suspects that his ophidian student cannot help but act the way she does, he writes his medical school professor a letter asking about Venner's case: "Do you think there may be predispositions, inherited or ingrafted, but at any rate constitutional, which shall take out certain apparently voluntary determinations from the control of the will, and leave them as free from moral responsibility as the instincts of the lower animals?"[54] His professor replies that his question "opens a very wide range of speculation":

> Automatic action in the moral world; the reflex movement which seems to be self-determination, and has been hanged and howled at as such (metaphorically) for nobody knows how many centuries: until somebody shall study this as Marshall Hall has studied reflex nervous action in the bodily system, I would not give much for men's judgments of each others' [sic] characters. Shut up the robber and the defaulter, we must. But what if your oldest boy had been stolen from his cradle and bred in a North-Street cellar? What if you are drinking a little too much wine and smoking a little too much tobacco, and your son takes after you, and so your poor grandson's brain being a little injured in physical texture, he loses the fine moral sense on which you

pride yourself, and doesn't see the difference between signing another man's name to a draft and his own?⁵⁵

The professor compares the issue of "automatic action in the moral world" to Marshall Hall's studies of the reflex arc, thus explicitly linking morality to physiology.⁵⁶ Like the theorists of what he calls "that great doctrine of moral insanity," which he says "has done more to make men charitable and soften legal and theological barbarism than any one doctrine that I can think of since the message of peace and good-will to men," the professor views physicians and physiologists as the proper arbiters of the nineteenth century's pressing new moral conundrums.⁵⁷ Crucially, the professor does not advocate letting criminals run free even if they should not be held morally responsible for their actions: society must protect itself. *"Treat bad men exactly as if they were insane,"* he tells Langdon later in the letter. "They are *in-sane*, out of health, morally."⁵⁸ Just as a society might restrain an insane man without holding him morally accountable for his actions, the professor asserts, it might restrain criminals not as retribution but as a practical action necessary for the public good.

The professor asks us to consider the ways that one's body might limit the range of one's behaviors in ways that challenge ideas like free will and moral responsibility. An image Holmes deploys in "The Autocrat of the Breakfast-Table" to explain the will's limits clarifies the point. The Autocrat describes the will as being like a drop of water imprisoned in a crystal.⁵⁹ In this image, the crystal—rigid yet arranged according to a given structure—stands in for the body, constituted according to a set of hereditary structures. The drop of water, or the will, has a certain amount of movement within its enclosure, but ultimately that enclosure binds and shapes it. This is not to deny free will and moral responsibility altogether, he writes; in describing the limits of the will, he wishes rather to "*define* moral obligations, and not weaken them."⁶⁰ His point is that probing how the body might limit one's moral agency can lead us to a better, more exact, more scientifically informed way of thinking about responsibility.

Thinking of "bad men" and, by extension, Venner as "out of health, morally" transforms sin into disease. That transformation, in turn, raises the question of reforming inherited traits: Can Venner be "cured" by changing her physiological makeup? In his letter to Stowe, Holmes identifies such a cure with "humanizing traits" that fight against "the lower organic tendencies" bequeathed by the venom: "To make the subject of this influence interest the reader, to carry the animalizing of her nature just as far as can be done without rendering her repulsive, to redeem the character in some measure by humanizing traits, which struggle through the lower organic tendencies, to carry her on to her inevitable fate by the natural machinery of circumstance, grouping many human interests around her, which find their natural solution in the train of events involving her doom, — such is the idea of this story."[61] The "subject of this influence," Venner, is just sympathetic enough to convince readers that she does not deserve to bear judgment for her immoral behavior. She stands in for everyone subject to influences out of their control. Holmes thus hopes that by "humanizing" Venner, he might convince his readers to adjust their ideas about the human body and responsibility. But, as Jane F. Thrailkill argues, the Elsie Venner readers come to know is not human; therefore, humanizing her "would be to deny or even destroy what makes her Elsie."[62] And that is precisely what happens in the novel. School friends include in a bundle of flowers sent to her leaves from the white ash, rumored to be deadly to snakes.[63] When she comes into contact with them, she flings the basket away and faints; thereafter, she loses her snaky traits—the "cold glitter" of her "diamond eyes," the "stormy scowl" that shades her face—and comes to resemble her mother.[64] At the same time, she becomes so weak that she cannot leave her bed. The leaves of the white ash purge the "lower nature" of the snake from her body, but Dr. Kittridge fears that the corruption has "involved the centres of life in its own decay" and is killing her.[65] Finally, what would seem to restore her supposedly "true," human self, if one could be said to exist, kills her.

The novel as a whole investigates what it means for someone's heredity to be so determinative that it lessens his or her moral responsibility. But Venner's death, puzzling in a novel focused on ways to improve the situation of people negatively affected by their inherited characteristics, asks what it means for a person's inherited traits to be plastic. The answer the novel gives—that changing Venner's inherited tendencies, however destructive they are, kills her—illuminates the destructive side of bioplasticity. The novel shows that if bodies might change for the better, as reformers of the antebellum decades optimistically affirmed, they can also change for the worse. By taking as the basis of his novel a young woman whose hereditary makeup is altered by a snake bite, Holmes opens up a provocative question about the links between one's body and one's identity: does changing one's body change who one is? In Venner's case, curing her by driving away the physiological influence of the snake venom alters her body in such a way that it transforms her identity—not to some occluded version of a putatively real self but, the novel suggests, to some version of her mother. That this process kills her underscores how such somatic interventions as therapy, treatment, and healing can do great harm.

In her book *The New Wounded*, Malabou discusses the brain's capacity for self-repair after trauma as a "type of plasticity" that *"creates a certain form of being by effacing a previously existing identity."*[66] Focusing on sufferers of brain lesions, Alzheimer's disease, and other neural conditions, she opens her study with the image of her grandmother, suffering from Alzheimer's — someone who "was not a diminished person" or "the same woman weaker than she used to be, lessened, spoiled," but rather *"someone else,"* another person, entirely.[67] Her plasticity allowed her to be "operated upon" by the disease in such a way, Malabou writes, that she became someone with a different identity. This destructive plasticity inheres also in treatment and repair more generally, which, as Catherine Kellogg notes, can in some cases "annihilate the form that it receives or creates."[68] In Holmes's context, such an annihilation extends to the body generally. To attempt to ameliorate a person's inherited characteristics, *Elsie Venner* suggests, is to risk destroying the person altogether.

Like Begets Like

Elsie Venner was successful enough that William Ticknor, partner in the company that published the *Atlantic Monthly*, asked Holmes to write another novel, a proposition to which he agreed. Throughout 1867, Ticknor led every issue of the magazine with an installment of the new work, *The Guardian Angel* (published in book form November 1867).[69] The first preface to the novel explains Holmes's view of its relation to *Elsie Venner*, which he writes was predicated on "an experiment which some thought cruel, even on paper."[70] The new tale "forms a natural sequence" to *Elsie Venner*, he writes, making *The Guardian Angel* a development of its sibling novel.[71] He says that although the earlier novel posed an outlandish situation to explore original sin, *The Guardian Angel* "comes more nearly within the range of common experience."[72] Instead of relying on a prenatal snakebite to demonstrate responsibility's limits, Holmes here draws on human heredity as such, or "inherited bodily aspects and habitudes," the existence and effects of which are obvious (so he says) to all who observe them.[73]

Though the premise of *The Guardian Angel* is more grounded in reality as Holmes found it than that of its sibling novel, both might still be called, he writes, "Studies of the Reflex Function in its higher sphere" or "protests against the scholastic tendency to shift the total responsibility of all human action from the Infinite to the finite."[74] But doing so, he jokes, "might alarm the jealousy of the cabinet-keepers of our doctrinal museums."[75] As his poke at "doctrinal museums" suggests, Holmes anticipated a backlash similar to that inspired by his earlier writing. He attempts to nip in the bud the familiar complaint that he abolishes moral responsibility: anyone, he insists, who confuses his "doctrine of limited responsibility" for a denial of self-determination and responsibility altogether is, as he puts it in what might be a pun on the subject of heredity, one of the country's many "intellectual half-breeds."[76] If we "cannot follow the automatic machinery of nature into the mental and moral world," he asserts, we might as well embrace our backwardness and "return at once to our old demonology."[77] *The Guardian Angel*, then, promises to depict the machinery of heredity as limiting but not eliminating responsibility.

It is, as Boewe writes, "very difficult to establish any exact sources for Holmes's scientific knowledge of heredity."[78] In his preface to *The Guardian Angel*, Holmes insists that the "successive development of inherited bodily aspects and habitudes" are "well known to all who have lived long enough to see families grow up under their own eyes."[79] Here, I am less interested in determining Holmes's "exact sources" than I am in inquiring into the broader epistemic conditions under which Holmes could understand his view of heredity as the "successive development of inherited bodily aspects and habitudes" as obvious. In doing so, I wish to emphasize the conceptual indeterminacy that made heredity such a powerful engine of conservation for Hawthorne, on the one hand, and such a pliable force for Holmes, on the other. What does it mean biologically, spiritually, and morally to inherit traits from one's ancestors? How are those characteristics transmitted? What sorts of traits are passed down? And, most importantly for the broader story of concepts of bioplasticity in the nineteenth century, to what extent are those traits mutable, what does it mean to change them, and what forms of choice, if any, might be found within the biological confines of inheritance? These questions, and the ways Holmes's novels turn to them again and again, form a crucial turning point toward the postwar decades' popular theories of biological determinism.

Although the concept of heredity as the biological transmission of traits from parents to offspring seems as self-evident today as it did to Holmes, it did not take shape as a coherent way of explaining similarities between parents and offspring until well into the nineteenth century. Historian of science Carlos López-Beltrán writes that "for those living under different physiological and theological frames," including those prior to Holmes, similarities

Tricks of the Blood 115

between parents and children "could be accounted for in different ways or dismissed as accidental or irrelevant."[80] Before the 1830s, when French physiologists established the foundation of the modern model of heredity, the transmission of traits was understood to be dependent on the environmental circumstances surrounding "conception, pregnancy, embryonic development, parturition, and lactation."[81] Whatever similarities inhered between parents and offspring were understood as a function of "the similarity in the constellation of causes," whether environmental or social, "involved in each act of generation."[82] Historians Staffan Müller-Wille and Hans-Jörg Rheinberger turn to Laurence Sterne's *Tristram Shandy* (1760) as an illustration of this mindset: during the act of conceiving Shandy, his mother suddenly asks his father whether he had wound their clock for the night.[83] The distracting question hampers the man's ejaculation, which consequently "scattered and dispersed the animal spirits" that transmit the stuff of a "man's sense or his nonsense, his successes and miscarriages in this world," from father to child. The question of the clock dooms Shandy to an absurd life.[84] He can only wish that "either my father or my mother, or indeed both of them, as they were in duty both equally bound to it, had minded what they were about when they begot me; had they duly consider'd how much depended upon what they were then doing."[85] For Sterne and his eighteenth-century contemporaries, the transmission of characteristics is contingent on the circumstances of conception, "understood as an individual, separate act," not as a multigenerational pattern of inheritance.[86] The stuff of inheritance inheres not just in the animal spirits themselves but also in the conditions of their emission.

Two poems, one written in the first decade of the nineteenth century and one written after the Civil War, clarify some of the distinctions between environmental and biological models of heredity. In 1803, Charles Darwin's grandfather, the naturalist and poet Erasmus Darwin, published *The Temple of Nature; Or, the Origin of Society: A Poem, with Philosophical Notes*, an epic didactic poem exploring topics as varied as psychology, botany, reproduction, and materialism. Of heredity he writes:

> The clime unkind, or noxious food instills
> To embryon nerves hereditary ills;
> The feeble births acquir'd diseases chase,
> Till Death extinguish the degenerate race.[87]

In Darwin's poem, environmental factors such as climate and "noxious food" afflict the embryo's nerves with "hereditary ills" that are hereditary not because its parents have passed on their innate biological structures but because its uterine environment was affected by external factors in such a way that the child will be born "feeble." Historian Philip K. Wilson notes that Darwin, like his mentors William Hunter and William Cullen, understands certain environmental factors as transmitting to an embryo or a fetus "the predisposition of disease," resulting in "feeble births" susceptible to "acquir'd diseases."[88] The venom of Elsie Venner's nature, injected in utero, exemplifies this viewpoint.

A stanza of "Dorothy Q.," a poem written by Holmes about a portrait of his great-grandmother Dorothy Quincy, published in the January 1871 issue of the *Atlantic Monthly*, illustrates how profoundly prevailing ideas about heredity changed over the century:

> What if a hundred years ago
> Those close-shut lips had answered NO,
> When forth the tremulous question came
> That cost the maiden her Norman name,
> And under the folds that look so still
> The bodice swelled with the bosom's thrill?
> Should I be I, or would it be
> One tenth another, to nine tenths me?[89]

Holmes wonders in his poem who he would be had Quincy refused her soon-to-be husband's offer of marriage. He construes the question as tied to his very identity: "Should I be I" (would he be exactly who he is) were one-tenth (one-eighth, really) of his ancestry different? Or would he be only "nine tenths" the person he currently is, the other tenth being drawn from "another" ancestor? Heredity, for Holmes, is not a matter of the environmental circumstances of conception and pregnancy but of traits that are inherent to his progenitors. Because Holmes's conception of heredity is not founded on such environmental circumstances, he understands his traits as inherited not only from his parents but also from their parents, theirs, and so on. He — and the midcentury model of heredity that makes his poem possible — thus understands heredity as involving a temporal scope larger than that of earlier models, which focus on the nine-month span between conception and birth.

Darwin's and Holmes's poems also reflect a shift, driven by an intervening biological model of heredity, from conceiving of inheritance primarily in terms of abnormalities and illnesses to conceiving of it in terms of characteristics and dispositions. Not only one's ailments but one's entire makeup, then, came to be understandable as heritable over the course of the nineteenth

Tricks of the Blood 117

century. The implications of this shift are twofold: first, heredity became understandable as the transference of putatively normal rather than abnormal traits. Language tracked that change: Müller-Wille and Rheinberger write that whereas "the adjective *hereditary* can be dated back to antiquity in the context of nosography (*maladies héréditaires*), a transition to a nominal use (*hérédité*) took place only from the 1830s onward, first among French physiologists and physicians, then in other European scientific circles."[90] López-Beltrán agrees; he writes that although traits such as hair color were sometimes construed as hereditary prior to the 1830s, "the reference to the hereditary nature of a trait occurred . . . with much more frequency and consistency when anomalies, moral or physical, were the subject."[91] The second set of implications arises from the first: if putatively "normal" traits, not just abnormalities or diseases, are inherited, then one's entire being, including one's temperament and personality, is inherited. Holmes can thus imagine himself simultaneously as a mixture of his progenitors and as "I" and "me," for he understands himself as the sum of his antecedents.

López-Beltrán identifies the entry for "*Héréditaire*" in the sixty-volume *Dictionnaire des Sciénces Médicales* (1812–20) as a key step toward the emergence of a biological theory of heredity.[92] The entry includes physician Antoine Petit's *Essai sur les Maladies Héréditaires* (1817), in which he argues that the reproductive transmission of characteristics "has to be based on particular states of the bodily constitution communicated to children by parents."[93] As the title of Petit's essay makes clear, his understanding of heredity draws on the prevailing focus on disease as the primary subject of hereditary transmission even as it seeks to account for family similarities in constitution. Understanding a child's "bodily constitution" (its biological makeup or, in an analogous term of the time, "organization") as derived from its parents' bodies rather than environmental circumstances made it thinkable as a biological concept that explains both the transmission of pathology from parents to offspring and the transmission of normal bodily characteristics. And once heredity cohered as a biological concept, an avalanche of speculations about its mechanisms and boundaries followed. Gabriel Andral, one of Holmes's professors at Paris's *École de Médicine* and the man who succeeded François Broussais's chair at the same institution, lectured to Holmes and his classmates "on the possibility of hereditary characteristics and weaknesses" in 1833 and 1834.[94] Yet when Holmes wrote *The Guardian Angel*, heredity was not a settled concept. On the one hand, as we have seen in chapter 1, certain ways of understanding heredity had taken on qualities that anticipated the brutal determinism of eugenicism; on the other, heredity as a concept was indeterminate enough in the middle decades of the nineteenth century that its powers were not certain. Part of the cultural work that *The Guardian Angel* and other literary works accomplish is discovering those powers and attaching meaning to them.

Whereas dietary reformers sought to put the tools of self-determination in the hands of individuals, Holmes depicts heredity in *The Guardian Angel* as not being a matter of self-control. The vision of reform that Holmes proposes in the novel is one that involves neither the sorts of somatic self-fashioning embraced by Thoreau and Whitman nor the sorts of harmful therapeutic interventions explored in *Elsie Venner*; rather, he focuses on the role of local communities in guiding those whose inherited tendencies drive them to immorality. The afflicted individual cannot help him- or herself because a person who is affected enough to need help, so goes Holmes's logic, probably does not have the willpower necessary to exercise Thoreauvian self-determination. In *The Guardian Angel*, it falls to the community to provide treatment, which consists of protecting the afflicted from harm until his or her hereditary influences cohere with his or her own personality, forming an individual self. A community should thus approach a person with inherited immoral tendencies with patient mercy, not punishment or derision. By depicting the ways that those with such tendencies might change, given time and guidance, Holmes pushes back against what he views as the biological determinism of his age—a determinism that, despite his efforts, only grew stronger after he published *The Guardian Angel*, as his 1880 essay on Jonathan Edwards suggests.

Like Holmes's other novels, *The Guardian Angel* takes place in a bucolic New England village (here, Oxbow) populated by charming if one-dimensional characters. Readers are introduced to Myrtle Hazard, the novel's case study in biological heredity, through her ancestors. This is because, as the narrator asserts, it is not "certain that our individual personality is the single inhabitant of these our corporeal frames": some of us "have cotenants in this house we live in," and it is best to familiarize oneself with as much of the household as possible.[95] The dead, Holmes writes, might find within their descendants "a kind of secondary and imperfect, yet self-conscious life," which leads to our detecting at one time "the look, at another the tone of voice, at another some characteristic movement of this or that ancestor."[96] To know Hazard, then, is to know Ann Holyoake, a sixteenth-century Protestant burned at the stake by Catholics; Major Gideon Withers, a pompous, bombastic American of the eighteenth century; his son David, a sensitive aesthete of Poe's mold; his wife, Judith Pride, a flirtatious beauty; her daughter-in-law,

Virginia Wild, who is part American Indian; and Wild's son-in-law, Captain Charles Hazard, Myrtle's dead father, who loves the sea.[97] Candace, Wild's daughter and Charles Hazard's wife, gives birth to Myrtle in India, and while she is still an infant, both parents die of disease.[98] A relative in India brings her back to America to be raised in New England. Hazard, then, is subject to the influence of an extraordinarily varied family tree. At few points in the story does Holmes make it clear which ancestors predominate at which times; he keeps their influence subtle enough that the reader must keep them all in mind to distinguish one's characteristics from another's.

According to the narrator, these ancestors' "instincts and qualities" lie within Hazard "in embryo," in much the same way as when a tree bears grafts from many others: "It is as when several grafts, bearing fruit that ripens at different times, are growing upon the same stock. Her earlier impulses may have been derived directly from her father and mother, but all the ancestors who have been mentioned, and more or less obscurely many others, came uppermost in their time, before the absolute and total result of their several forces had found its equilibrium in the character by which she was to be known as an individual. These inherited impulses were therefore many, conflicting, some of them dangerous."[99] Key to Holmes's figure of the grafted tree is the idea that the different grafts bear fruit that "ripens at different times" despite "growing upon the same stock."[100] This image dramatizes the biological concept of latent heredity, in which inherited traits express themselves at different points of their descendants' lives.[101] Even Hazard's more distant ancestors might thus, in Holmes's words, come "uppermost in their time," before their descendant attains "equilibrium."[102] That her "inherited impulses" are "many, conflicting, some of them dangerous" makes her inner life a site of conflict and incoherence.[103] Her personal development depends on cohering her inherited tendencies into a stable character while operating under the constant threat of a latent characteristic showing itself. The process of learning how to do so drives the plot. Holmes here poses a biological heredity problem in that it affects Hazard in ways that limit her responsibility, but it is a problem with a solution: by attaining "equilibrium," Hazard might assimilate her competing hereditary traits into a whole and autonomous personality. This means that just as Holmes creates new ways of thinking about heredity's ethical and religious ramifications, he also makes it possible to think of the body as trainable and malleable in ways that mitigate heredity's effects. In *The Guardian Angel*, then, Holmes posits heredity as a sort of temporary determinism, one strong enough to raise potent questions about responsibility but plastic enough that it can be guided. Because the effects of one's inherited tendencies are temporary, they do not need the sorts of dramatic interventions portrayed in *Elsie Venner*; as the novel suggests, they need instead communal understanding and support.

Secondary characters abound in the novel, including the wannabe poet Gifted Hopkins and Hazard's naive friend Susan Posey, but the most important character other than Hazard (and perhaps the novel's real protagonist) is Byles Gridley, an "old Master of Arts" and a bachelor who retires to Oxbow after a career as a professor.[104] Holmes invests many of his own traits into Gridley: both are men of letters, great talkers, and critics of theological dogma.[105] For example, Gridley goes to the local Calvinist church precisely because he disagrees with its doctrines: he "liked to go there so as to growl to himself through the sermon, and go home scolding all the way about it."[106] Despite his cantankerous personality, he develops a grandfatherly affection for Hazard after learning of her difficulties. As the novel progresses, he guides her through the challenges raised by her inherited tendencies, and he rallies others in Oxbow to do the same. The conclusion reveals him to be the eponymous guardian angel.

The plot of *The Guardian Angel* concerns a series of challenges Hazard encounters due to her inherited tendencies. The novel begins with Gridley finding in his newspaper an advertisement placed by Hazard's guardian and aunt, Silence Withers, "a shadowy, pinched, sallow, dispirited, bloodless woman."[107] The advertisement says that Hazard, "tall and womanly for her age," has gone missing.[108] Withers and her maiden second cousin, Cynthia Badlam, live with their Irish servant, Kitty Fagan, and Hazard in their ancestral home, the Poplars. Withers worries that Hazard has run away with a man, but her worry is not for her ward's sake but for her own: she would rather "know that she was dead, and had died in the Lord," than for her to be "living in sin, or dead in wrong-doing," because she thinks the sin would reflect on herself.[109] What will happen, she wonders, "when 'He maketh inquisition for blood'?"[110] Her "engine," the narrator later remarks, is "*responsibility,* — her own responsibility, and the dreadful consequences which would follow to her, Silence, if Myrtle should in any way go wrong."[111] To protect her responsibility, her spiritual training of Hazard consists of "going to meeting three times every Sabbath day, and knowing the catechism by heart, and reading of good books, and the best of daily advice."[112] Withers's unceasing concern for her own responsibility even at the cost of her ward's life dramatizes what Holmes views as the folly and cruelty of the doctrine of original sin: Withers's belief that Hazard's responsibility might fall on her shoulders makes her callous about the young woman's well-being in a way that mirrors theologians' damning of children to perdition. In her desperation to be Godly, Holmes suggests, Withers forgets to be good.

Readers discover in time that Hazard has run away from the Poplars because of a sudden urge to go to sea. She spends her days gazing at a river visible from her home, and one day "it appeared all at once as a *Deliverer*."[113] Like all rivers, it leads to the ocean, "the great highway of the world," and eventually to "the gates of those cities from which she could take her departure unchallenged."[114] Her urge to travel is sparked by her discovery a few months before of "some sea-shells and coral-fans, and dried star-fishes and sea-horses, and a natural mummy of a rough-skinned dogfish."[115] These items strike a "dangerous chord" within her, and she feels "impelled" to examine them; when she does so, the smell of the sea clinging to them reaches "the very inmost haunts of memory" and stirs her urge to go to sea.[116] Soon after, Withers comments that she is beginning to look like her father, a ship's captain.[117] Here, Holmes suggests that the hereditary legacy of Hazard's seagoing father becomes a powerful influence on her behavior after her discovery of the seashells triggers its emergence. She flees her home by cutting her hair short, which masculinizes her and makes her look even more like her father, and stealing a boat.[118]

As Hazard drifts, her boat wanders into a marsh known by locals as the "Witches' Hollow," where she experiences a vision that dramatizes how her heredity affects her. She sees a burning cross and the ghostly figures of her ancestors, each one solid in proportion to how closely he or she is related to her: her parents' figures are more clear than her grandparents', for example.[119] She sees them silently mouthing the word "Breath," as if "they wanted to breathe the air of the world again in my shape, which I seemed to see as it were empty of myself and of these other selves, like a sponge that has water pressed out of it."[120] Soon, "it seemed to me that I returned to myself, and then those others became part of me by being taken up, one by one, and so lost in my own life."[121] She inherits the tendencies of several ancestors in particular. Her parents become part of her, imparting to her their "longing to live over the life they had led, on the sea and in strange countries."[122] Major Withers, the boisterous, hard-drinking eighteenth-century American, possesses characteristics of which Hazard does not want any part, but "there was some right he had in me through my being of his blood, and so his health and his strength went all through me, and I was always to have what was left of his life in that shadow-like shape, forming a portion of mine."[123] She feels the influence of Judith Pride, famous for her beauty and flirtatiousness; Ruth Bradford, burned as a witch in the seventeenth century;

an unnamed American Indian woman, whose ghost is "wild-looking" and wearing a "head-dress of feathers"; and Ann Holyoake, "burned long ago by the Papists," whom Hazard feels is her "guardian and protector."[124] Each of these figures, Hazard says, "really live over some part of their past lives in my life."[125]

This scene points up Holmes's shift to the realist mode, for he refuses to let Hazard's mysterious experience remain mysterious. An explanatory note by Gridley follows Hazard's vision, which he says "must be accounted for in some way, or pass into the category of the supernatural."[126] This accounting models Holmes's approach to heredity in *The Guardian Angel*—his strategy is to ensure that the events of the novel are explainable in the terms offered by biology. To leave the seemingly supernatural unexamined by science would be to leave it entirely in the hands of mystics and theologians, those who Holmes views as obfuscating rather than illuminating reality. Gridley guesses that her vision "was one of those intuitions, with *objective projection*, which sometimes comes to imaginative young persons, especially girls, in certain exalted nervous conditions."[127] He proceeds to translate the supernatural into the natural, articulating his view of heredity:

> The lives of our progenitors are, as we know, reproduced in different proportions in ourselves. Whether they as individuals have any consciousness of it, is another matter. It is possible that they do get a second as it were [of] fractional life in us. It might seem that many of those whose blood flows in our veins struggle for the mastery, and by and by one or more get the predominance, so that we grow to be like father, or mother, or remoter ancestor, or two or more are blended in us, not to the exclusion, however, it must be understood, of a special personality of our own, about which these others are grouped. Independently of any possible scientific value, this "Vision" serves to illustrate the above-mentioned fact of common experience, which is not sufficiently weighed by most moralists.[128]

Gridley, Holmes's avatar in the novel, makes two points. One is that Hazard's vision is not mystical but rather a psychological projection of the fact of inherited influences, a fact, he says, established by both science and experience. The entire vision, then, can be understood in a way that does not ask us "to suppose any exceptional occurrence outside of natural laws."[129] Acknowledging the presence of "a special personality of our own" around which one's inherited tendencies "are grouped" provides a normative picture of heredity that provides a possible endpoint for Hazard's story. The second point Gridley makes, articulated by Holmes elsewhere, is that inherited influences are not sufficiently acknowledged by moralists and theologians as factors that limit the will. Here, Holmes argues that the very thing Calvinists say preserves Adam's responsibility for his sin—that is, the nature he and his descendants share—instead mitigates that responsibility.

Hazard's escape by boat, which concludes when she hit rapids and ends up unconscious on a downriver bank, sets a pattern repeated throughout the novel. Her inexplicably dangerous actions seem to the community at large the work of a sinful nature, but readers hear from various sources—Gridley, the village physician, the narrator, or some other person learned in science—that she acts the way she does because of her heredity. And theologians, these characters assert, ought to recognize that physical condition as something that mitigates her responsibility. The novel presents her inherited tendencies as being part of her physical, not her spiritual, makeup, so what at first appears to be a moral corruption of her nature is actually a natural, physiological limitation. The issue, as the narrator of *The Guardian Angel* complains, is that ministers think "that the treatment of all morbid states of mind short of raving madness belongs to them and not to the doctors."[130] After all, Cotton Mather attributed New England's preponderance of "*Splenetic* Maladies" and "*Melancholy* Indispositions" to the "*unsearchable Judgments of God.*"[131] Hazard, not totally mentally incompetent yet not totally in control, is somewhere in between. Her responsibility, then, ought to be likewise partial.

The novel charts the effects of Hazard's inherited tendencies throughout, but I will examine only a few episodes, the first being when her tendency toward hysteria, inherited from the women in her family, leads her to the edge of sexual indiscretion. After returning from her nautical adventure she requires convalescence, and Withers calls on the services of Lemuel Hurlbut, a ninety-two-year-old physician.[132] Due to his age, he has seen five generations of Hazard's family in his lifetime ("same thing over and over again," he remarks), and he immediately discerns in her features a predisposition to nervousness and hysteria.[133] He comments that he has seen similar nervous disorders in her ancestors, for the living "are only dead folks warmed over."[134] As he predicts, Hazard soon begins showing signs of hysteria, or a "morbid condition, accompanied with a series of mental and moral perversions, which in ignorant ages and communities is attributed to the influence of evil spirits."[135] At this point, the narrator asserts, "the reader, if such there be, who believes in the absolute independence and self-determination of the will, and the consequent total responsibility of every human being for every irregular nervous action and ill-governed muscular contraction, may as well lay down this narrative."¹³⁶ Otherwise, "he may lose all faith in poor Myrtle Hazard, and all patience with the writer who tells her story."¹³⁷

Hazard's hysteria manifests as an attraction to Dr. Hurlbut's middle-aged son, Fordyce, also a doctor. She becomes subject to strong headaches, and only his touch removes her pain; when he soothes "her strange, excited condition," she fixes "her wandering thoughts upon him."¹³⁸ Soon, her will loses its "power," and "'I cannot help it'—the hysteric motto—" becomes her refrain.¹³⁹ Her hysteria causes her to undergo "a singular change of her moral nature": whereas before she "had been a truthful child," at this point "she seemed to have lost the healthy instincts for veracity and honesty. She feigned all sorts of odd symptoms, and showed a wonderful degree of cunning in giving an appearance of truth to them" so that she might see Fordyce more often.¹⁴⁰ She comes to depend on the doctor's constant care, and in time the two begin to have romantic feelings for each other. Nurse Byloe, Fordyce's assistant, goes to Gridley for his help, telling him that "this gal ain't Myrtle Hazard no longer" and that the younger Hurlbut is "gettin' a little bewitched" by her.¹⁴¹ Gridley solves the problem by inviting Hurlbut to his home, reading the Oath of Hippocrates to him, and asking him bluntly whether he is "in danger of violating the sanctities of [his] honorable calling, and leading astray a young person committed to [his] sacred keeping."¹⁴² The physician agrees that he has been careless, and from that point his elderly father sees the teenager instead; after three days of nervous attacks, she returns to a healthy state.¹⁴³ In this episode, as in others, the novel suggests that part of the role of community is to guide those less in control of their inclinations and actions—here, Hazard and, to a certain degree, the younger Hurlbut—in ways that prevent harm.

After Hazard develops "the instincts of the coquette, or at least of the city belle," due to the influence of her worldly ancestor Judith Pride, she becomes "conscious of her gifts of fascination, and seemed to please herself with the homage of her rustic admirers."¹⁴⁴ She, Withers, and Gridley agree that she should leave the village for more schooling, and Gridley offers some money to send her to "Madam Delacoste's institution for young ladies," where she will find no "rustic admirers."¹⁴⁵ But there she imbibes the ways of the rich and fashionable, and her inclination to flaunt her beauty grows. Pride's influence only wanes when that of Hazard's American Indian ancestor grows. The school holds a party featuring living tableaux, and Hazard is chosen to play the part of Pocahontas in a few scenes.¹⁴⁶ As she dresses for the part, her Native ancestor surfaces in her consciousness:

She felt herself carried back into the dim ages when the wilderness was yet untrodden save by the feet of its native lords. Think of her wild fancy as we may, she felt as if that dusky woman of her midnight vision on the river were breathing for one hour through her lips. If this belief had lasted, it is plain enough where it would have carried her. But it came into her imagination and vivifying consciousness with the putting on of her unwonted costume, and might well leave her when she put it off. It is not for us, who tell only what happened, to solve these mysteries of the seeming admission of unhoused souls into the fleshly tenements belonging to air-breathing personalities.[147]

Hazard's first scene as Pocahontas, in which she holds a knife to cut the cords binding John Smith's hands, is so well-received that someone in the audience throws a wreath to her, which enrages another student who had expected the accolade.[148] In "a spasm of jealous passion," the student tears the wreath from Hazard's hands and stomps on it just as the curtain rises for the next scene.[149] Screaming "a cry which some said had the blood-chilling tone of an Indian's battle-shriek," Hazard pins her assailant to the ground and raises the knife to strike her, but she suddenly flings the knife away.[150] If the incident had gone further, the narrator comments, the evening "would have been treated in full in all the works on medical jurisprudence published throughout the limits of Christendom."[151] Unlike the other incidents, though, Gridley is not around to help her; she has learned through experience how to limit her ancestors' deleterious influence on her own. The movement of *The Guardian Angel*, then, is toward a greater, not a lesser, degree of self-determination. If Calvinism "assumes the necessity of the extermination of instincts which were given to be regulated," then Holmes seeks to delineate how they might be molded and governed.[152]

Hazard gains full self-determination only through her work as a nurse in the Civil War. It is surprising, given that the novel spans roughly 1859–65, that the Civil War does not take up a larger share of the text. Only fifty of its roughly four hundred and twenty pages remain when, in a chapter titled "Just as You Expected," the narrator announces that "the spring of 1861 had now arrived,—that eventful spring which was to lift the curtain and show the first scene of the first act in the mighty drama which fixed the eyes of mankind during four bloody years."[153] After the fall of Fort Sumter, the men of Oxbow organize and march to war.[154] By this point, Hazard has been guided through many problems caused by her inherited tendencies and has learned how to regulate her impulses, and the outbreak of the war completes the harmonization of Hazard's competing ancestral influences. She acquires "womanly endurance" in the face of conflict, for "a great cause makes great souls."[155] Her only wish thereafter is to "help the soldiers and their families."[156] In only two paragraphs, her beau Clement Lindsay, a pleasant albeit colorless man from a nearby town, rises from the rank of captain to major and then to colonel, and Hazard marries him and follows him to the front.[157] From that point until the war's conclusion, she becomes a nurse and "passe[s] her time between the life of the tent and the life of the hospital."[158] Her ministrations "performed for the sick and the wounded and the dying" remove the last traces of "the dross of her nature"; "the conflict of mingled lives in her blood had ceased."[159]

The conclusion of *The Guardian Angel* suggests connections among a unified community (which learns to accommodate Hazard), a unified Hazard (who coheres many identities into one), and a unified nation (newly united after its own inner conflict).[160] We might read Hazard as an embodiment of the postbellum ideology of national unity—cohered and coherent as a new and better whole, unbound by her past, and able to determine her future. Doing so underscores how Holmes understands reform as the communal work of individuals striving for a better society. By dramatizing how even the most combative "conflict of mingled lives" might be stilled with communal support and the acquisition of new habits, Holmes calls into question whether those damned by heredity need remain so during a historical moment suspended between Calvinist and eugenicist hereditary determinisms. Two years after the publication of *The Guardian Angel*, J. Bruce Thompson, surgeon at Scotland's General Prison and an early eugenicist, wrote in his article "The Hereditary Nature of Crime" that crime is "generally committed by criminals hereditarily disposed to it"; therefore, he writes, it is incurable.[161] Concluding that crime is "a moral disease of a chronic and congenital nature, intractable in the extreme, because transmitted from generation to generation," he asserts that heredity is fate.[162] But in *The Guardian Angel*, Holmes seeks to show how even those traits most conducive to immorality might be contained and guided. If *The Guardian Angel* translates *Elsie Venner*'s environmental model of heredity into what is for Holmes a more scientifically current model, so too does it attempt to revise the earlier novel's depiction of the deadly effects of treatment. By presenting the management of inherited traits not as a matter of biological intervention but as a matter of social support and ongoing self-reflection, the novel cuts a path between a bioplasticity so malleable that it risks the integrity of the subject and varieties of determinism that deny the subject's ability to change at all.

By focusing on the novels Holmes published between Darwin and Galton, I have sought to recover the productive unsettledness and indeterminacy of conceptions of heredity in the middle of the nineteenth century. I find in the novels a sensitive exploration of the risks of somatic change, whether that of one's own body or another's; that *The Guardian Angel* emphasizes social rather than physiological interventions into the situations of those whom Holmes calls "moral monsters" suggests his sense that the sometimes dangerous, irrational impulses of the human body are to be accommodated and gently guided, not directly reformed. In this way, he seems to echo Hawthorne's notion that bodily refinement takes place naturally, through the intervention of Providence rather than of humankind. Yet the two authors disagree about many aspects of heredity: How does heredity work? What characteristics do children inherit from their parents? Can heredity be yoked to the betterment of humanity? What are the moral ramifications of doing so?

These questions, explored by both Hawthorne and Holmes, set the stage for debates about what would come to be known as eugenics in the last decades of the nineteenth century and beyond. The same conceptual fluidity that allowed novels published only ten years apart to offer substantially different depictions of heredity also catalyze the rise of ever more restrictive visions of how and why to harness it. Darwin himself professed not to understand the intricacies of hereditary transmission: in the first chapter of *The Origin of Species*, he writes that "the laws governing inheritance are quite unknown; no one can say why the same peculiarity in different individuals of the same species, and in individuals of different species, is sometimes inherited and sometimes not so."[163] In his 1865 essay on "Hereditary Talent and Character," Galton admits the same: "In investigating the hereditary transmission of talent," he writes, "we must ever bear in mind our ignorance of the laws which govern the inheritance even of physical features."[164] Yet in the rest of the essay, Galton wastes little time in proposing "a Utopia—or a Laputa, if you will," in which the state selects ten men and ten women to marry and bring forth "an extraordinarily talented issue." Such a joining might yield, over time, "a galaxy of genius," a new governing caste of "prophets and high priests of civilization." Of those individuals whom he, along with Holmes, terms "moral monsters," Galton notes with pride that "the law puts them out of the way, by the prison or the gallows, and so prevents them from continuing their breed." Preventing purported "monsters"—moral, physical, intellectual, racial—from reproducing would become one of the signature reform projects of the Progressive Era.

Galton appears here as Hawthorne's Holgrave, whose zest for reform leaves him blinkered and naive; as Thoreau's philanthropist, who mistakes his own sour stomach for that of the world; as Melville's graham cracker–eating bohemians, whose efforts at self-perfection leave them disconnected from the society they would see renewed. This is not to villainize Galton more than is warranted or to make him the patsy for the whole sordid history of eugenics; in the late nineteenth century, eugenicism was no less an unsettled and debated concept than heredity was in the antebellum period, and such atrocities as forced sterilization did not occur on a mass scale until the early twentieth century. Rather, this is to say that antebellum literature, as much as it celebrates the perfecting of nature, prophesizes the rise of reformers whose ambitions outstrip their fellow feeling.

Coda
Literature and Neurological Selfhood

> Is the body as linked to a particular subject position anything more than a particular embodiment *of* ideology? Where has the potential for change gone?
>
> —BRIAN MASSUMI, *Parables for the Virtual*

"Where has the potential for change gone?" Brian Massumi posed this question in 2002, and as of this writing, we humanists seem no closer to answering it. In general, we still reflexively regard attempts to think of bodies as anything other than permutations of ideology with querulous suspicion. Yet ideological analysis of embodiment, as Massumi notes, asks us to think of bodies as positioned at fixed, defined, predetermined points on a cultural grid. The problem with doing so, as he writes, is that "positionality begins by subtracting movement from the picture. This catches the body in a cultural freeze-frame."[1] When we analyze historical bodies, our disciplinary impulse to freeze them is all the stronger. I have sought in this book to foreground antebellum Americans' sense that their bodies were unfixed; as Fuller writes, bodies are where "fluid hardens to solid, solid rushes to fluid."[2] *The Perfecting of Nature* has brought into conversation writers with a shared commitment to thinking through the possibilities and the perils of bioplasticity. These writers imagined into being the sorts of subjectivity that might lead someone like Ishmael to wonder if too much chowder might affect his mental state. In a variety of ways, literature was an important point at which culture and the body met and intermingled. To read Fuller, Melville, and Whitman is to rediscover a "potential for change" that humanists seem to have lost.

At the same time, we find ourselves in a moment when the question of plasticity is as salient as it has ever been. Confronted with a rapidly expanding range of somatic interventions (gene editing, tailored pharmaceuticals, cybernetic implants), we face a choice: Do we shy away from them and close our bodies' borders? (Can we ever exercise such sovereignty?) Or do we make what is perhaps the harder choice: to imagine more freely what our bodies might be capable of doing? Embracing change runs the risk of harm, as

Holmes makes clear; it also means affirming Fuller's notion that our bodies need not always be burdened with meanings and capacities that are natural in name only.

Just as nineteenth-century physiology provides the conceptual backdrop of the varieties of bioplasticity addressed by the writers this book studies, so too does the neuroscientific revolution of the early twenty-first century inform our understanding of how we might shape our selves in the present day. Each of us could be said to possess what Nikolas Rose and Joelle Abi-Rached, among others, call a "neurological self": a "neurological dimension to our self-understanding" engendered by neuroscientific ideas.[3] Working from Charles Taylor's argument that the self is historically and culturally constituted, they write that the neurological self provides "a new register to understand, speak, and act upon ourselves—and on others—as the kinds of beings whose characteristics are shaped by neurobiology."[4] As they note, such a concept provokes comparisons to eugenics and forced lobotomization by many in the humanities and social sciences; but, as they remind us, this neurobiology "is not a biology of fate or destiny . . . but a biology that is open for intervention and improvement, malleable and plastic," and it conceptualizes the embodied self as subject to the demands of its biology yet able to meet those demands deliberately and rationally.[5] Just as Whitman imagined exercise and training as placing the body's form under deliberate control, a variety of new interventions promise to make it possible to "predict, modify, and control" the brain.[6] These interventions, as political scientist Robert Blank notes, "run the gamut from physical techniques that act directly on the brain to psychotropic drugs and biologics, to noninvasive virtual reality and neural imaging, to neural grafting and neurogenetics research."[7] The first response of many humanists to these interventions is, justifiably, to critique them as making the brain available to influence by governmental and corporate power. That attention itself has emerged as a valuable resource for social media companies suggests that marketers, if they could access something like a neural implant, would harvest our data directly from our neurons. But interventions into the brain also allow it to be conceived, as Rose and Abi-Rached put it, as "a site of choice, prudence, and responsibility for each individual."[8]

Bruno Latour encapsulates the Foucauldian counterargument to the idea that individuals might freely intervene in their biology: those who think themselves free to participate in projects of self-creation are "entirely determined by the action of powerful causalities coming from objective reality they don't see," including "economic infrastructure, fields of discourse, [and] social domination."⁹ The claim is that any promise of freedom and autonomy encrypts governmental, social, and corporate efforts to shape what individuals might imagine themselves to be free to do, causing them to internalize the regulatory state. Yet I ask, along with Massumi, whether bodies might not be thinkable in alternative terms: What happens when we "set aside the intemperate arrogance of debunking," rise past suspicion, and take seriously what other fields of inquiry, including neuroscience, might be able to tell us about ourselves?[10] More to the point, how might literary scholars address the neurological self and the conceptual structures that support it: the emerging ways of thinking about the mind and body brought about by neuroscience?

Henry David Thoreau and Oliver Wendell Holmes Sr. might provide some answers. These and other nineteenth-century American writers, as I have argued, took antebellum conceptions of bodily plasticity as opportunities to create imaginative spaces in which readers might discover new forms of embodied subjectivity. Having done so, they offer readers insight into forms of bodily change and motion now being called to attention by queer theory, new materialism, posthumanism, cinema studies, neovitalism, and animal studies. In their landmark book *Animacies*, Mel Y. Chen argues for attuning ourselves to the ways that the forms of material agency highlighted by these fields are themselves "shaped by race and sexuality"; what better elucidates this idea than little Ned gulping his Jim Crow gingerbread or Dough-Boy's fear that the *Pequod*'s harpooners might eat him?[11] In these instances, lines of demarcation between eater and eaten, human and foodstuff, animate and inanimate, do not exist in the ways that most of us intuitively understand them to exist in the present day. Rather, they are part of a historical and cultural moment that assumed not only the agency of matter in relation to the ever-changing human body but also the racial and sexual dimensions of ingestion, digestion, and other modes of assemblage. Those of us who hope to better understand the human body's future might first look to its past. Doing so, we might find what Thoreau found gazing at a thawing bank: a profusion of forms—lungs, brains, excreta—in the process of becoming.

Notes

Introduction

1. Channing, "Self-Culture," 5.
2. Channing, "Self-Culture," 9.
3. Channing, "Self-Culture," 10.
4. Channing, "Self-Culture," 10.
5. Channing, "Self-Culture," 9.
6. Emerson, *Selected Lectures*, 263.
7. Whitman, "Manly Health," 275.
8. Rosenberg, *Right Living*, 2. Rosenberg writes that homeopathy and hydropathy "flourished through the antebellum years," not least because they "assumed an oppositional role in defining their claims vis-à-vis regular medicine—with advocates of hydropathy and homeopathy emphasizing the unnatural and physiologically debilitating aspects of regular medical practice" (9). And in *The Politics of Anxiety in Nineteenth-Century American Literature*, Justine Murison notes that the decades preceding the Civil War were "the nadir of medical professionalism in the United States" (3). She offers a compelling reminder that many practices that we now condemn as "pseudoscience," including hydrotherapy and mesmerism, "were explicit responses to the potentially deadly hand of the physician," whose techniques of bloodletting and purging were popularly considered dangerous (4).
9. Jacques, *Hints toward Physical Perfection*, xvi (Jacques's emphasis).
10. Morantz-Sanchez, *Sympathy and Science*, 32.
11. Gura, *Man's Better Angels*, 4.
12. Gura, *Man's Better Angels*, 3.
13. Tyler, William S. to Edward Tyler, 190.
14. Altschuler, *Medical Imagination*, 8.
15. See Murison, *Politics of Anxiety in Nineteenth-Century American Literature*; Wazana Tompkins, *Racial Indigestion*; Altschuler, *Medical Imagination*; Schuller, *Biopolitics of Feeling*; Rusert, *Fugitive Science*; Thrailkill, *Affecting Fictions*.
16. Emerson, *Complete Works*, 2:185.
17. Felski, *Limits of Critique*, 12.
18. Felski, *Limits of Critique*, 12.
19. Jacques, *Hints toward Physical Perfection*, xvi.
20. Malabou, "You Are (Not) Your Synapses," 31.
21. Malabou, *What Should We Do with Our Brain?*, 6.
22. Thoreau, *Walden*, 148.
23. Foucault, *Use of Pleasure*, 10–11.
24. In her study of health discourses in nineteenth-century America, Burbick writes that "ruthless attempts are made to differentiate bodies into hierarchies of sexual,

racial, and class differences" at historical points at which the body emerges "as that which society must confront and explain." She continues: "To read the narratives of the healthy body is to begin to understand the relationships of power and subordination that societies attempt to render invisible." Burbick, *Healing the Republic*, 3.

25. Coviello, "Wild Not Less Than the Good," 510.
26. Coviello, "Wild Not Less Than the Good," 513.
27. Coviello, "Wild Not Less Than the Good," 513.
28. L. M. Alcott, *Eight Cousins*, 209.
29. L. M. Alcott, *Eight Cousins*, 209.
30. L. M. Alcott, *Eight Cousins*, 217.
31. Schuller, *Biopolitics of Feeling*, 12, 4.
32. Schuller, *Biopolitics of Feeling*, 3–4.
33. Schuller, *Biopolitics of Feeling*, 26–27.
34. Lane and Alcott, "Consociate Family Life," 440.
35. Lane and Alcott, "Consociate Family Life," 440.
36. L. M. Alcott, "Transcendental Wild Oats," 1570.
37. L. M. Alcott, "Transcendental Wild Oats," 1570.
38. Lane and Alcott, "Consociate Family Life," 448.
39. The argument I make in chapter 2, that Herman Melville speaks back to health reform by framing white rather than nonwhite bodies as being more unruly, addresses these distinctions in greater detail.
40. Stone, *Black Well-Being*, 57.
41. Stone, *Black Well-Being*, 57.
42. Rusert, *Fugitive Science*, 23, 198.
43. Rusert, *Fugitive Science*, 114.
44. In *Forgotten Readers*, Elizabeth McHenry turns to the archive of early African American print culture in her argument that not only fiction and poetry "were included in early African Americans' definition of literature, so too were treatises, declarations, letters, appeals, and, perhaps most significantly, journalism of every variety" (12). Britt Rusert in *Fugitive Science* recovers how African American periodicals "produced a dynamic space for cross-fertilization and exchange between literary and scientific texts" by publishing scientific works alongside fiction and poetry (22). For more on Harriet Jacobs's encounters with medicine, see Sarah L. Berry's and Mary Titus's work on the subject. For more on the diversity of early African American literary production, see especially Lara Langer Cohen and Jordan Alexander Stein's edited collection *Early African American Print Culture*.
45. J. Tompkins, *Sensational Designs*, xi, xiii.
46. Rose and Abi-Rached, *Neuro*, 223.

Chapter One

1. Channing, "Self-Culture," 9.
2. A. B. Alcott, *Doctrine and Discipline of Human Culture*, 71.
3. A. B. Alcott, *Doctrine and Discipline of Human Culture*, 7.
4. A. B. Alcott, *Doctrine and Discipline of Human Culture*, 23–24.

5. A. B. Alcott, *Doctrine and Discipline of Human Culture*, 24.

6. Emerson, *Complete Works*, 6:7; Thoreau, *Walden*, 206.

7. With regard to Hawthorne's attitude toward abolition, see his remarks in his *Life of Franklin Pierce*, a biography of Pierce written in support of his successful presidential campaign. Against abolitionists' fervor, he asks his readers to consider another view, one that "looks upon slavery as one of those evils which divine Providence does not leave to be remedied by human contrivances, but which, in its own good time, by some means impossible to be anticipated, but of the simplest and easiest operation, when all its uses shall have been fulfilled, it causes to vanish like a dream. There is no instance, in all history, of the human will and intellect having perfected any great moral reform by methods which it adapted to that end; but the progress of the world, at every step, leaves some evil or wrong on the path behind it, which the wisest of mankind, of their own set purpose, could never have found the way to rectify" (113).

8. For an overview of transcendentalist views on the human body, see Mary Lamb Sheldon's entry on "Health and the Body" in *The Oxford Handbook of Transcendentalism*, edited by Joel Myerson, Sandra Harbert Petrulionis, and Laura Dassow Walls. A great deal of work has been done on transcendentalist writers and science generally, but not on the body specifically. For scholarship on science in transcendentalism, see especially Lee Rust Brown's *The Emerson Museum: Practical Romanticism and the Pursuit of the Whole*; Eric Wilson's *Emerson's Sublime Science*; Walls's *Seeing New Worlds: Henry David Thoreau and Nineteenth-Century Natural Science*; Walls's *Emerson's Life in Science: The Culture of Truth*; Peter Obuchowski's *Emerson and Science: Goethe, Monism, and the Search for Unity*.

9. Hurst, "Bodies in Transition," 3.

10. Blumenthal, "Margaret Fuller's Medical Transcendentalism," 565.

11. Fuller, *Woman in the Nineteenth Century*, 103.

12. Fuller, *Woman in the Nineteenth Century*, 9.

13. Fuller, *Woman in the Nineteenth Century*, 103.

14. Murison, *Politics of Anxiety*, 2–3.

15. Mayo, *Letters on the Truths*, 146–47.

16. Blumenthal, "Margaret Fuller's Medical Transcendentalism," 567–68.

17. Blumenthal, "Margaret Fuller's Medical Transcendentalism," 568.

18. Fuller, *Woman in the Nineteenth Century*, 149.

19. Fuller, *Woman in the Nineteenth Century*, 149.

20. Thoreau, *Walden*, 5.

21. Thoreau, *Walden*, 65.

22. Thoreau, *Walden*, 150.

23. Thoreau, *Walden*, 150.

24. Thoreau, *Walden*, 150.

25. Thoreau, *Walden*, 150–51.

26. Thoreau, *Walden*, 150.

27. Neely, "Embodied Politics," 38. Neely argues that Gilmore and Bercovitch "have dismissed *Walden*'s ability to reform its society on the grounds that despite his vocal critique of the economic and political status quo, Thoreau merely replicates the conditions of his society while at Walden instead of imagining a substantive alternative" (34).

28. Neely, "Embodied Politics," 34.
29. Neely, "Embodied Politics," 34.
30. Neely, "Embodied Politics," 42, 44.
31. Neely, "Embodied Politics," 35.
32. Thoreau, *Journal*, 165.
33. Thoreau, *Journal*, 166.
34. Walls, *Emerson's Life in Science*, 112.
35. Walls, *Emerson's Life in Science*, 112.
36. Walls, *Emerson's Life in Science*, 118.
37. Thoreau, *Walden*, 204.
38. Thoreau, *Walden*, 205.
39. Thoreau, *Walden*, 205.
40. Thoreau, *Walden*, 205.
41. Thoreau, *Walden*, 205.
42. Thoreau, *Walden*, 206 (Thoreau's emphasis).
43. Thoreau, *Walden*, 206.
44. Thoreau, *Walden*, 206.
45. Thoreau, *Walden*, 206.
46. Thoreau, *Walden*, 206–7.
47. Thoreau, *Walden*, 207.
48. Thoreau, *Walden*, 207.
49. Thoreau, *Walden*, 83.
50. Thoreau, *Walden*, 238.
51. Thoreau, *Walden*, 239.
52. Thoreau, *Walden*, 239.
53. Thoreau, *Walden*, 151.
54. Thoreau, *Walden*, 151.
55. Thoreau, *Walden*, 56.
56. Thoreau, *Walden*, 56.
57. Thoreau, *Walden*, 56.
58. Gura, *American Transcendentalism*, 139.
59. Gura, *American Transcendentalism*, 139.
60. Lamarck, *Zoological Philosophy*, 122.
61. Lamarck, *Zoological Philosophy*, 119 (Lamarck's emphasis).
62. Lamarck, *Zoological Philosophy*, 339.
63. Lamarck, *Zoological Philosophy*, 339.
64. Quoted in López-Beltrán, "Cradle," 51–52.
65. Brown, *Domestic Individualism*, 79.
66. Brown, *Domestic Individualism*, 95.
67. Baldwin, "Specters of Servitude," 57.
68. Baldwin, "Specters of Servitude," 58.
69. Baym, "Heroine," 608.
70. Hawthorne, *House of the Seven Gables*, 3.
71. Hawthorne, *House of the Seven Gables*, 6.

72. See especially Genesis 1:11–12: "And God said, Let the earth bring forth grass, the herb yielding seed, and the fruit tree yielding fruit after his kind, whose seed is in itself, upon the earth: and it was so. And the earth brought forth grass, and herb yielding seed after his kind, and the tree yielding fruit, whose seed was in itself, after his kind: and God saw that it was good."

73. Hawthorne, *House of the Seven Gables*, 6.
74. Hawthorne, *House of the Seven Gables*, 4.
75. Hawthorne, *House of the Seven Gables*, 6.
76. Baym, "Heroine," 607.
77. Hawthorne, *House of the Seven Gables*, 6.
78. Hawthorne, *House of the Seven Gables*, 8.
79. Hawthorne, *House of the Seven Gables*, 8.
80. Hawthorne, *House of the Seven Gables*, 8.
81. Hawthorne, *House of the Seven Gables*, 16–17.
82. Hawthorne, *House of the Seven Gables*, 21.
83. Hawthorne, *House of the Seven Gables*, 21.
84. Hawthorne, *House of the Seven Gables*, 8, 21.
85. Hawthorne, *House of the Seven Gables*, 21.
86. Hawthorne, *House of the Seven Gables*, 30.
87. Hawthorne, *House of the Seven Gables*, 28–29.
88. Brazier, "History of the Electrical Activity of the Brain," 1.
89. Brazier, "History of the Electrical Activity of the Brain," 1.
90. Hawthorne, *House of the Seven Gables*, 29.
91. Brown, *Domestic Individualism*, 69.
92. Hawthorne, *House of the Seven Gables*, 29.
93. Hawthorne, *House of the Seven Gables*, 31.
94. Murison, *Politics of Anxiety*, 2.
95. Hawthorne, *House of the Seven Gables*, 31.
96. Murison, *Politics of Anxiety*, 3.
97. Hawthorne, *House of the Seven Gables*, 32.
98. Hawthorne, *House of the Seven Gables*, 32.
99. Hawthorne, *House of the Seven Gables*, 32.
100. Hawthorne, *House of the Seven Gables*, 34.
101. Hawthorne, *House of the Seven Gables*, 34.
102. Hawthorne, *House of the Seven Gables*, 34.
103. Hawthorne, *House of the Seven Gables*, 37.
104. Kyla Wazana Tompkins offers a compelling reading of Ned's consumption of the Jim Crow gingerbread as at once subjecting "the black body to total dehumanization, as it allows the consumer to digest and symbolically destroy that body," and as "anything but passive, especially in a world such as that of the novel, in which objects are so relentlessly animated for their symbolic value." Tompkins, *Racial Indigestion*, 95.
105. Brown, *Domestic Individualism*, 83.
106. Hawthorne, *House of the Seven Gables*, 39.
107. Hawthorne, *House of the Seven Gables*, 39.

108. Hawthorne, *House of the Seven Gables*, 34.
109. Hawthorne, *House of the Seven Gables*, 39.
110. Hawthorne, *House of the Seven Gables*, 39.
111. Peripatetic and Cosmopolite, "Quackery," 458.
112. Peripatetic and Cosmopolite, "Quackery," 458.
113. "Medical Matters," 276.
114. Hawthorne, *House of the Seven Gables*, 40.
115. Hawthorne, *House of the Seven Gables*, 40.
116. Hawthorne, *House of the Seven Gables*, 50.
117. Hawthorne, *House of the Seven Gables*, 50.
118. Hawthorne, *House of the Seven Gables*, 53–54.
119. Hawthorne, *House of the Seven Gables*, 58.
120. Hawthorne, *House of the Seven Gables*, 97.
121. Sklar, *Catharine Beecher*, 151.
122. C. Beecher, *Treatise*, 5.
123. C. Beecher, *Treatise*, 6.
124. C. Beecher, *Treatise*, 131; Hawthorne, *House of the Seven Gables*, 98.
125. Hawthorne, *House of the Seven Gables*, 128.
126. Hawthorne, *House of the Seven Gables*, 128.
127. Hawthorne, *House of the Seven Gables*, 128.
128. Hawthorne, *House of the Seven Gables*, 128.
129. Hawthorne, *House of the Seven Gables*, 128.
130. Hawthorne, *House of the Seven Gables*, 62.
131. Hawthorne, *House of the Seven Gables*, 87.
132. Hawthorne, *House of the Seven Gables*, 87.
133. Hawthorne, *House of the Seven Gables*, 87.
134. Hawthorne, *House of the Seven Gables*, 132.
135. Hawthorne, *House of the Seven Gables*, 132.
136. Hawthorne, *House of the Seven Gables*, 20.
137. Hawthorne, *House of the Seven Gables*, 20.
138. Hawthorne, *House of the Seven Gables*, 20.
139. Hawthorne, *House of the Seven Gables*, 222.
140. Hawthorne, *House of the Seven Gables*, 222.
141. Hawthorne, *House of the Seven Gables*, 222.
142. Hawthorne, *House of the Seven Gables*, 131.
143. Hawthorne, *House of the Seven Gables*, 222.
144. Hawthorne, *House of the Seven Gables*, 222.
145. Hawthorne, *House of the Seven Gables*, 223.
146. Hawthorne, *House of the Seven Gables*, 65.

Chapter Two

1. Parker, *Herman Melville*, 228.
2. Parker, *Herman Melville*, 228.
3. Kelley, "'I'm Housewife Here,'" 7.

4. Domestic guides and cookbooks provided ways for women to intervene in emerging discourses about the changeable body. In doing so, they often connected somatic malleability with women's domestic role as guardians of their family's health. Even such a mainstream publication as Catharine Beecher's *Domestic Receipt Book* (1846) could caution that serving too many dishes at a dinner party "overloads the stomach, and thus stupefies the brain" (241). In this and similar texts, restrictive dietary practices and female empowerment intersect.

5. Pullan, *Modern Housewife's Receipt Book*, iii.
6. Delbanco, *Melville*, 44.
7. Graham, *Lecture to Young Men*, 50.
8. Shelley, "Vindication," 16.

9. Other literary scholars who have addressed dietary reform include Michelle C. Neely, whose recent work on Thoreau's vegetarian dietary practices, themselves borrowed from reformer Sylvester Graham, asks us to reevaluate *Walden's* (1854) "embodied politics." When we do so, she argues, we understand how antebellum theories of diet and digestion are situated within "consequential debates over capitalism, citizenship, freedom, and the body." Neely, "Embodied Politics," 34. Likewise, Sean Ross Meehan draws on the history of physiology and medicine to describe what he calls "the poetics of digestion" in Emerson's and Whitman's writing. For Meehan, digestion's ability to break down matter and assimilate it into new forms "offers a paradox of identity through change" that complicates prevailing ways of thinking about Emerson's influence on Whitman. Meehan, "'Nature's Stomach,'" 101. And Kyla Wazana Tompkins studies the ways that nineteenth-century writers figure racially black bodies as both edible and prodigiously hungry.

10. Bennett, *Vibrant Matter*, 49.
11. Bennett, *Vibrant Matter*, 49.
12. Melville, *Moby-Dick*, 196.
13. Melville, *Moby-Dick*, 196–97.
14. Forget, "Evocations of Sympathy," 282.
15. Forget, "Evocations of Sympathy," 291.

16. For outstanding histories of studies of the nervous system, see especially Mary Brazier, *A History of Neurophysiology in the Nineteenth Century* (New York: Raven Press, 1988); Edwin Clarke and L. S. Jacyna, *Nineteenth-Century Origins of Neuroscientific Concepts* (Berkeley: University of California Press, 1987); Sidney Ochs, *A History of Nerve Functions: From Animal Spirits to Molecular Mechanisms* (Cambridge: Cambridge University Press, 2004).

17. Philip, *Treatise on Indigestion*, 87.
18. Philip, *Treatise on Indigestion*, 75.
19. Philip, *Treatise on Indigestion*, 76.
20. Philip, *Treatise on Indigestion*, 295.
21. Philip, *Treatise on Indigestion*, 125.
22. Philip, *Treatise on Indigestion*, 126.
23. Philip, *Treatise on Indigestion*, 128.
24. Philip, *Treatise on Indigestion*, 129.
25. Philip, *Treatise on Indigestion*, 130.

26. Fish, Philip writes, is less easily digestible than "the flesh of land animals," and less nutritive. Philip, *Treatise on Indigestion*, 130. Because any food that might create a paste-like consistency in the stomach is difficult to digest, Philip recommends avoiding new bread, "all articles composed of strong jellies, and food carefully mashed" (132). Fresh vegetables, which, he writes, ferment in the stomach, are "injurious," but "mealy potatoes, turnips, and broccoli" may be boiled and eaten. He also counsels avoiding fruit, butter, milk, oil, anything fried, alcohol, coffee, tea, and iced drinks (136-37, 145, 153).

27. Philip, *Treatise on Indigestion*, 4.
28. Philip, *Treatise on Indigestion*, 4.
29. Philip, *Treatise on Indigestion*, 42.
30. Johnson, *Essay on Morbid Sensibility of the Stomach and Bowels*, 36.
31. Johnson, *Essay on Morbid Sensibility of the Stomach and Bowels*, 36.
32. Johnson, *Essay on Morbid Sensibility of the Stomach and Bowels*, 43.
33. Johnson, *Essay on Morbid Sensibility of the Stomach and Bowels*, 61.
34. Johnson, *Essay on Morbid Sensibility of the Stomach and Bowels*, 69.
35. Johnson, *Essay on Morbid Sensibility of the Stomach and Bowels*, 43.
36. Parker, *Herman Melville*, 49.
37. Johnson, *Essay on Morbid Sensibility of the Stomach and Bowels*, 60 (Johnson's emphasis).
38. Johnson, *Essay on Morbid Sensibility of the Stomach and Bowels*, 60.
39. Johnson, *Essay on Morbid Sensibility of the Stomach and Bowels*, 60-61.
40. Johnson, *Essay on Morbid Sensibility of the Stomach and Bowels*, 61.
41. Johnson, *Essay on Morbid Sensibility of the Stomach and Bowels*, 61.
42. Johnson, *Essay on Morbid Sensibility of the Stomach and Bowels*, 61.
43. Johnson, *Essay on Morbid Sensibility of the Stomach and Bowels*, 61.
44. In a December 1850 letter to Evert Augustus Duyckinck, Melville writes about the pleasure he receives watching his cow ruminate: "It's a pleasant sight to see a cow move her jaws—she does it so mildly & with such sanctity." Melville, *Correspondence*, 174.
45. Johnson, *Essay on Morbid Sensibility of the Stomach and Bowels*, 60-61.
46. Johnson, *Essay on Morbid Sensibility of the Stomach and Bowels*, 61.
47. Johnson, *Essay on Morbid Sensibility of the Stomach and Bowels*, 62.
48. Johnson, *Essay on Morbid Sensibility of the Stomach and Bowels*, 62.
49. Johnson, *Essay on Morbid Sensibility of the Stomach and Bowels*, 1.
50. Johnson, *Essay on Morbid Sensibility of the Stomach and Bowels*, i.
51. Melville, "Melville's Marginalia," 132 (Melville's emphasis).
52. Emerson, *Complete Works*, 1:6.
53. Melville, *Poems*, 280.
54. Melville, *Correspondence*, 193-94.
55. Melville, *Correspondence*, 194.
56. Melville, *Correspondence*, 194.
57. In a February 1851 letter to Duyckinck, Melville notes that Hawthorne himself is worryingly incorporeal: "There is something lacking—a good deal lacking—to the plump sphericity of the man. What is that?—He does'nt patronize the butcher—he

needs roast-beef, done rare." Melville, *Correspondence*, 181. For Melville, food—"roast-beef, done rare"—can fill the bodily lack he sees in Hawthorne.

58. Browner, *Profound Science and Elegant Literature*, 71.
59. Tally, "Whale as a Dish," 73.
60. Crain, "Lovers of Human Flesh," 26.
61. Boren, "What's Eating Ahab," 9.
62. K. W. Tompkins, *Racial Indigestion*, 2–3.
63. K. W. Tompkins, *Racial Indigestion*, 5.
64. Philip, *Treatise on Indigestion*, 133.
65. Orson Fowler and his brother, Lorenzo, are possibly the most influential figures in nineteenth-century health reform. Their publishing house, Fowler and Wells, published their own works on phrenology, marriage, and health, others' works, and periodicals such as the *Phrenological Journal*. Their interests ranged from vegetarianism to hydropathy to education. Gura, *Man's Better Angels*, 157–58. Because of their considerable impact and the breadth of their interest, works written by and published by the Fowlers play a large role in this study. The most authoritative biography of the brothers is Madeleine B. Stern's *Heads and Headlines: The Phrenological Fowlers* (1971). For a learned exploration of the Fowlers' influence in nineteenth-century America, especially in the context of health reform, please see Philip F. Gura's *Man's Better Angels*. As Gura notes, the brothers analyzed such nineteenth-century luminaries as "sculptor Hiram Powers; daguerreotypist Matthew Brady; authors William Cullen Bryant, Lydia Maria Child, John Greenleaf Whittier, Oliver Wendell Holmes, and Walt Whitman" (138–39).
66. Fowler, *Practical Phrenology*, 30.
67. Fowler, *Practical Phrenology*, 30.
68. Fowler, *Practical Phrenology*, 30.
69. Fowler, *Practical Phrenology*, 30.
70. Fowler, *Practical Phrenology*, 30.
71. Fowler, *Practical Phrenology*, 30.
72. Fowler, *Practical Phrenology*, 30.
73. Rose and Abi-Rached, *Neuro*, 2.
74. Rose, *Politics of Life Itself*, 27.
75. Smith, *Eating History*, 31.
76. Smith, *Eating History*, 29.
77. Smith, *Eating History*, 33–34.
78. Smith, *Eating History*, 34.
79. Graham, *Lecture on Epidemic Diseases Generally*, 78–80.
80. Smith, *Eating History*, 34; Graham, *Lecture on Epidemic Diseases Generally*, 78.
81. Graham, *Lecture on Epidemic Diseases Generally*, 79.
82. Graham, *Lecture on Epidemic Diseases Generally*, 80.
83. Graham, *Lecture to Young Men*, 36.
84. Graham, *Lecture to Young Men*, 37.
85. Graham, *Lecture to Young Men*, 38.
86. Graham, *Lecture to Young Men*, 40–41.
87. Graham, *Lecture to Young Men*, 134.

88. Mann, *Christianity in the Kitchen*, 2.
89. Mann, *Christianity in the Kitchen*, 2.
90. Mann, *Christianity in the Kitchen*, 2. Philip F. Gura notes that reformers' habitual condemnations of others' lack of self-discipline and general moral laxity is a consequence of their emphasis on individual effort as the foundation of reform: "Many nineteenth-century reformers willfully or not ignored that there was a more threatening side to this habit of reform logic. If we all have it in us to be better, and our unwillingness to do the work necessary to realize that perfection is what stands in the way of universal harmony, then a harsh judgment is certainly called for." Gura, *Man's Better Angels*, 3.
91. Mann, *Christianity in the Kitchen*, 2–3.
92. Mann, *Christianity in the Kitchen*, 3.
93. Mann, *Christianity in the Kitchen*, 163.
94. Rose and Abi-Rached, *Neuro*, 14.
95. Rose and Abi-Rached, *Neuro*, 223.
96. Johnson, *Essay on Morbid Sensibility of the Stomach and Bowels*, 1.
97. Rose and Abi-Rached, *Neuro*, 2.
98. Rose and Abi-Rached, *Neuro*, 223.
99. Rose and Abi-Rached, *Neuro*, 52.
100. Rose and Abi-Rached, *Neuro*, 22.
101. Rose and Abi-Rached, *Neuro*, 52.
102. Rose and Abi-Rached, *Neuro*, 22–23.
103. Graham, *Lectures on the Science of Human Life*, 4.
104. Graham, *Lectures on the Science of Human Life*, i.
105. Graham, *Lectures on the Science of Human Life*, i.
106. Graham, *Lectures on the Science of Human Life*, i.
107. Graham, *Lectures on the Science of Human Life*, 6.
108. Savarese, "Nervous Wrecks and Ginger-Nuts," 30.
109. Melville, "Bartleby," 16.
110. Melville, *Pierre*, 300.
111. Melville, *Pierre*, 300.
112. Melville, *Pierre*, 299.
113. Melville, *Moby-Dick*, 3.
114. Melville, *Moby-Dick*, 3.
115. Ryan, "Ishmael's Recovery," 33.
116. Murison, *Politics of Anxiety*, 33.
117. An anonymous review of two treatises on hypochondriasis in an 1844 issue of the *Medico-Chirurgical Review* charts an array of disagreements about the disease: James Johnson views it as originating in overstimulation of the brain, leading to a "morbid sensibility of the digestive organs"; German physician Christoph Hufeland claims that it originates in the nervous system generally and the digestive organs more particularly; William Cullen understands it as primarily a neurosis (421–23). In the midst of the controversy, though, physicians agreed that the two most common symptoms of the disorder are digestive troubles and despondency.
118. Johnson, *Essay on the Morbid Sensibility of the Stomach and Bowels*, 63.

119. Johnson, *Essay on the Morbid Sensibility of the Stomach and Bowels*, 65, 69.
120. Johnson, *Essay on the Morbid Sensibility of the Stomach and Bowels*, 72.
121. Melville, *Moby-Dick*, 3.
122. Melville, *Moby-Dick*, 6.
123. Rush, *Medical Inquiries*, 10.
124. Melville, *Moby-Dick*, 3.
125. Melville, *Moby-Dick*, 226.
126. Melville, *Moby-Dick*, 66–67.
127. Melville, *Moby-Dick*, 67.
128. Graham, *Lectures on the Science of Human Life*, 223.
129. Graham, *Lectures on the Science of Human Life*, 223–24.
130. Philip, *Treatise on Indigestion*, 133.
131. Melville, *Moby-Dick*, 67.
132. Melville, *Moby-Dick*, 50.
133. Melville, *Moby-Dick*, 50.
134. Melville, *Moby-Dick*, 50.
135. Melville, *Moby-Dick*, 50.
136. Johnson, *Essay on the Morbid Sensibility of the Stomach and Bowels*, 63.
137. Melville, *Moby-Dick*, 83.
138. Melville, *Moby-Dick*, 85.
139. Melville, *Moby-Dick*, 85.
140. Melville, *Moby-Dick*, 85.
141. Melville, *Moby-Dick*, 85.
142. Otter, *Melville's Anatomies*, 154.
143. Melville, *Moby-Dick*, 55.
144. K. W. Tompkins, *Racial Indigestion*, 7.
145. K. W. Tompkins, *Racial Indigestion*, 7.
146. K. W. Tompkins, *Racial Indigestion*, 7.
147. Melville, *Moby-Dick*, 121.
148. Melville, *Moby-Dick*, 295.
149. Melville, *Moby-Dick*, 150.
150. Melville, *Moby-Dick*, 150–51.
151. Melville, *Moby-Dick*, 151.
152. Melville, *Moby-Dick*, 151.
153. Melville, *Moby-Dick*, 152.
154. Melville, *Moby-Dick*, 152.
155. Graham, *Lectures on the Science of Human Life*, 178.
156. Melville, *Moby-Dick*, 151.
157. Melville, *Moby-Dick*, 153.
158. Melville, *Moby-Dick*, 152.
159. Melville, *Moby-Dick*, 153.
160. Melville, *Moby-Dick*, 153.
161. Melville, *Moby-Dick*, 152.
162. Melville, *Moby-Dick*, 292.
163. Graham, *Lectures on the Science of Human Life*, 141.

164. Melville, *Moby-Dick*, 293.
165. Melville, *Moby-Dick*, 293.
166. Melville, *Moby-Dick*, 294.
167. Melville, *Moby-Dick*, 294.
168. Melville, *Moby-Dick*, 294.
169. Melville, *Moby-Dick*, 295.
170. Melville, *Moby-Dick*, 296.
171. Melville, *Moby-Dick*, 296.
172. Melville, *Moby-Dick*, 296.
173. Melville, *Moby-Dick*, 297.
174. Melville, *Typee*, 125.
175. Melville, *Moby-Dick*, 301.
176. Melville, *Moby-Dick*, 302.
177. Melville, *Moby-Dick*, 302.
178. Melville, *Moby-Dick*, 89.
179. Melville, *Moby-Dick*, 79.
180. Melville, *Moby-Dick*, 183–84.
181. Melville, *Moby-Dick*, 163–64.
182. Melville, *Moby-Dick*, 164.
183. Melville, *Moby-Dick*, 408.
184. Melville, *Moby-Dick*, 408.
185. Melville, *Moby-Dick*, 409.
186. Cheever, *Whale and His Captors*, 115.
187. Cheever, *Whale and His Captors*, 115.
188. Melville, *Moby-Dick* 409. See 1 Corinthians 15: 42–45: "So also is the resurrection of the dead. It is sown in corruption; it is raised in incorruption: It is sown in dishonour; it is raised in glory: it is sown in weakness; it is raised in power: It is sown a natural body; it is raised a spiritual body. There is a natural body, and there is a spiritual body. And so it is written, The first man Adam was made a living soul; the last Adam was made a quickening spirit" (King James Version).
189. W. A. Alcott, *Lectures*, 67.
190. Melville, *Moby-Dick*, 440.
191. Melville, *Moby-Dick*, 441.
192. Melville, *Moby-Dick*, 439.
193. Melville, *Moby-Dick*, 441.
194. Melville, *Moby-Dick*, 441.
195. Ishmael notes that whales are able to maintain their internal temperatures: "Oh, man! admire and model thyself after the whale! Do thou, too, remain warm among ice. Do thou, too, live in this world without being of it. Be cool at the equator; keep thy blood fluid at the Pole. Like the great dome of St. Peter's, and like the great whale, retain, O man! in all seasons a temperature of thine own." Melville, *Moby-Dick*, 307. Yet the question raised by Bunger is whether the whale can regain its physiological equilibrium once it has been disturbed.
196. Melville, *Moby-Dick*, 441.
197. Melville, *Moby-Dick*, 347.

198. Otter, *Melville's Anatomies*, 155.
199. Melville, *Moby-Dick*, 3.
200. Melville, *Moby-Dick*, 3.
201. Melville, *Moby-Dick*, 185.
202. *New York Albion*, November 22, 1851, quoted in Selby, *Herman Melville*, 29.
203. *Bell's Weekly Messenger* (London), November 2, 1851, quoted in Selby, *Herman Melville*, 29.

Chapter Three

1. Hungerford, "Walt Whitman," 369.
2. Fowler, *Practical Phrenology*, 365.
3. Fowler, *Practical Phrenology*, 365.
4. Whitman, *Leaves of Grass* (1860), 25.
5. Aspiz, *Walt Whitman and the Body Beautiful*, 38.
6. Whitman, "Manly Health," 186.
7. Douglass, "Claims of the Negro," 21. Douglass met and was impressed by Combe in his Edinburgh home during the fugitive's first visit to Europe in the 1840s. For more on Douglass's relationship with Combe, see James Poskett, *Materials of the Mind*, 129–30.
8. Rusert, *Fugitive Science*, 125. In her compelling reading of what she calls Frederick Douglass's "pro-phrenology agenda," pursued in "many of his publications—including *My Bondage and My Freedom*, the *North Star*, and *Frederick Douglass' Paper*," Rusert argues that "Douglass mobilized phrenology as a fugitive science that destabilized the racist science of craniology from within its own methodology" (125–26).
9. Douglass, "Claims of the Negro," 32.
10. Douglass, "Claims of the Negro," 32–33.
11. Douglass, "Claims of the Negro," 34.
12. Edwin Clarke and J. S. Jacyna write that Gall was actually the first to insist that the mind is situated within the brain, "to us a very obvious conclusion," and later note that Gall's concept of brain localization is "generally accepted" today (*Nineteenth-Century Origins*, 4, 213). Mary Brazier argues that Gall "may be regarded as a pioneer in emphasizing the importance of the grey matter for intellectual processes" ("Electrical Activity" 199). Robert Young argues that the founders of modern psychology owe a "direct debt" to Gall (250). Denis Leigh agrees, writing that Gall's map of the human skull "was an early forerunner of the magnificent work on localization of nervous functions which still continues" (245).
13. Gall never approved of the word "phrenology" to describe his system, preferring instead the terms "*Schädellehre*" or "*organologie*." Spurzheim popularized the term "phrenology" in America with his many lectures and public demonstrations. (Clarke and Jacyna, *Nineteenth-Century Origins*, 9). For the sake of simplicity, I will use the term "phrenology" to refer to Gall's neuroanatomical system and the popular scientific methods stemming from it.
14. Some historians argue that only later phrenologists, not Gall, claimed that these mental organs were made legible from examining bumps on one's head and

that Gall believed that only individuals with extraordinarily large neural bumps would have bumps that are discernible (Clarke and Jacyna, *Nineteenth-Century Origins*, 223–24). However, he writes in the first volume of *Sur les fonctions du cerveau et sur celles de chacune de ses parties* (1822)—his systematic treatise on the brain and skull—that "the form of the head or cranium should represent, in most cases, the form of the brain, and should suggest various means to ascertain the fundamental qualities and faculties, and the seat of their organs" (Gall, *Sur les fonctions du cerveau et sur celles de chacune de ses parties*, 55).

15. Fowler, *Practical Phrenology*, 5 (Fowler's emphasis).
16. Fowler, *Practical Phrenology*, 5.
17. Fowler, *Practical Phrenology*, 10 (Fowler's emphasis).
18. Fowler, *Practical Phrenology*, 22.
19. Fowler, *Practical Phrenology*, 365 (Fowler's emphasis).
20. Fowler, *Practical Phrenology*, 366 (Fowler's emphasis).
21. Fowler, *Practical Phrenology*, 367.
22. Fowler, *Practical Phrenology*, 369 (Fowler's emphasis).
23. Fowler, *Practical Phrenology*, 369–70.
24. Fowler, *Practical Phrenology*, 23 (Fowler's emphasis).
25. Fowler, *Fowler on Memory*, 9 (Fowler's emphasis).
26. Fowler, *Self-Culture*, 85.
27. Fowler, *Self-Culture*, 85, 104.
28. Fowler, *Self-Culture*, 108.
29. Todd, *Physical Culture and the Body Beautiful*, 3.
30. Todd, *Physical Culture and the Body Beautiful*, 3, 7.
31. Hungerford, "Walt Whitman," 355.
32. Hungerford, "Walt Whitman," 356.
33. Turpin, "Introduction," 149.
34. Turpin, "Introduction," 149.
35. Turpin, "Introduction," 156, 159.
36. Turpin, "Introduction," 157.
37. Turpin, "Introduction," 161.
38. Whitman, "Manly Health," 186.
39. Reynolds, *Walt Whitman's America*, 249.
40. Reynolds, *Walt Whitman's America*, 249.
41. Reynolds, *Walt Whitman's America*, 249.
42. Whitman, "Manly Health," 195 (Whitman's emphasis).
43. Whitman, "Manly Health," 196.
44. Whitman, "Manly Health," 235.
45. Thoreau, *Walden*, 56.
46. Whitman, "Manly Health," 235.
47. Whitman, "Manly Health," 212.
48. Whitman, "Manly Health," 210.
49. Whitman, "Manly Health," 210.
50. Whitman, "Manly Health," 210.
51. Whitman, "Manly Health," 210.

52. Whitman, "Manly Health," 210.
53. Whitman, "Manly Health," 269.
54. Whitman, "Manly Health," 194.
55. Whitman, "Manly Health," 194.
56. Whitman, "Manly Health," 211.
57. Whitman, "Manly Health," 194.
58. Whitman, "Manly Health," 184.
59. Whitman, "Manly Health," 184.
60. Whitman, "Manly Health," 190.
61. Whitman, "Manly Health," 252.
62. Whitman, "Manly Health," 185.
63. Whitman, "Manly Health," 221.
64. Whitman, "Manly Health," 221.
65. Whitman, "Manly Health," 221.
66. Whitman, "Manly Health," 222.
67. Whitman, "Manly Health," 222.
68. Whitman, *Leaves of Grass* (1860), 415.
69. Whitman, "Manly Health," 289, 308.
70. The nature of Whitman's attitudes toward African Americans has long been a subject of study and debate. For a comprehensive overview of this subject from the perspective of African American scholars, please see Ivy Wilson's edited collection *Whitman Noir*. See also Martin Klammer's *Whitman, Slavery, and the Emergence of "Leaves of Grass."*
71. Turpin, "Introduction," 170.
72. For a comprehensive discussion of the links between the changeability of poetry and that of the human body in Whitman's work, see especially Michael Moon's *Disseminating Whitman*. Moon makes the compelling case that Whitman's ideas about the human body evolve from the 1855 to the 1867 editions of *Leaves of Grass* in ways that chart a transition from understanding textual and biological bodies as "fluid" to understanding them as in need of both stability and the capacity for revision (vii–viii). My argument locates the concept of bodily discipline as the site at which fluidity and structure meet.
73. Whitman, *Leaves of Grass* (1855), 14.
74. Whitman, *Leaves of Grass* (1856), 167.
75. Eiselein, "*Leaves of Grass*, 1860 edition," 363.
76. Eiselein, "*Leaves of Grass*, 1860 edition," 363.
77. Aspiz, *Walt Whitman and the Body Beautiful*, 117.
78. Whitman, "Manly Health," 276.
79. Aspiz, *Walt Whitman and the Body Beautiful*, 24.
80. Hunt, "Observations on the Cause of the Disease Known as Sun-Stroke," 200.
81. Reynolds, *Walt Whitman's America*, 375.
82. Aspiz, *Walt Whitman and the Body Beautiful*, 24.
83. Whitman, *Leaves of Grass* (1856), 181.
84. Whitman, *Democratic Vistas*, 257.
85. Whitman, *Democratic Vistas*, 257.

86. Folsom, "'Spirt of My Own Seminal Wet,'" 591–92.
87. Trall, *Illustrated Family Gymnasium*, 18.
88. Whitman, *Democratic Vistas*, 204.
89. Whitman, *Democratic Vistas*, 218.
90. Whitman, *Democratic Vistas*, 208.
91. Whitman, *Democratic Vistas*, 245.
92. Whitman, *Democratic Vistas*, 257.
93. Whitman, *Leaves of Grass* (1860), 344, 346.
94. Folsom, "'Spirt of My Own Seminal Wet,'" 592.
95. Whitman, *Leaves of Grass* (1860), 341.
96. Whitman, *Leaves of Grass* (1860), 341.
97. Whitman, *Leaves of Grass* (1860), 357.
98. Whitman, *Leaves of Grass* (1860), 357.
99. Whitman, "Manly Health," 185 (Whitman's emphasis).
100. Whitman, *Leaves of Grass* (1860), 225.
101. Whitman, *Leaves of Grass* (1860), 225.
102. For an analysis of Whitman's theories about the healthful effects of reading from the perspective of disability studies, see Libow, "Song of My Self-Help."
103. Aspiz, *Walt Whitman and the Body Beautiful*, 10.
104. Warner, introduction, xix.
105. Whitman, *Leaves of Grass* (1860), 418.
106. Whitman, *Leaves of Grass* (1860), 418.
107. Whitman, *Leaves of Grass* (1860), 418.
108. Whitman, *Leaves of Grass* (1860), 418.
109. Whitman, *Leaves of Grass* (1860), 419.
110. Whitman, "Manly Health," 220.
111. Jacques, *Hints towards Physical Perfection*, 68.
112. Jacques, *Hints towards Physical Perfection*, 67.
113. Jacques, *Hints towards Physical Perfection*, 67 (Jacques's emphasis).
114. Whitman, *Leaves of Grass* (1860), 419.
115. Thoreau, *Walden*, 150.
116. Whitman, *Leaves of Grass* (1860), 420.
117. Whitman, "Manly Health," 195 (Whitman's emphasis).
118. Whitman, "Manly Health," 195 (Whitman's emphasis).
119. Fowler, *Education and Self-Improvement*, 25 (Fowler's emphasis).
120. Fowler, *Education and Self-Improvement*, 26 (Fowler's emphasis).
121. Whitman, *Leaves of Grass* (1860), 420.
122. Whitman, *Leaves of Grass* (1860), 38.
123. Mancuso, "*Leaves of Grass* (1867 edition)," 365.
124. Mancuso, "*Leaves of Grass* (1867 edition)," 365.
125. Mancuso, "*Leaves of Grass* (1867 edition)," 366.
126. Warren, "Cluster Arrangements in *Leaves of Grass*," 58.
127. Whitman, *Leaves of Grass* (1855), 85.
128. Whitman, *Leaves of Grass* (1856), 242.

Chapter Four

1. Holmes, *Works*, 8:366–67.
2. Holmes, *Works*, 8:380.
3. Holmes, *Works*, 8:380.
4. Holmes, *Works*, 8:344.
5. Boewe, "Reflex," 303.
6. For scholarship on the intersection of Holmes's medical and literary practices, see especially Altschuler, *Medical Imagination*; Davis, *Bodily and Narrative Forms*; Thrailkill, *Affecting Fictions*. My argument owes much to these scholars' insights into the ways that Holmes's novels intervene in, rather than merely reflect, contemporary scientific and medical debates. For general introductions to Holmes's writing in prose, please see Gibian, *Oliver Wendell Holmes and the Culture of Conversation*; Weinstein, *Imaginative Prose of Oliver Wendell Holmes*. The best available biography of Holmes remains Tilton's *Amiable Autocrat*.
7. Tilton, *Amiable Autocrat*, 10.
8. Hoyt, *Improper Bostonian*, 34.
9. Hoyt, *Improper Bostonian*, 34.
10. Tilton, *Amiable Autocrat*, 10.
11. Tilton, *Amiable Autocrat*, 6.
12. Tilton, *Amiable Autocrat*, 7, 9.
13. *New England Primer*, 8.
14. *New England Primer*, 33.
15. *New England Primer*, 33.
16. *New England Primer*, 34. Calvinist theologians emphasized that while "the want of original righteousness" is a *negative* quality (a lack of righteousness), "the corruption of [Adam's] whole nature" is a *positive* quality (corruption is added to Adam's nature). The state of misery is the "lost communion with God" that deprives humans of what Edwards calls the "spiritual sense" by which the elect perceives God's goodness. *New England Primer*, 34.
17. Hodge, *Systematic Theology*, 218.
18. Hodge, *Systematic Theology*, 219–20.
19. Hodge, *Systematic Theology*, 229–30.
20. Hodge, *Systematic Theology*, 230.
21. Hodge, *Systematic Theology*, 230.
22. Hodge, *Systematic Theology*, 230–31.
23. Morse, *Life and Letters of Oliver Wendell Holmes*, 38.
24. Morse, *Life and Letters of Oliver Wendell Holmes*, 38.
25. Morse, *Life and Letters of Oliver Wendell Holmes*, 44.
26. Morse, *Life and Letters of Oliver Wendell Holmes*, 44. Wigglesworth's poem, published in 1662, describes the Day of Judgment.
27. Morse, *Life and Letters of Oliver Wendell Holmes*, 44. Holmes refers here to one of Aesop's fables. In it, a wolf decides to eat a lamb, so he accuses the lamb of insulting him the previous year to have an excuse to do so. The lamb replies that he is only six

months old, so he could not have done as the wolf says. The wolf responds that if the lamb did not do it, then it must have been his father, so he eats him anyway. The moral is that someone seeking to abuse power will always find a reason to do so, including blaming a child for its father's infractions.

28. Morse, *Life and Letters of Oliver Wendell Holmes*, 39.
29. Tilton, *Amiable Autocrat*, 235.
30. Tilton, *Amiable Autocrat*, 235.
31. Holmes, *Works*, 1:29.
32. Hoyt, *Improper Bostonian*, 186.
33. Hoyt, *Improper Bostonian*, 187.
34. Tilton, *Amiable Autocrat*, 249–50.
35. Holmes, *Works*, 2:114.
36. Holmes, *Works*, 2:114.
37. Holmes, *Works*, 2:108; Hoyt, *Improper Bostonian*, 215.
38. Tilton, *Amiable Autocrat*, 249.
39. Holmes, *Works*, 5:313.
40. Holmes, *Works*, 5:321 (Holmes's emphasis).
41. Holmes, *Works*, 5:323.
42. Holmes, *Works*, 5:323.
43. Holmes, *Works*, 5:322.
44. Holmes, *Works*, 5:322.
45. Morse, *Life and Letters of Oliver Wendell Holmes*, 263–64 (Holmes's emphasis).
46. Holmes, *Works*, 5:51, 5:147.
47. Holmes, *Works*, 5:193.
48. Holmes, *Works*, 5:v.
49. Holmes, *Works*, 5:v.
50. Holmes, *Works*, 1:89.
51. Holmes, *Works*, 5:247–48.
52. Holmes, *Works*, 5:247.
53. Holmes, *Works*, 5:247.
54. Holmes, *Works*, 5:220.
55. Holmes, *Works*, 5:227.
56. Holmes was more than familiar with Hall's work, for he and his colleague Jacob Bigelow prepared the first American edition of Hall's *Principles of the Theory and Practice of Medicine* for publication in 1839 (Boewe, "Heredity," 122). In the 1830s, Hall articulated the theory of the reflex arc, according to which nerves can communicate without the mediation of the brain. Hall's work laid the foundation for physiological studies of unconscious thought and movement.
57. Holmes, *Works*, 5:227.
58. Holmes, *Works*, 5:228 (Holmes's emphasis).
59. Holmes, *Works*, 1:86.
60. Holmes, *Works*, 1:86.
61. Morse, *Life and Letters of Oliver Wendell Holmes*, 264–65.
62. Thrailkill, *Affecting Fictions*, 79.
63. Holmes, *Works*, 5:439.

64. Holmes, *Works*, 5:441.
65. Holmes, *Works*, 5:445.
66. Malabou, *New Wounded*, xv (Malabou's emphasis).
67. Malabou, *New Wounded*, xi.
68. Kellogg, "Plasticity and the Cerebral Unconscious," 117.
69. Tilton, *Amiable Autocrat*, 284.
70. Holmes, *Works*, 6:v.
71. Holmes, *Works*, 6:v.
72. Holmes, *Works*, 6:vi.
73. Holmes, *Works*, 6:vi.
74. Holmes, *Works*, 6:vii.
75. Holmes, *Works*, 6:vii.
76. Holmes, *Works*, 6:vii.
77. Holmes, *Works*, 6:vii.
78. Boewe, "Heredity," 113.
79. Boewe, "Heredity," 113; Holmes, *Works*, 6:vi.
80. López-Beltrán, "Medical Origins," 105.
81. Müller-Wille and Rheinberger, "Heredity," 3.
82. Müller-Wille and Rheinberger, "Heredity," 3.
83. Müller-Wille and Rheinberger, "Heredity," 4.
84. Müller-Wille and Rheinberger, "Heredity," 4.
85. Müller-Wille and Rheinberger, "Heredity," 4.
86. Müller-Wille and Rheinberger, "Heredity," 4.
87. E. Darwin, *Temple of Nature*, 56.
88. P. K. Wilson, "Erasmus Darwin," 137.
89. Holmes, *Works*, 13:48–49.
90. Müller-Wille and Rheinberger, "Heredity," 12.
91. López-Beltrán, "Medical Origins," 106.
92. López-Beltrán, "Cradle," 47.
93. López-Beltrán, "Cradle," 48.
94. Tilton, *Amiable Autocrat*, 105.
95. Holmes, *Works*, 6:22.
96. Holmes, *Works*, 6:22.
97. Holmes, *Works*, 6:24–26.
98. Holmes, *Works*, 6:26.
99. Holmes, *Works*, 6:26–27. Boewe notes that Holmes explores the figure of the grafted tree even more forcefully in *The Poet at the Breakfast-Table*: "You have seen a tree with different grafts upon it, an apple or a pear tree we will say. . . . It is the same thing with ourselves, but it takes us a long while to find it out. The various inherited instincts ripen in succession. You may be nine tenths paternal at one period of your life, and nine tenths maternal at another. All at once the traits of some immediate ancestor may come to maturity unexpectedly on one of the branches of your character, just as your features at different periods of your life betray different resemblances to your nearer or more remote relatives" (Holmes, *Works* 3:165–66, quoted in Boewe, "Heredity," 190).

100. Holmes, *Works*, 6:26.

101. The concept of latent heredity helps enable late-century discourses about atavism, or the regression to behaviors and mental states characteristic of evolutionary anterior species.

102. Holmes, *Works*, 6:27.

103. Holmes, *Works*, 6:27.

104. Holmes, *Works*, 6:2.

105. Holmes, *Works*, 6:3.

106. Holmes, *Works*, 6:3.

107. Holmes, *Works*, 6:13. That Hazard and Withers do not resemble each other could be attributed to Wither's being only a half sister to Hazard's mother.

108. Holmes, *Works*, 6:6.

109. Holmes, *Works*, 6:14.

110. Holmes, *Works*, 6:14. See Psalm 9:12 (King James Version): "When he maketh inquisition for blood, he remembereth them: he forgetteth not the cry of the humble."

111. Holmes, *Works*, 6:76.

112. Holmes, *Works*, 6:14.

113. Holmes, *Works*, 6:73.

114. Holmes, *Works*, 6:73.

115. Holmes, *Works*, 6:75.

116. Holmes, *Works*, 6:75.

117. Holmes, *Works*, 6:76.

118. Holmes, *Works*, 6:82–83.

119. Holmes, *Works*, 6:90.

120. Holmes, *Works*, 6:90.

121. Holmes, *Works*, 6:90.

122. Holmes, *Works*, 6:90.

123. Holmes, *Works*, 6:90.

124. Holmes, *Works*, 6:90–91. Ann Holyoake's name is spelled as "Anne" once and "Ann" twice in the novel; here, I use "Ann."

125. Holmes, *Works*, 6:91.

126. Holmes, *Works*, 6:92.

127. Holmes, *Works*, 6:92 (Holmes's emphasis).

128. Holmes, *Works*, 6:92.

129. Holmes, *Works*, 6:93.

130. Holmes, *Works*, 6:142.

131. Quoted in Holmes, *Works*, 6:154. See also Mather, *Magnalia Christi Americana*, 3:153.

132. Holmes, *Works*, 6:124.

133. Holmes, *Works*, 6:126.

134. Holmes, *Works*, 6:127.

135. Holmes, *Works*, 6:129.

136. Holmes, *Works*, 6:129.

137. Holmes, *Works*, 6:129.

138. Holmes, *Works*, 6:131, 133.

139. Holmes, *Works*, 6:133.
140. Holmes, *Works*, 6:133.
141. Holmes, *Works*, 6:137.
142. Holmes, *Works*, 6:140.
143. Holmes, *Works*, 6:141.
144. Holmes, *Works*, 6:253.
145. Holmes, *Works*, 6:253.
146. Holmes, *Works*, 6:271.
147. Holmes, *Works*, 6:272.
148. Holmes, *Works*, 6:273.
149. Holmes, *Works*, 6:273.
150. Holmes, *Works*, 6:274.
151. Holmes, *Works*, 6:272.
152. Holmes, *Works*, 1:42.
153. Holmes, *Works*, 6:367.
154. Holmes, *Works*, 6:373.
155. Holmes, *Works*, 6:405.
156. Holmes, *Works*, 6:406.
157. Holmes, *Works*, 6:406–7.
158. Holmes, *Works*, 6:407.
159. Holmes, *Works*, 6:407.
160. Holmes, *Works*, 6:407.
161. Thompson, "Hereditary Nature of Crime," 164.
162. Thompson, "Hereditary Nature of Crime," 157.
163. C. Darwin, *Origin of Species*, 13.
164. Galton, "Hereditary Talent and Character," 157.

Coda

1. Massumi, *Parables for the Virtual*, 3.
2. Fuller, *Woman in the Nineteenth Century*, 103.
3. Rose and Abi-Rached, *Neuro*, 223.
4. Rose and Abi-Rached, *Neuro*, 223.
5. Rose and Abi-Rached, *Neuro*, 223.
6. Blank, *Intervention in the Brain*, 26.
7. Blank, *Intervention in the Brain*, 26.
8. Rose and Abi-Rached, *Neuro*, 52.
9. Latour, "Why Has Critique Run Out of Steam?," 239, 238.
10. Massumi, *Parables for the Virtual*, 13.
11. Chen, *Animacies*, 5.

Bibliography

Alcott, Amos Bronson. *The Doctrine and Discipline of Human Culture.* Boston: James Munroe and Co., 1836.

Alcott, Louisa May. *Eight Cousins; or, The Aunt-Hill.* London: Sampson Low, Marston, Low, and Searle, 1875.

———. "Transcendental Wild Oats." *Independent*, December 18, 1873, 1569–71.

Alcott, William Andrus. *Lectures on Life and Health; or, The Laws and Means of Physical Culture.* Boston: Philips, Sampson, 1853.

Altschuler, Sari. *The Medical Imagination: Literature and Health in the Early United States.* Philadelphia: University of Pennsylvania Press, 2018.

Aspiz, Harold. *Walt Whitman and the Body Beautiful.* Champaign: University of Illinois Press, 1980.

Baldwin, Martha. "'The Ghosts of Departed Cook-Maids Looked Wonderingly On': Specters of Servitude in Nathaniel Hawthorne's *The House of the Seven Gables*." *Nathaniel Hawthorne Review* 41, no. 1 (2015): 57–74.

Baym, Nina. "The Heroine of *The House of the Seven Gables*; or, Who Killed Jaffrey Pyncheon?" *New England Quarterly* 77, no. 4 (2004): 607–18.

Beecher, Catharine. *A Treatise on Domestic Economy, for the Use of Young Ladies at Home, and at School.* New York: Harper and Brothers, 1848.

———. *Miss Beecher's Receipt Book: Designed as a Supplement to Her Treatise on Domestic Economy.* New York: Harper and Brothers, 1846.

Beecher, Jonathan. *Charles Fourier: The Visionary and His World.* Berkeley: University of California Press, 1990.

Bennett, Jane. *Vibrant Matter: A Political Ecology of Things.* Durham, NC: Duke University Press, 2010.

Berry, Sarah L. "'[No] Doctor but My Master': Health Reform and Antislavery Rhetoric in Harriet Jacobs's *Incidents in the Life of a Slave Girl*." *Journal of Medical Humanities* 35 (2014): 1–18.

Bhandar, Brenda, and Jonathan Goldberg-Hiller. "Introduction. Staging Encounters." In *Plastic Materialities: Politics, Legality, and Metamorphosis in the Work of Catherine Malabou*, edited by Brenda Bhandar and Jonathan Goldberg-Hiller, 1–33. Durham, NC: Duke University Press, 2015.

Blank, Robert H. *Intervention in the Brain: Politics, Policy, and Ethics.* Cambridge, MA: MIT Press, 2013.

Blumenthal, Rachel A. "Margaret Fuller's Medical Transcendentalism." *ESQ: A Journal of the American Renaissance* 61, no. 4 (2015): 553–95.

Boewe, Charles. "Heredity in the Writings of Hawthorne, Holmes, and Howells." PhD diss., University of Wisconsin, 1955.

———. "Reflex Action in the Novels of Oliver Wendell Holmes." *American Literature* 26 (1954): 313–19.

Boren, Mark Edelman. "What's Eating Ahab? The Logic of Ingestion and the Performance of Meaning in *Moby-Dick*." *Style: A Quarterly Journal of Aesthetics, Poetics, Stylistics, and Literary Criticism* 34 (2000): 1–24.

Brazier, Mary. "The History of the Electrical Activity of the Brain as a Method for Locating Sensory Function." *Medical History* 7, no. 3 (1963): 199–211.

Brillat-Savarin, Jean Anthelme. *The Physiology of Taste; or, Transcendental Gastronomy*. Translated by Fayette Robinson. Philadelphia: Lindsay and Blakiston, 1854.

Brodtkorb, Paul. *Ishmael's White World: A Phenomenological Reading of "Moby-Dick."* New Haven, CT: Yale University Press, 1965.

Brown, Gillian. *Domestic Individualism: Imagining Self in Nineteenth-Century America*. Berkeley: University of California Press, 1990.

Browner, Stephanie P. *Profound Science and Elegant Literature: Imagining Doctors in Nineteenth-Century America*. Philadelphia: University of Pennsylvania Press, 2005.

Burbick, Joan. *Healing the Republic: The Language of Health and the Culture of Nationalism in Nineteenth-Century America*. Cambridge: Cambridge University Press, 1994.

Castiglia, Christopher. *Interior States: Institutional Consciousness and the Inner Life of Democracy in the United States*. Durham, NC: Duke University Press, 2008.

Channing, William Ellery. *Self-Culture: An Address Introductory to the Franklin Lectures, Delivered at Boston, September, 1838*. Boston: J. Munroe, 1839.

Cheever, Henry T. *The Whale and His Captors; or, The Whaleman's Adventures, and The Whale's Biography*. New York: Harper and Brothers, 1850.

Chen, Mel Y. *Animacies: Biopolitics, Racial Mattering, and Queer Affect*. Durham, NC: Duke University Press, 2012.

Clarke, Edwin, and L. S. Jacyna. *Nineteenth-Century Origins of Neuroscientific Concepts*. Berkeley: University of California Press, 1987.

Early African American Print Culture, eds. Lara Langer Cohen and Jordan Alexander Stein, Philadelphia, PA: University of Pennsylvania Press, 2012.

Coviello, Peter. "The Wild Not Less Than the Good: Thoreau, Sex, Biopower." *GLQ: A Journal of Lesbian and Gay Studies* 23, no. 4 (2017): 509–32.

Crain, Caleb. "Lovers of Human Flesh: Homosexuality and Cannibalism in Melville's Novels." *American Literature* 66 (1994): 25–53.

"Crisis, n." *OED Online*. December 2019. Oxford University Press. https://www.oed.com/view/Entry/44539 (accessed October 11, 2019).

Critique and Postcritique, eds. Elizabeth S. Anker and Rita Felski, Durham, NC: Duke University Press, 2017.

D'Amore, Maura. "Hawthorne and the Suburban Romance." *Studies in American Fiction* 37, no. 2 (2010): 155–80.

Darnton, Robert. *Mesmerism and the End of Enlightenment in France*. Cambridge, MA: Harvard University Press, 1968.

Darwin, Charles. *On the Origin of Species by Means of Natural Selection, or The Preservation of Favoured Races in the Struggle for Life*. London: J. Murray, 1859.

Darwin, Erasmus. *The Temple of Nature; Or, the Origin of Society. A Poem, with Philosophical Notes*. London: J. Johnson, St. Paul's Churchyard, 1803.

Davis, Cynthia. *Bodily and Narrative Forms: The Influence of Medicine on American Literature, 1845–1915*. Palo Alto, CA: Stanford University Press, 2000.

Delano, Sterling. *Brook Farm: The Dark Side of Utopia*. Cambridge, MA: Belknap Press, 2004.

Delbanco, Andrew. *Melville: His World and Work*. New York: Vintage Books, 2006.

Douglass, Frederick. *The Claims of the Negro, Ethnologically Considered: An Address, Before the Literary Societies of Western Reserve College, At Commencement, July 12, 1854*. Rochester: Lee, Mann, 1854.

Eiselein, Gregory. "Leaves of Grass, 1860 edition." In *Walt Whitman: An Encyclopedia*, edited by J. R. LeMaster and Donald D. Kummings. Shrewsbury, MA: Garland, 1998.

Emerson, Ralph Waldo. *The Complete Works of Ralph Waldo Emerson*. Edited by Robert E. Spiller and Alfred R. Ferguson. 10 vols. Cambridge, MA: Harvard University Press, 1971–2013.

———. "New England Reformers." *Essays: Second Series*. Boston: James Munroe, 1844.

———. *The Selected Lectures of Ralph Waldo Emerson*, edited by Ronald A. Bosco and Joel Myerson. Athens: University of Georgia Press, 2005.

Fairclough, Mary. *The Romantic Crowd: Sympathy, Controversy, and Print Culture*. Cambridge: Cambridge University Press, 2013.

Felski, Rita. *The Limits of Critique*. Chicago: University of Chicago Press, 2015.

Folsom, Ed. "'A Spirt of My Own Seminal Wet': Spermatoid Design in Walt Whitman's 1860 *Leaves of Grass*." *Huntingdon Library Quarterly* 73, no. 4 (2010): 585–600.

Forget, Evelyn. "Evocations of Sympathy: Sympathetic Imagery in Eighteenth-Century Social Theory and Physiology." *History of Political Economy* 35 (2003): 282–308.

Foucault, Michel. *The Use of Pleasure*. Translated by Robert Hurley. New York: Vintage Books, 1990.

Fowler, Orson. *Education and Self-Improvement, Founded on Physiology and Phrenology: Or, What Constitutes Good Heads and Bodies, and How to Make them Good, by Enlarging Deficiencies and Diminishing Excesses*. 2nd ed. New York: O. S. and L. N. Fowler, 1844.

———. *Fowler on Memory: or, Phrenology Applied to the Cultivation of Memory; The Intellectual Education of Children, and the Strengthening and Expanding of the Intellectual Powers*. New York: O. S. Fowler and L. N. Fowler, 1842.

———. *Fowler's Practical Phrenology: Giving a Concise Elementary View of Phrenology*. New York: O. S. Fowler and L. N. Fowler, 1840.

———. *Self-Culture, and Perfection of Character: Including the Management of Youth*. New York: Fowlers and Wells, 1847.

Fuller, Margaret. *Woman in the Nineteenth Century*. New York: Greeley and McElrath, 1845.

Gall, Franz Joseph. *Sur les fonctions du cerveau et sur celles de chacune de ses parties, avec des observations sur la possibilité de reconnaitre les instincts, les penchans, les talens, ou les dispositions morales et intellectuelles des hommes et des animaux, par la configuration de leur cerveau et de leur tête*. In *Gall's Works*, edited by J. B. Baillière, translated by Winslow Lewis. 6 vols. Boston: Marsh, Capon, and Lyon, 1835.

Galton, Francis. "Hereditary Talent and Character." *Macmillan's Magazine* 12 (1865): 157–66.

Gibian, Peter. *Oliver Wendell Holmes and the Culture of Conversation*. Cambridge: Cambridge University Press, 2009.

Graham, Sylvester. *A Lecture on Epidemic Diseases Generally, and Particularly the Spasmodic Cholera*. New York: Mahlon Day, 1833.

———. *A Lecture to Young Men on Chastity*. 4th ed. Boston: George W. Light, 1838.

———. *Lectures on the Science of Human Life*. London: Horsell, Aldine Chambers, 1849.

Gura, Philip F. *American Transcendentalism: A History*. New York: Hill and Wang, 2007.

———. *Man's Better Angels: Romantic Reformers and the Coming of the Civil War*. Cambridge, MA: Belknap Press, 2017.

Halliday, Sam. *Science and Technology in the Age of Hawthorne, Melville, Twain, and James: Thinking and Writing Electricity*. New York: Palgrave Macmillan, 2007.

Hawthorne, Nathaniel. *The Centenary Edition of the Works of Nathaniel Hawthorne*. Vol. 16, *The Letters, 1843–1853*. Edited by Thomas Woodson, L. Neal Smith, and Norman Holmes Pearson. Columbus: Ohio State University Press, 1985.

———. *The House of the Seven Gables*. Edited by Robert S. Levine. New York: W. W. Norton, 2006.

———. *Life of Franklin Pierce*. Boston: Ticknor, Reed, and Fields, 1852.

Hodge, Charles. *Systematic Theology*. 2 vols. New York: Charles Scribner, 1870.

Holmes, Oliver Wendell. *The Works of Oliver Wendell Holmes*. 13 vols. Boston: Houghton Mifflin, 1892.

Hoyt, Edwin P. *The Improper Bostonian: Dr. Oliver Wendell Holmes*. New York: William Morrow, 1979.

Hungerford, Edward. "Walt Whitman and His Chart of Bumps." *American Literature* 2, no. 4 (1931): 350–84.

Hunt, Sanford B. "Observations on the Cause of the Disease Known as Sun-Stroke." *New Hampshire Journal of Medicine* 5 (1855): 200–206.

Hurst, C. Michael. "Bodies in Transition: Transcendental Feminism in Margaret Fuller's *Woman in the Nineteenth Century*." *Arizona Quarterly: A Journal of American Literature, Culture, and Theory* 66, no. 4 (2010): 1–32.

Jacques, Daniel Harrison. *Hints toward Physical Perfection: or, The Philosophy of Human Beauty*. New York: Fowler and Wells, 1859.

Johnson, James. *An Essay on Morbid Sensibility of the Stomach and Bowels, as the Proximate Cause, or Characteristic Condition of Indigestion, Nervous Irritability, Mental Despondency, Hypochondriasis, &c. &c*. 4th ed. London: Thomas and George Underwood, 1827.

Kelley, Wyn. "'I'm Housewife Here': Herman Melville and Domestic Economy." *Melville Society Extracts* 98 (1994): 7–10.

Kellogg, Catherine. "Plasticity and the Cerebral Unconscious: New Wounds, New Violences, New Politics." In *Plastic Materialities: Politics, Legality, and*

Metamorphosis in the Work of Catherine Malabou, edited by Brenda Bhandar and Jonathan Goldberg-Hiller, 111–32. Durham, NC: Duke University Press, 2015.

Klammer, Martin. *Whitman, Slavery, and the Emergence of "Leaves of Grass."* University Park: Pennsylvania State University Press, 1995.

Lamarck, Jean-Baptiste. *Zoological Philosophy: An Exposition with Regard to the Natural History of Animals.* Translated by Hugh Elliot. London: Macmillan, 1914. Originally published as *Philosophie Zoologique* (Paris: Musée d'Histoire Naturelle, 1809).

Lane, Charles, and Amos Bronson Alcott. "The Consociate Family Life." In *Transcendentalism: A Reader*, edited by Joel Myerson, 435–42. Oxford: Oxford University Press, 2000.

Latour, Bruno. "Why Has Critique Run Out of Steam? From Matters of Fact to Matters of Concern." *Critical Inquiry* 30, no. 2 (2004): 225–48.

Leigh, Denis. "Recurrent Themes in the History of Psychiatry." *Medical History* 1, no. 3 (1957): 237–48.

Libow, Jess. "Song of My Self-Help: Whitman's Rehabilitative Reading." *Commonplace: The Journal of Early American Life* 19, no. 1 (Spring 2019). http://commonplace.online/article/song-self-help-whitmans-rehabilitative-reading/.

López-Beltrán, Carlos. "In the Cradle of Heredity; French Physicians and L'Hérédité Naturelle in the 19th Century." *Journal of the History of Biology* 37 (2004): 39–72.

———. "The Medical Origins of Heredity." In *Heredity Produced: At the Crossroads of Biology, Politics, and Culture, 1500–1970*, edited by Staffan Müller-Wille and Hans-Jörg Rheinberger, 105–32. Cambridge: MIT Press, 2007.

Malabou, Catherine. *The New Wounded: From Neurosis to Brain Damage.* Translated by Steven Miller. New York: Fordham University Press, 2012.

———. *What Should We Do with Our Brain?* Translated by Sebastian Rand. New York: Fordham University Press, 2008.

———. "You Are (Not) Your Synapses: Toward a Critical Approach to Neuroscience." In *Plasticity and Pathology: On the Formation of the Neural Subject*, edited by David Bates and Nima Bassiri, 20–34. New York: Fordham University Press, 2016.

Mancuso, Luke. "*Leaves of Grass* (1867 edition)." In *The Routledge Encyclopedia of Walt Whitman*, edited by Donald Kummings and J. R. LeMaster, 365–68. New York: Routledge, 1998.

Mann, Mary Tyler Peabody. *Christianity in the Kitchen: A Physiological Cook-Book.* Boston: Ticknor and Fields, 1858.

Massumi, Brian. *Parables for the Virtual: Movement, Affect, Sensation.* Durham, NC: Duke University Press, 2002.

Mather, Cotton. *Magnalia Christi Americana.* London: Thomas Parkhurst, 1702.

Mayo, Herbert. *Letters on the Truths Contained in Popular Superstitions.* Edinburgh: John David Sauerlander and Messrs. Blackwood, 1849.

McHenry, Elizabeth. *Forgotten Readers: Recovering the Lost History of African American Literary Societies.* Durham, NC: Duke University Press, 2002.

"Medical Matters in the United States." *Lancet*, September 2, 1848, 276.

Meehan, Sean Ross. "'Nature's Stomach': Emerson, Whitman, and the Poetics of Digestion." *Walt Whitman Quarterly Review* 28, no. 3 (2011): 97–121.

Melville, Herman. "Bartleby, the Scrivener." In *The Piazza Tales and Other Prose Pieces*, edited by Harrison Hayford, Hershel Parker, and G. Thomas Tanselle, 13–46. Evanston, IL: Northwestern University Press, 1987.

———. *Correspondence*. Edited by Lynn Horth. Evanston, IL: Northwestern University Press, 1993.

———. "Melville's Marginalia in Ralph Waldo Emerson's *Essays: First Series*." In *Melville's Marginalia Online*, edited by Steven Olsen-Smith, Peter Norberg, and Dennis C. Marnon. http://melvillesmarginalia.org/Share.aspx?DocumentID=62&PageID=22724 (Accessed September 4, 2014.)

———. *Moby-Dick, or The Whale*. Edited by Harrison Hayford, Hershel Parker, and G. Thomas Tanselle. Evanston, IL: Northwestern University Press, 1988.

———. *Pierre; or, The Ambiguities*. Edited by Harrison Hayford, Hershel Parker, and G. Thomas Tanselle. Evanston, IL: Northwestern University Press, 1971.

———. *Published Poems*. Edited by Robert C. Ryan, Harrison Hayford, Alma MacDougall Reisling, and G. Thomas Tanselle. Evanston, IL: Northwestern University Press, 2009.

———. *Typee: A Peep at Polynesian Life*. Edited by Harrison Hayford, Hershel Parker, and G. Thomas Tanselle. Evanston, IL: Northwestern University Press, 1968.

Moon, Michael. *Disseminating Whitman: Revision and Corporeality in "Leaves of Grass."* Cambridge, MA: Harvard University Press, 1993.

Morantz-Sanchez, Regina. *Sympathy and Science: Women Physicians in American Medicine*. Chapel Hill: University of North Carolina Press, 2000.

Morse, John Torrey. *Life and Letters of Oliver Wendell Holmes*. 2 vols. New York: Houghton, Mifflin, 1896.

Müller-Wille, Staffan, and Hans-Jörg Rheinberger. "Heredity—the Formation of an Epistemic Space." In *Heredity Produced: At the Crossroads of Biology, Politics, and Culture, 1500–1870*, edited by Staffan Müller-Wille and Hans-Jörg Rheinberger, 3–34. Cambridge, MA: MIT Press, 2007.

Murison, Justine. *The Politics of Anxiety in Nineteenth-Century American Literature*. Cambridge: Cambridge University Press, 2011.

Neely, Michelle. "Embodied Politics: Antebellum Vegetarianism and the Dietary Economy of *Walden*." *American Literature* 85 (2013): 33–60.

The New England Primer. Boston: Manning and Loring, 1803.

Nissenbaum, Stephen. *Sex, Diet, and Debility in Jacksonian America: Sylvester Graham and Health Reform*. Westport, CT: Greenwood Press, 1980.

Ochs, Sidney. *A History of Nerve Functions: From Animal Spirits to Molecular Mechanisms*. Cambridge: Cambridge University Press, 2004.

Otter, Samuel. *Melville's Anatomies*. Berkeley: University of California Press, 1999.

"Outbreak, n." *OED Online*. December 2019. Oxford University Press. https://www.oed.com/view/Entry/133458?rskey=RFyQ8Z&result=2&isAdvanced=false (accessed April 14, 2016).

Parker, Hershel. *Herman Melville: A Biography*. Vol. 2, *1851–1891*. Baltimore: Johns Hopkins University Press, 2002.

Peabody, Elizabeth Palmer. "Plan of the West Roxbury Community." *The Dial: A Magazine for Literature, Philosophy, and Religion* 7 (January 1842): 361–72.

A Peripatetic and Cosmopolite. "Quackery in New York." *Boston Medical and Surgical Journal*, July 8, 1846, 456–59.

Philip, Alexander Philip Wilson. *A Treatise on Indigestion and Its Consequences, Called Nervous and Bilious Complaints; with Observations on the Organic Diseases in Which They Sometimes Terminate*. 4th ed. London: Thomas and George Underwood, 1824.

Poskett, James. *Materials of the Mind: Phrenology, Race, and the Global History of Science, 1815–1920*. Chicago: University of Chicago Press, 2019.

Pullan, Matilda Marian. *The Modern Housewife's Receipt Book: A Guide to All Matters Connected with Household Economy with Receipts Tested by John Sayer, the Medical and Other Portions of the Work Revised by J. Baxter Langley*. London: Aird and Hutton, 1854.

Reynolds, David S. *Walt Whitman's America: A Cultural Biography*. New York: Vintage Books, 1996.

Rose, Nikolas. *The Politics of Life Itself: Biomedicine, Power, and Subjectivity in the Twenty-First Century*. Princeton, NJ: Princeton University Press, 2007.

Rose, Nikolas, and Joelle M. Abi-Rached. *Neuro: The New Brain Sciences and the Management of the Mind*. Princeton, NJ: Princeton University Press, 2013.

Rosenberg, Charles, ed. *Right Living: An Anglo-American Tradition of Self-Help Medicine and Hygiene*. Baltimore: Johns Hopkins University Press, 2003.

Rusert, Britt. *Fugitive Science: Empiricism and Freedom in Early African American Culture*. New York: New York University Press, 2017.

Rush, Benjamin. *Medical Inquiries and Observations upon the Diseases of the Mind*. 5th ed. Philadelphia: Grigg and Elliot, 1835.

Ryan, James Emmett. "Ishmael's Recovery: Injury, Illness, and Convalescence in *Moby-Dick*." *Leviathan: A Journal of Melville Studies* 8, no. 1 (2006): 17–34.

Savarese, Ralph James. "Nervous Wrecks and Ginger-Nuts: Bartleby at a Standstill." *Leviathan: A Journal of Melville Studies* 5, no. 2 (2003): 19–49.

Schuller, Kyla. *The Biopolitics of Feeling: Race, Sex, and Science in the Nineteenth Century*. Durham, NC: Duke University Press, 2017.

Selby, Nick. *Herman Melville: "Moby-Dick."* Columbia Critical Guides. New York: Columbia University Press, 1998.

Sheldon, Mary Lamb. "Health and the Body." In *The Oxford Handbook of Transcendentalism*, edited by Joel Myerson, Sandra Harbert Petrulionis, and Laura Dassow Walls, 241–48. Oxford: Oxford University Press, 2010.

Shelley, Percy Bysshe. "A Vindication of Natural Diet." London: J. Callow, 1813.

Sklar, Kathryn Kish. *Catharine Beecher: A Study in American Domesticity*. New York: Norton, 1976.

Smith, Andrew F. *Eating History: 30 Turning Points in the Making of American Cuisine*. New York: Columbia University Press, 2009.

Stern, Madeleine B. *Heads and Headlines: The Phrenological Fowlers*. Norman, OK: University of Oklahoma Press, 1971.

Stone, Andrea. *Black Well-Being: Health and Selfhood in Antebellum Black Literature*. Gainesville: University of Florida Press, 2016.

Tally, Robert T., Jr. "Whale as a Dish: Culinary Rhetoric and the Discourse of Power in *Moby-Dick*." In *Culinary Aesthetics and Practices in Nineteenth-Century American Literature*, edited by Monika Elbert and Marie Drews, 73–88. New York: Palgrave Macmillan, 2009.

Thompson, Bruce J. "The Hereditary Nature of Crime." *Journal of Mental Science* 15 (1970): 487–98. In *The Origins of Criminology: A Reader*, edited by Nicole Rafter, 163–68. New York: Routledge, 2009.

Thoreau, Henry David. *Walden*. Edited by William Rossi. New York: W. W. Norton, 2008.

———. *Journal*. Vol. 2, 1842–1848. In *The Writings of Henry D. Thoreau*, edited by John C. Broderick. Princeton, NJ: Princeton University Press, 1984.

Thrailkill, Jane F. *Affecting Fictions: Mind, Body, and Emotion in American Literary Realism*. Cambridge, MA: Harvard University Press, 2007.

Tilton, Eleanor M. *Amiable Autocrat: A Biography of Dr. Oliver Wendell Holmes*. New York: Henry Schuman, 1947.

Titus, Mary. "'This Poisonous System': Social Ills, Bodily Ills, and *Incidents in the Life of a Slave Girl*." In *Harriet Jacobs and* Incidents in the Life of a Slave Girl*: New Critical Essays*, edited by Deborah M. Garfield and Rafia Zahar, 199–215. Cambridge: Cambridge University Press, 1996.

Todd, Jan. *Physical Culture and the Body Beautiful: Purposive Exercise in the Lives of American Women 1800–1875*. Macon, GA: Mercer University Press, 1998.

Tompkins, Jane. *Sensational Designs: The Cultural Work of American Fiction, 1790–1860*. Oxford: Oxford University Press, 1985.

Tompkins, Kyla Wazana. *Racial Indigestion: Eating Bodies in the 19th Century*. New York: New York University Press, 2012.

Trall, Russell Thacher. *The Illustrated Family Gymnasium*. New York: Fowler and Wells, 1857.

Turpin, Zachary. "Introduction to Walt Whitman's 'Manly Health and Training.'" *Walt Whitman Quarterly Review* 33, nos. 3–4 (2016): 147–83.

Tyler, William S. William S. to Edward Tyler, Amherst College, October 10, 1833. In Thomas H. Le Duc, "Grahamites and Garrisonites," in *New York History*, vol. 20, no. 2 (Albany, NY: Association, April 1939), 189–91.

Walls, Laura Dassow. *Emerson's Life in Science: The Culture of Truth*. Ithaca, NY: Cornell University Press, 2003.

Warner, Michael. Introduction to *The Portable Walt Whitman*, by Walt Whitman, xi–xxxvii. Edited by Michael Warner. New York: Penguin Books, 2004.

Warren, James Perrin. "The 'Paths to the House': Cluster Arrangements in *Leaves of Grass*, 1860–1881." *ESQ* 31, no. 1 (1984): 51–70.

Weinstein, Michael A. *The Imaginative Prose of Oliver Wendell Holmes*. Columbia: University of Missouri Press, 2006.

Whitman, Walt. *Democratic Vistas*. Washington, DC: J. S. Redfield, 1871.

———. *Leaves of Grass*. New York: Walt Whitman, 1855.

———. *Leaves of Grass*. New York: Fowler and Wells, 1856.

———. *Leaves of Grass*. Boston: Thayer and Eldridge, 1860.

———. [Mose Velsor, pseud.]. "Manly Health and Training, with Off-Hand Hints toward their Conditions." Edited by Zachary Turpin. *Walt Whitman Quarterly Review* 33, nos. 3–4 (2016): 184–310. Originally published in weekly serial form in the *New York Atlas*, September 12, 1958–December 26, 1858.

Wilson, Ivy, ed. *Whitman Noir: Black America and the Good Gray Poet.* Iowa City: University of Iowa Press, 2014.

Wilson, Philip K. "Erasmus Darwin on Human Reproductive Generation: Placing Heredity within Historical and *Zoonomian* Contexts." In *The Genius of Erasmus Darwin*, edited by C. U. M. Smith and Robert Arnott, 113–32. Burlington, VT: Ashgate, 2005.

Young, Robert M. *Mind, Brain and Adaptation in the Nineteenth Century: Cerebral Localization and its Biological Context from Gall to Ferrier.* Oxford: Oxford University Press, 1990.

Index

Abi-Rached, Joelle M., 15, 43–44, 53, 56, 68, 131. *See also* Neurotechnology
alcohol, 13, 43, 54, 64, 80, 86, 140n26
Alcott, Abby May, 10
Alcott, Amos Bronson, 10, 16–17, 20
Alcott, Louisa May, on gender and reform, 8–10; Works: *Eight Cousins, or The Aunt-Hill*, 8–9; "Transcendental Wild Oats," 10
Alcott, William Andrus, 71
Altschuler, Sari, 4, 133n15, 149n6
Andral, Gabriel, 118
Aspiz, Harold, 76, 87–88, 92
Atlantic Monthly, The, 106, 107–08, 114, 117

Baldwin, Martha, 30
Beecher, Catharine, *A Treatise on Domestic Economy*, 37–38, 42, 82, 139n4
Beecher, Lyman, 104
Bennett, Jane, 44
Bercovitch, Sacvan, 21, 135n27
Bhandar, Brenda, 6
bioplasticity, 5–9, 12–18, 29, 44, 77, 85, 98–100, 102, 113–15, 130–31; and neuroplasticity, 6–7, 15, 43–44, 53, 131–32
Blank, Robert, 131
Blumenthal, Rachel, 18, 20
Boewe, Charles, 103, 115, 151n99
brain, 6, 23, 74–80, 93, 103; as connected to stomach, 42–49, 52, 58
Brillat-Savarin, Jean Anthelme, 42, 61
Broussais, François J. V., 53, 118
Brown, Gillian, 29, 33, 36–37, 39
Brown, Lee Rust, 135n8
Brown, William Wells, 11
Browner, Stephanie, 50
Brownson, Orestes, 13, 27

Bunyan, John, 104
Burbick, Joan, 8, 133n24

caffeine, 36, 54, 64, 140n26
Calvinism, 101–08, 121, 124, 126–27, 149n16. *See also* Predestination, Theological
cannibalism, 51, 61, 64–70
Channing, William Ellery, 1–2, 16–17, 27
Cheever, Henry Theodore, 71
Chen, Mel Y., 132
Chesnutt, Charles, 12
Christian Science, 2
Civil War, 98, 126–28
coffee. *See* caffeine
Coleridge, Samuel Taylor, 23
Combe, George, 77, 145n7
Coviello, Peter, 8
Crain, Mark, 51
Craniometry, 2, 57, 76
Cullen, William, 45

Dale, Philip Marshall, 88
Darwin, Charles, 12, 14, 95, 99–100, 102–03, 128
Darwin, Erasmus, 116–17
Delany, Martin, 11–12
destructive plasticity, 102–03, 113–14
dietary reform, 3–7, 10, 13–14, 21–22, 43–44, 49–58, 60–64, 71–72, 83–84, 139n4, 139n9; and race, 64–70. *See also* digestion
digestion, 7, 14, 42–49, 58–63; cognitive effects of, 42–49; indigestion, 44–49, 70–72; as narrative mode, 59–60, 63–64; as opposed to eating, 50–51; and race, 64–70. *See also* brain, as connected to stomach; dietary reform

165

discipline, 14, 75–77, 81, 84–85, 87–88, 98
domestic advice. *See* domestic guides
domestic guides, 37–38, 42–43, 139n4
Douglass, Frederick, 76–77, 145n7, 145n8
Douglass, Sarah Mapps, 11
Duyckinck, George, 47, 140n44, 140n57
Dyspepsia. *See* Digestion

Easton, Hosea, 11
Edwards, Jonathan, 101, 103, 105–07, 149n16
Eiselein, Gregory, 87–88
Embodiment, historicizing of, 5–9
Emerson, Ralph Waldo, 13, 23, 38, 93, 135n8, 139n9; on materiality, 17–18, 49–50, 62, 72; Works: "Brahma," 106; "Circles," 5; "Fate," 16–17, "Reform," 2; "Spiritual Laws," 49–50, 62, 72
Euclid, 57
Eugenics, 80, 100, 102, 118, 127–29, 131

Felski, Rita, 5
Folsom, Ed, 90–91
Forget, Evelyn L., 45
Foucault, Michel, 8, 131–32
Fowler, Lorenzo, 74, 78–80, 84, 93, 95, 98, 141n65
Fowler, Orson, 80–82, 84–85, 88–90, 92–95, 97–98, 141n65; on diet and digestion, 52–53, 63; on exercising the brain, 78–80; on phrenology, 52–53, 74–75, 78–80
Fruitlands, 10. *See also* Amos Bronson Alcott; Louisa May Alcott; Charles Lane
Fuller, Margaret, 2, 6, 13, 16–18, 130–131; and gender, 19–20; and mesmerism, 20; and physiology, 19–20; Works: "The Great Lawsuit. Man versus Men. Woman versus Women," 18; *Woman in the Nineteenth Century*, 18–20

Galenic medicine, 2
Gall, Franz Joseph, 77–78, 145n12, 145n13, 135n14. *See also* Phrenology
Galton, Francis, 100, 102–03, 128–29
Galvani, Luigi, 32
Galvanic rings, 36
Garrison, William Lloyd, 4, 54
Gilmore, Michael, 21
Goethe, Johann Wolfgang von, 49–50, 62, 97
Goldberg-Hiller, Jonathan, 6
Graham, Sylvester, 3–4, 7, 10, 14, 21–22, 43–44, 53–58, 60, 64, 66, 68–70, 75, 79, 82–84, 95; and self-culture, 57
Greely, Horace, 54
Gura, Philip F., 3, 27, 141n65, 142n90

Hawthorne, Nathaniel 2, 13, 14, 16–17, 50, 103, 115, 128–29, 135n7, 140n57; Works: "The Birthmark," 30; *The Blithedale Romance*, 17; *The House of the Seven Gables*, 13, 17, 27–41; "The Marble Faun," 30
Hawthorne, Sophia, 55
Health reform, 1–4; contemporary critiques of, 3–4; and gender, 8–10; and literature, 2, 4–5; and national flourishing, 3; predominantly white and male audience of, 11–12; and race, 10–12; universalizing rhetoric of, 34–35. *See also* Dietary reform; Heredity, and reform; Physical training
Hereditary depravity. *See* Heredity, as vehicle of original sin
Heredity, 12–14, 41, 95–96, 99–103, 110–15, 120–24; changing conceptions of, 27–29, 115–119; and reform 30–31, 37–38, 127–29; as vehicle of original sin, 104–08. *See also* Eugenics; Predestination, Biological
Hodge, Charles, 105–06
Holmes, Oliver Wendell, Sr.: theological training of, 103–06. Works: "Autocrat

at the Breakfast-Table," 106–07, 110, 112; "The Chief End of Man," 107; "Crime and Automatism," 102; "Dorothy Q," 117; *Elsie Venner: A Romance of Destiny*, 14–15, 102–04, 108–14, 117, 119, 121, 127; *The Guardian Angel*, 14–15, 102, 114–15, 118–28; "The Professor at the Breakfast-Table," 107
Holmes, Abiel, 104–06
Hopkins, Pauline, 12
Hunt, Sanford B., 88
Hunter, William, 117
Hurst, Michael C., 18
Hypochondriasis, 58–60, 142n117

Indigestion. *See* Digestion

Jacobs, Harriet, 11, 134n44
Jacques, Daniel Harrison, 3, 6, 95
Jim Crow, 35, 64, 132, 137n104
Johnson, James, 43, 46–49, 51–54, 59, 62, 71, 142n117

Kelley, Wyn, 42
Kellogg, Catherine, 114

Lamarck, Jean-Baptiste, 27–28
Lane, Charles, 10
Langley, J. Baxter, 42–43
Latour, Bruno, 131–32
Lereboullet, Dominique August, 28–30
Lewis, Robert Benjamin, 11
López-Beltrán, Carlos, 115, 118

Malabou, Catherine, 6–7, 103, 114. *See also* Destructive plasticity
Mancuso, Luke, 98
Mann, Mary Peabody, 55, 60
Massumi, Brian, 130, 132
Mather, Cotton, 124
Mayo, Herbert, 20
McHenry, Elizabeth, 134n44
Melville, Elizabeth, 42

Melville, Herman, 2, 4, 13–14; 42–43, 47, 49–50, 58, 129; Works: "Art," 50; "Bartleby, the Scrivener," 58; *Moby-Dick*, 13–14, 44–45, 49–51, 58–73; *Pierre: Or, The Ambiguities*, 58, 129; *Typee*, 69
Mesmerism, 4, 20, 133n8
Morantz-Sanchez, Regina, 3
Morewood, Sarah, 47
Morse, John T., 106
Müller-Wille, Staffan, 116–18
Murison, Justine, 4, 19, 33–34, 59, 133n8, 133n15
Myers, Fredric, 93

Neely, Michelle, 4, 21, 135n27, 139n9
Neovitalism, 132
Nervous sympathy, 45–48
Nervous system, 4, 6, 9, 18–20, 32–35, 43–48, 52–55, 58–59, 66–67, 111–12, 116–17, 123–25, 139n16, 142n117, 145n12, 150n56. *See also* Digestion; Nervous sympathy
Neuroplasticity, 6–7
Neurotechnology, 53, 56–57, 130–32
New England Primer, The, 104, 149n16
New materialism, 7, 132
Nicholson, Asenath, 4, 54

Obuchowski, Peter, 135n8

Panic of 1837, 27
Pennington, James W. C., 11
Petit, Antoine, 118
Phrenology, 2–4, 11–12, 52–53, 63, 72, 74–81, 141n65, 145n8, 145n13, 145n14
Physical training, 2–3, 14, 75, 78–85, 88–91, 98
Physiognomy, 2, 57, 63, 72
Pitts-Taylor, Victoria, 9–10
Predestination: biological, 101–03, 108–14, 127–29; theological, 103–08. *See also* Heredity
Pullan, Matilda Marian, 42–43

Index 167

Queer theory, 132

Reynolds, David S., 81, 88
Rheinberger, Hans-Jörg, 116–18
Rose, Nicholas, 6, 15, 43–44, 53, 56, 131. See also Neurotechnology
Rush, Benjamin, 59
Rusert, Britt, 4, 11, 77, 133n15, 134n44, 145n8
Ryan, James Emmett, 59

Saturday Club, 107
Savarese, Ralph James, 58
Schuller, Kyla, 4, 9–10, 133n15
Self-culture, 1–3, 9–12, 16–17, 26–27, 29, 38
Shadd, Mary Ann, 11
Shelley, Percy Bysshe, 43
Sklar, Kathryn, 37
Smith, Andrew F., 53–54
Spurzheim, Johann, 77, 145n13. See also Phrenology
Stern, Madeleine B., 141n65
Sterne, Laurence, 116
Stowe, Harriet Beecher, 109, 112
Symonds, John Addington, 92–93

Tally, Robert T., Jr., 50–51
Taylor, Charles, 131
Tea. See Caffeine
Thompson, J. Bruce, 127
Thomsonian medicine, 11
Thoreau, Henry David: and philanthropy, 26–27, 82, 129; and self-culture, 20–26; Works: *Walden*, 1, 8, 17, 20–26
Thrailkill, Jane F., 4, 33, 113, 133n15, 149n6
Ticknor, William, 114
Tilton, Eleanor, 104, 149n6
Todd, Jan, 79

Tompkins, Jane, 12
Tompkins, Kyla Wazana, 4, 11, 51, 64, 133n15, 137n104, 139n9
Trall, Russell Thatcher, 90
Turpin, Zachary, 80–81, 86
Tyler, William, 4

Vegetarianism, 21, 43, 66, 82, 139n9, 141n65
Velsor, Mose. See Walt Whitman

Walls, Laura Dassow, 23, 135n8
Warner, Michael, 93
Warren, James Perrin, 98
Wells, Samuel R., 80
Whitman, Walt, interest in physical training, 75; personal health of, 75, 88–89; relationship with Fowler brothers, 74–75, 80; theory of reading as training, 89–91. Works: "Calamus" cluster, 87, 91–93; *Democratic Vistas*, 89–91; "Enfans d'Adam" cluster, 99; "A Hand Mirror," 85–87; "I Sing the Body Electric," 87; "Manly Health and Training, with Off-Hand Hints toward their Conditions," 75–76, 80–95, 97–99; *Leaves of Grass*, 1855 edition, 80–81, 87, 147n72; *Leaves of Grass*, 1856 edition, 2, 14, 75, 81, 85, 87–89, 99; *Leaves of Grass*, 1860 edition, 2, 14, 75, 85–99; "A Poem of the Body," 87; "Poem of Procreation," 80, 99; "Says" cluster, 93–98; "Song of Myself," 87. See also Physical training
Wigglesworth, Michael, 106
Wilson Philip, Alexander Philip, 43, 45–47, 52–53, 61, 71. See also Digestion
Wilson, Eric, 135n8
Wilson, Ivy, 147n70
Wilson, Philip K., 117

www.ingramcontent.com/pod-product-compliance
Lightning Source LLC
Chambersburg PA
CBHW021858230426
43671CB00006B/443